Walter A

Walter Alston

*The Rise of a Manager
from the Minors to
the Baseball Hall of Fame*

ALAN H. LEVY

McFarland & Company, Inc., Publishers
Jefferson, North Carolina

This book has undergone peer review.

ISBN (print) 978-1-4766-8210-5
ISBN (ebook) 978-1-4766-4205-5

LIBRARY OF CONGRESS AND BRITISH LIBRARY
CATALOGUING DATA ARE AVAILABLE

Library of Congress Control Number 2021003327

Front cover: Dodgers manager Walter Alston (National Baseball
Hall of Fame and Museum, Cooperstown, New York)

Printed in the United States of America

McFarland & Company, Inc., Publishers
Box 611, Jefferson, North Carolina 28640
www.mcfarlandpub.com

Contents

Introduction

Walter Alston was one of the most successful managers in the history of baseball, one of only ten managers to win more than 2,000 games. His lifetime win/loss percentage was a remarkable .558. (Of the ten managers with 2,000 wins, only Joe McCarthy's mark of .615 and John McGraw's .586 were higher.) Among baseball fans, common images of Alston involve a quiet man who was thoroughly congenial and non-combative. "The Quiet Man" was indeed the phrase that many journalists repeatedly clacked into stories about Alston and his leadership of the Los Angeles Dodgers. The sobriquet resonated among fans as it was also the title of a John Wayne movie that came out at the time Alston first emerged in the baseball public's eyes as the Dodgers' manager. The John Wayne movie introduced audiences to a man who, while once a proficient boxer, preferred to pursue all subsequent issues in life while avoiding all fighting and violence. (Few knew that Alston could be quite adept at boxing too.)

Many aspects of Walter Alston appeared to underscore the "quiet" image. Along with the others who ran the Dodgers, like owners Walter and Peter O'Malley, general manager Emil "Buzzie" Bavasi, and radio/television broadcaster Vin Scully, Alston greatly preferred that the team's day-to-day relations with the media and the fans be kept at a calm level ("laid-back," as many late 1970s Los Angeles natives preferred to phrase it). This trait would be unsettling to some fans and sports writers who preferred, and sometimes thought superior, the rambunctious, yelling, scrapping styles of other skippers who have dotted the baseball landscape. Among those within the Dodgers' management, most notably Walter O'Malley and "Buzzie" Bavasi, Alston's outward appearance suited everyone just fine, however, and O'Malley and Bavasi were too smart ever to hire a mere fool as their field manager. Alston's managerial record, building and refining young talent as he did for over a decade in the Dodgers' valuable farm system, showed how smart a baseball man he was.

Alston's "quiet" image could convey an impression among some casual observers that he was not fully in charge of the team. Often, whenever Brooklyn or LA came up short in a campaign, such grousing about Alston would permeate barber shops, bar rooms, and the media. His image certainly cast a stark contrast to the styles of such younger, bombastic contemporaries as Billy Martin or Earl Weaver. Still, as Weaver, Martin, and other managers of the day knew all too well, beneath the calm exterior, Alston was a manager who did not miss a trick and who was anything but even a trifle disengaged from the details of any game in which he was involved.

Another of Alston's contemporaries, Fred Hutchinson of the Cincinnati Reds, noted to a few surprised reporters a few things that most informed men in baseball knew all too well: "Never challenge him to anything involving a gun," Hutchinson first noted with a smirk. "He'll hit more bull's eyes than any ten men you know." Alston's skills were top-notch at both hunting and skeet shooting. (In skeet competition, of 25 shots, a score of 24, or a perfect 25, was a typical mark for him.) Hutchinson also advised never to challenge Alston to any game involving "a billiard stick [as] he's an amateur with an old pro's skill and cunning." By his own modest account, Alston was capable of running 100 balls in straight pool, and he occasionally played with the legendary Willie Mosconi.

The other area Hutchinson advised people to avoid challenging Alston on concerned "his fists: He's hard as nails," chuckled Hutchinson, "and he'll snap your head off with a single punch." Challenging Alston in any such endeavors was indeed risky, and real baseball men knew it. One hot afternoon, with the Dodgers en route to the Pittsburgh airport after a sweaty, irritating loss to the Pirates, many of the players were grumbling about the heat and the discomfort of the substandard bus they were riding. After a few minutes of this, Alston ordered the driver to stop the bus. He turned to the team and asked anyone who wished to air any further comments about the bus to step outside. All complaining immediately ceased.[1]

In his long tenure as the manager of the Dodgers, Alston astutely helped build several dynasties. The first was the team he inherited after the 1953 season, and to which he had contributed strongly in his managing of several of the Dodgers' minor league teams over the previous ten seasons. This work also included important contributions Alston made to Branch Rickey and the Dodgers as they famously led the successful integration of professional baseball.

Amidst Alston's quiet contributions to the Dodgers, in the early 1950s, Charlie Dressen had been very successful in his managing of the Brooklyn Dodgers. Other Brooklyn managers had done well too. In every season since World War II, under several managers, Brooklyn had either won the National League pennant, tied for it, or at least been in the thick of the race. Winning pennants in 1952 and 1953, Dressen had every reason to feel proud of his accomplishments. Unfortunately, and to the excruciating dismay of both the Dodgers' ownership and their legendary, rabid fans, Dressen's squads had failed to win the World Series. Aggravating this was the oh so more painful fact that every time Brooklyn had captured the NL flag in these years (1941, 1947, 1949, 1952, and 1953), they not only lost the World Series, they lost it to the _____ Yankees. Contemplating wider meaning in these heartbreaking losses, comedian/Dodger fanatic Sid Caesar surmised what thousands of other Brooklyn fans knew (and utterly detested): "It wasn't that we were the second-best team in baseball," Caesar sighed. "It was that we were the second-best team in New York!"

The result was that in late October of 1953, albeit after piloting the Dodgers to two consecutive pennants, the moment Charlie Dressen asked owner Walter O'Malley for a multi-year contract, O'Malley fired him. Amidst cries of "Who's He?" (and since it was Brooklyn, the more accurate, though unprintable recounting of Flatbush's cry should be: "Who the _____ is he?"), up came Walter Alston, who had been managing Brooklyn's top farm club in Montreal.

Alston inherited the great Brooklyn team he had quietly helped construct, and in 1955 he took them to their only World Series win. (And it was against the Yankees!) From there, amidst the even more excruciating pain of the team's uprooting and relocation to Los Angeles, a matter that never bothered Alston one bit, he won it all again in 1959. With but a few remnants from the legendary teams of the final Brooklyn years, Alston managed a second dominant club that won three pennants from 1963 through 1966. (Having Sandy Koufax on his pitching staff certainly helped here.) From there, after several painful years of rebuilding, Alston produced yet a third consistent winner in the 1970s. These Dodgers contended season after season, won the NL pennant in 1974, and continued to win after Alston had retired in 1976 and turned the club over to his protégé and successor, Tommy Lasorda.

The development of three dynasties marked quite an achievement. To many casual onlookers it all looked so easy. As with many feats in athletic competition, the very best performers do indeed convey a sense of ease. Fans watch great players, and since most have played ball at one time or another, any sense of how easy greatness may appear is something readily set aside. Anyone who ever played the game knows how difficult it is to achieve a level of play remotely resembling any sort of

grace. In contrast, the finer arts of coaching or managing do not easily resonate among as many fans. While most have played, very few ever
coached or managed, let alone at such refined tactical and strategic levels as practiced among that elite fraternity of major league professionals.

Senses of how "anyone can do that," or such dismissive phrases
as "push button manager" or "a team that runs itself" can all too easily
implant themselves in the minds of casual fans and even, sadly, among
some less-than-sharp scribes whose mental imprecision further enables
the ingratitude. Several great managers, including Connie Mack, Joe
McCarthy, Casey Stengel, and Earl Weaver, had to endure such superficial, dismissive castings. For obvious reasons, none cared one bit for any
such simple-minded reductions. Alston faced this too. As well or better than anyone, he was always able to smile and nod along with most
less-than-sharp critics, preferring, quite sensibly, not to waste a hint of
time or energy on such peripheral matters as the outlooks (one could
not call them "perceptions"; there was nothing "perceptive" about them)
of ignorant fans and glib reporters. Only rarely did any reporter ever
"get to" Walter Alston.

While manager Charlie Dressen had demanded a multi-year contract from Walter O'Malley, when Walter Alston first signed to manage
the Brooklyn Dodgers in late October of 1953, he received a one-year
contract. This short tenure implied an obvious and stern directive from
the owner—win now! It also underscored the point that Alston's tenure
as manager could indeed be brief. (That autumn, one could have certainly secured rather long odds that Walter Alston would last even five
years as the Dodgers' manager; any notion that he would last 23 seasons would have been dismissed as utterly preposterous.) While such a
single-year contract clearly denoted the fact that he could be immediately fired after a disappointing season, Alston was quite content with
such terms. Operating within them, he appeared to feel no undue pressure and would certainly succeed remarkably well. Throughout his subsequent decades at the helm with the Dodgers, Alston would never sign
any other sort of contract. Every agreement between Walter Alston and
the Dodgers was for a single season.

By the latter half of his long tenure managing the Dodgers, Alston's
series of one-years had become legendary. Indeed, in 1976 Alston poignantly entitled a memoir *One Year at a Time*.[2] Alston worked so well
with the O'Malley family and with GM Buzzie Bavasi that he had no
fear of anything arising, no matter the clear legal implications of his
one-season contracts. Making absolutely no false postures, Alston genuinely meant it when he affirmed that he would never want to stay on with
any club where he was not wanted. Assessing Alston, Walter O'Malley

once declared, no doubt a trifle selfishly, how pleasant Alston always was to work with: "Do you realize," he declared, "how important it is to have a manager who doesn't irritate you?"[3]

Alston's affable manner with the rest of the Dodgers' management was certainly important in regard to all "inside" office matters, but that alone would not have enabled him, or anyone, to last very long as manager were there no success on the field. Winning was what really counted, of course, with the team, as well as with the press and the fans. Here Alston's work could not be denied, although, as with many managers, no matter how highly baseball posterity would come to place him, many criticisms came forth anyway. Alston did indeed make it look easy.

One feature of Alston's success lay in the fact that he did not merely take the leadership position of the team from the outside, as do so many who are hired as managers. Alston's career, in effect, involved a variation on the classic tale of a man "working his way up the ladder to the top." First under Branch Rickey, and from there under Walter O'Malley, Alston rose in the ranks from a player at the lowest levels of the minor leagues, to the middle and higher minor league circuits, and briefly (in last weeks of the 1936 season) to the majors. From there he succeeded at minor league managerial posts and ultimately reached the top level of the Dodgers' minor league system in Montreal.

He excelled wherever he went, somewhat as a player, always as a manager, and he did so under the all-seeing eye of "the Mahatma," Branch Rickey. Under Rickey, the quality of any manager's work would never go unnoticed. Along the way, a few fortuitous points of timing certainly helped Alston as well. Especially important here was Rickey's decision, early in World War II, to leave the St. Louis Cardinals' organization to run the Brooklyn Dodgers. The Rickey-led Cardinals' farm system had first signed Alston, both as a player and subsequently as a player-manager. Rickey would later acquire him for the Dodgers' system. Alston indeed owed much of his early managerial career to Rickey, but equally important here was the fact that he never failed to meet, and sometimes exceeded, any expectations Rickey held out to him.

As he managed for many seasons at the lower minor league levels, Alston often had to handle many of the duties which, in the big leagues, a manager can delegate. This would prove a subtle but important part of his success within the Dodgers' organization. At the minor league levels, Alston often had to spend time handling the details of so many sub-managerial tasks—batting practice pitcher, trainer, first/third base coach, traveling secretary, press spokesman, accountant, equipment handler, even bus driver (he did this a few times in Trenton, New Jersey, during some of the severe labor-shortage days of World War II). Alston had personal experiences at so many minute levels of what goes into the running of a ball club, and he often did it all while batting third and playing first base every day. Alston could then bring to his later management a full understanding and appreciation of the value of all elements, big and small, that contribute to the running of a successful club.

Nothing escaped his comprehension, and any job well done, no matter how low or high the level, was something he understood and appreciated. Here, beyond his natural conviviality, both the substance and the tone of his management contained an added depth and subtlety, something which another manager could not simply copy via the pedestrian following of any how-to management manual. Even if they could not precisely put their finger on any such little factors, players and others in the organization generally felt the ambience and responded positively to it all. "If you can't play for Alston," noted both pitcher Tommy Lasorda and Hall of Fame pitcher Don Drysdale, "you can't play for anybody."[4]

As far back as Plato's *Republic*, there lies the deceptively simple dictum that the greatest justice comes forth in a society, or in any organization, in which each person does his or her own job. The implication here is that each part of an organization functions best within its own particular realm; others should not try to act or interfere in the job of anyone else, lest there then emerge unneeded levels of malfunction, ultimately leading to greater injustice. Alston's Dodgers embodied that outwardly simple maxim as well as any organization in sports. O'Malley's mention of Alston's non-irritating ways may have indeed revealed more than a bit of self-centeredness, but it underscored, even if unwittingly, the wisdom in the ways that he allowed the organization, which he first took over from Branch Rickey, to go forth with little internal tinkering, re-staffing, or interference. Devoid of any conscious patterning, Plato's wisdom then rolled forth, regardless of, even in spite of, any egos that may have intervened.

Later, with the occasional presence of some clearly interfering, disruptive egos, notably that of Leo Durocher, the Dodgers' *republican* virtues (Platonic, not GOP; if the latter, only coincidentally) withstood all the pressures and endured. Under Alston and the Dodgers' organization, the positive culture not only endured, it prevailed. The proof was simple: they were consistent winners like few other teams of the era.

Beyond the elements of personality, knowledge, and virtue that Alston brought to the manner and tonality with which the Dodgers' organization ran, there was in Alston a solid grounding of his spirit and nature, and this was essential to the man and his work. It was also a key factor in his ability to function, without a hint of stress, under the legal/

contractual structure of mere annual employment. This was another outwardly simple matter, but in Alston it was salient. Alston came from a community called Darrtown, a small township in Butler County, Ohio, near the Indiana border, about 50 miles north of Cincinnati. The town was (and still is) very small. Everyone knew everyone, and for those who lived there, the sense of calm solidity and happy acceptance subsumed everything. While baseball gave Alston a clear sense of what he did, the small-town Midwestern community of Darrtown gave him an even clearer sense of who he was.

Wherever he played or managed, from the time he first played ball professionally in Mississippi in 1935 to his last season at the helm in LA in 1976, Alston always knew that, no matter the outcome of a season, good or bad, and no matter what anyone said, thought, or wrote about him, he could and would always go home to Darrtown. Any prospect of being dismissed brought Alston only happy thoughts of life back in rural Ohio.

To the casual observer, any such praise of small-town Midwestern American values may sound trite. For something to become trite, however, there is usually some kernel of wisdom in the affirmation. Alston always displayed pride in his hometown and in his family, and he never cared one whit if anyone found it old-fashioned. Alston's life, like that of so many others across the Midwest, was never fancy. Financially, he had grown up rather poor. From this he developed a great deal of self-reliance and not a hint of bitterness. He needed little income to sustain himself and his life. All successes that came through what he later did professionally could never amount to anything more than the nicest of "extras" (skeet and hunting rifles, cameras, woodworking tools and equipment, pool tables, motorcycles), all on top of the life in Darrtown that he would always treasure and would (and could) never leave.

With Alston, the small-town Midwestern roots he held, along with such contemporaries as Woody Hayes, Paul Brown, and John Wooden, were values he felt little need to brag about or even articulate either as bases or as justifications for anything he said or did as a manager. Leaving his values implicit, Alston was always content to let his work speak for itself, and, with any success, to let the media fawn over the players and not him. Just as Plato's notion of how a just society operates manifested itself in the Dodgers' organization without any explicit modeling from Classical texts, Alston was directly conversant with few if any such philosophies implicitly at hand. He lived them without reading them. To that very end, indeed, beyond Plato, the French politician and intellectual Alexis de Tocqueville once observed a key matter, as he traveled and carefully studied the operation of democracy in America. Tocqueville visited the very region where Alston later lived, and in his effort to detail and explain how democracy operated in the United States, Tocqueville wrote:

> I discover that in most of the operations of the mind, each American appeals to the individual exercise of his own understanding alone. America is therefore one of the countries in the world where philosophy is least studied, and where the precepts of Descartes are best applied.

Tocqueville added that this came as no surprise. For Americans, he noted]

> do not read the works of Descartes, because their social condition deters them from speculative studies; but they follow his maxims because this very social condition naturally disposes their understanding to adopt them. ... The practice which obtains amongst the Americans of fixing the standard of their judgment in themselves alone.... Americans then have not required to extract their philosophical method from books; they have found it in themselves.[5]

Alston was indeed an example of someone able to follow many of the ideas of Descartes without directly reading them. His social grounding was the basis of his behavior with and treatment of all others; who they were or from where they came did not matter. That was how he treated anyone at a personal level. In the instrumentality of his work as a manager, it was similar: all that mattered was performance. In any wider terms, with reporters or fans, Alston would only talk baseball. He never philosophized, be it comically like Yogi Berra or Casey Stengel or seriously like such contemporaries as Vince Lombardi, Woody Hayes, or John Wooden. Alston would never consider such a matter as to how the institution of the Infield Fly Rule exemplified any sort of baseball version of the political philosophy of Progressive Era reform; he would only consider its utility in the context of the game in itself. No wider speculations crossed his mind, nor did they need to. Any implicit philosophical method did not come from any text; it lay within the game itself.

One major point of extra-baseball speculation and philosophizing of a highly political nature did come forth during Alston's career. Indeed, among all sports organizations in the country, it came forth most strikingly with the Dodgers right after World War II. It was a matter that demanded, in the very name of Platonic ideals of justice, far more than everyone just doing his own job. This concerned Branch Rickey's clear, explicit desire to bring racial integration to major league baseball. In stark contrast to "straight baseball," the matter of race was certainly an issue where one could not be a Cartesian without being consciously so. Tocqueville himself had made explicit that *the* major challenge Americans would have to face in *their* democratic experiment involved facing and resolving questions regarding race.

History certainly proved, and continues to prove, Tocqueville to have been remarkably cogent here. Rickey's efforts after 1945 demonstrated a consciousness well beyond any mere mastery of the instrumentalities of baseball. Rickey simply ("simply" if only in moral terms, for there was nothing "simple" about the logistics or the politics at play here) made the judgment that, within the confines of that sector of American society where he had had undeniable success, and where he then held great prominence, he would utilize his position to pursue a greater good. Those who worked under him, and who did not exercise the option to leave, had to have the requisite commitment, understanding, and character to maximize the success that Rickey sought.

At the time Rickey initiated his integration efforts in 1946, the game's and the nation's eyes focused first on Rickey himself and even more on Jackie Robinson. While under less scrutiny, others in the Dodgers' organization played significant roles too. Alston was among those who quietly worked in a supporting role; Bavasi was another. Their successes were part of the now famous, but, thus far, not fully told history of baseball's role in the breakdown of Jim Crow in post–1945 America.

Alston's chief role in "Baseball's Great Experiment" first involved managing a team, the Nashua (NH) Dodgers, in the newly reestablished New England League. In 1946, Jackie Robinson had signed with Brooklyn, but Rickey had him play that initial season in Montreal. Rickey chose the French-Canadian city because of convictions among Dodgers officials, especially Bavasi, who was French on his father's side (*voilà* his actual first name—Emil), that Montreal, and the French-Canadian region in general, would be more conducive to and accepting of African American players. This proved true, and it certainly marked a contrast to what would have occurred had Robinson first played for a team in an American city, let alone for one in the Deep South.

In the International League circuit in which Robinson played in 1946, the southernmost city he visited in the regular season was Baltimore, and racial tensions surfaced even there. Two other African Americans who signed with Brooklyn that same year would also be assigned to minor league towns in Quebec. But Rickey signed two other African Americans, and he placed them under Alston's (and Bavasi's) care in Nashua. With Alston as manager, that little New England town became the first American community of the 20th century to have a racially integrated professional ball club. And they won.

In contrast to the cultural dynamics of more recent decades, the game of professional baseball, in 1945–1946, held vastly more social significance than any, likely more than all, other professional sports (certainly more than all other team sports). Individual sports like boxing, horseracing, and Olympic competitions, while often popular and possibly socially significant, came forth sporadically and as singular events. Baseball, meanwhile, was indeed the nation's true pastime, the game that was fully integrated into the spring/summer/fall rhythms of day-to-day life in small towns and big cities all over the nation.

Without question, Rickey was keenly aware of this broader social and political meaning in the context of what he was first attempting in 1946. His firm resolve was an undeniably significant part of the process of the nation's post–1945 racial advances. Walter Alston would play a role in the events that Rickey set into motion when he signed Jackie Robinson in 1946, and Alston's work would prove important too. He believed in the righteousness of what was taking place both in the Dodgers' system and in the nation as a whole. He never did anything to undermine the work of the organization in which he was managing, and when challenges arose, he stood up, sometimes amidst genuine challenges to his own physical safety, directly facing all people and points of hostility and resistance.

The spiritual roots that lay in Alston's small-town background contributed to the certainty he brought to the work placed before him in 1946, as well as in the years that both preceded and followed. As Alston faced such challenges as he encountered in New Hampshire in 1946, he always did so with an outward conviviality which overlay a rock-solid foundation of character that so many (not all, certainly) players, opponents, officials, reporters, and fans found appealing, sometimes even intimidating. The roots of the man's career are thus well worth studying, especially as they have, until now, not been fully researched.

The events surrounding Alston's career, once he started managing the Brooklyn Dodgers in 1954, are familiar to many fans of baseball history. There is no heretofore-secret cache of letters or other hidden archives that can revise the various views, let alone resolve the often-heated controversies, that lay all about the familiar and famous stories involving the Dodgers since 1954, be they about Jackie Robinson, Sandy Koufax, or other Dodgers immortals. It is Walter Alston's earlier work that has received little coverage, and it merits study too.

Alston's career grew very much out of the Midwestern small-town ethos that so many associate with ideals about the nation's heartland. Some may find aspects of this world oppressively stifling, parochial, even deplorable. Others see it as a culture devoid of immodesty, free of pomposity and posturing, rooted in values that always give ultimate sanction to the performance, as opposed to the mere identity, of a person in regard to what he does, and to the soul of a person, rather than to any outward appearance, in regard to what he may be.

For most Ohioans, as for people from any other locale, there is likely some mixture of both positive and negative attributes that contribute to this culture. The life and career of an exceptional baseball man like Walter Alston certainly appear to involve a preponderance of positives. It entails a man who quietly personified many of the nation's heartland values and who, just as quietly, helped the nation take on and begin fundamentally to alter and expunge vestiges of what are undeniably some of the country's very worst legacies.

As with other works I have researched and written on American sports, American music, and American politics, I am grateful to many friends and colleagues. As always, I say thank you to the many deeply knowledgeable and helpful members of the staff of the Library of Congress. I thank my colleague, Mr. Charles C. Alexander, for his original encouragement in regard to the idea of a study of Mr. Walter Alston. To Mr. Jim Gates and the staff of the National Baseball Hall of Fame and Museum, I am grateful for their many assists in the field of research. To my colleagues at Slippery Rock University—professors Bill Bergmann, Aaron Cowan, Melissa Ford, John Craig, and the late Richard Martin (a fine small-town Ohio lad himself), my sincere thanks for listening, for reading an occasional chapter, and for yielding me the time, space, and means to carry out my work.

1

A Small Town in Rural Ohio

The small towns of Middle America have a storied place in the nation's lore and culture. As far back as 1829, the French political philosopher, Alexis de Tocqueville, famously visited America and praised the essential goodness of spirit that subsumed American communities. Nearly 200 years later, the immensely popular writer David McCullough also praised the courage and democratic instincts of many of the "pioneers" who settled out in the Midwest.[1] Between Tocqueville and McCullough, Frederick Jackson Turner, along with scores of other writers of varying political and social casts, have extolled the strengths and virtues they see rooted in the communities and the people of Middle America. Others, however, have tried very hard to debunk any perceived mythologizing of this region with counter images of decidedly negative cast.

Such iconoclasts as Oscar Wilde, late-in-life Mark Twain, Sinclair Lewis, and H.L. Mencken saw little virtue and many traits worthy of ridicule. The disdain of many who live on either of the nation's seacoasts does have a long-standing place in the nation's social and political discourse. The contrasting outlooks can involve differing forms of parochialisms, including many parochialisms from within the self-designated elite classes. Even accepting various critiques, many senses of Middle America's essential solidity and virtue continue to resonate. The positive perceptions still come forth in countless books, movies, documentaries, and television programs. Aside from the positive images evoked by the Midwestern American town, perhaps the only other set of traditional sentiments that have endured as much in American culture would be those linked to the national pastime of baseball, and the two certainly overlap.

After so many tales and stories about small-town Mid-America and baseball, if a writer were to approach various publishing houses or film producers and pitch them an idea of a book or movie about a future baseball Hall of Famer, who came out of a small town in the Midwest and always displayed many of heartland America's best traditions and virtues during his long baseball career—that writer could encounter a great deal of skepticism. The presented portrait could easily appear too full of clichés and all too well-known images. As clichéd as many of the "small-town Midwestern boy" images and virtues may appear, they aptly apply to the life of baseball's managerial great, Walter Alston.

Alston was born on a farm near the township of Darrtown, Ohio, some 45 miles north of Cincinnati. In 1911, the year Alston was born, Darrtown was as typical a small Mid-American community as can be imagined. The town's size has not changed much in the decades since. Darrtown largely consists of 16 square blocks, formed by five straight-line streets going north/south, crossed by five equally straight streets going east/west. Beyond the town's 16 blocks lie farms where Alston's father once owned land. People who resided in such communities lived in a closely-knit social network. Folks all knew one another's comings and goings. The level of familiarity here can strike people of more modern urban/suburban sensibilities as claustrophobic, even a trifle creepy. In rural Ohio when Alston was growing up, local papers repeatedly printed such seemingly absurd little items as "on Tuesday Mr. and Mrs. Emmons Alston spent the evening with the Alexanders."[2] To families like the Alstons, such closeness and knowledge of one another's lives was not only acceptable, it was welcome. Community bonds were treasured. They gave a sense of stability and security with no sorts of neuroses that many outsiders may wish to presume, possibly via their own projections. Community membership was not merely narrative, it was evaluative. Late in his life, Walter Alston wrote unapologetically of his keen attachment to his town and region: "There's something about going home to Darrtown that spells peace, security, and solitude. ... To me it's God's country. ... I was born and raised and will probably die amid that rolling farm land."[3] He did.

Alston's ancestors were among the farmers who had populated Butler County, Ohio, in the early and mid–19th century. They were the Southern Ohioans known as the "Butternuts." The nickname came from these farmers' habit of using the oil from butternuts (and walnuts) to dye their homespun clothing. In their origins, the Butternuts were largely Southerners who had moved west, mainly out of Virginia, Maryland, and parts of Western Pennsylvania, settling on the open lands of Ohio, Indiana, and Illinois. Out in Ohio, the Butternuts largely settled south of the National Road, today's route 40/Interstate 70. They survived and earned a living raising hogs, growing corn, and making their own whiskey. Their religious links were largely with the Baptists and Methodists. The Alstons were Methodists. In 19th-century state and national politics, the Butternuts tended strongly to the conservative side. The early settlers of Ohio had voted to keep slavery out of the region, but the vote was very close. A mix of views on key 19th-century issues was always present. The Butternuts were first more Democrat than Whig; in the mid–19th century, more Democrat than Republican. In the mid– and late–20th century and ever since, their descendants have generally become Republicans.

In the 19th century, the Butternuts tended to resist, or were at least quite slow to accept, economic advances in such areas as banking, commerce, and technology. These were developments more readily accepted among those who settled upper Ohio, as well as northern Indiana and Illinois, hailing from upstate New York and New England. These "Yankees" populated the northern half of the state, above the National Road. Arriving a little later, they tended more eagerly to adapt to various innovations, both economic and political. Their trade flowed to and from points East via the use of new canals and railroads. The Butternuts relied on the traditional usage of the Ohio and Mississippi Rivers, with their trade then generally running through New Orleans. In addition to being slower to adopt various economic, commercial, and technological innovations, many Butternuts were not as much affected by the various religious awakenings that swept through the North. Not coincidentally, the Butternuts also divided with the Yankee Ohioans in politics over such rising social reforms as "temperance" in regard to alcohol consumption.

Another part of the Butternuts' political legacy involved some of them resisting various pre–Civil War reforms, including some of the agitation against the institution of slavery. In the 1860 Presidential election, while the state of Ohio voted decidedly for the Republican Abraham Lincoln, a clear majority of Darrtown's Butler County voted for Democrat Stephen Douglas (the County's margin was: Lincoln: 2,867; Douglas: 4,109; a one-on-one balance of 41.2 percent to 58.8 percent).[4] During the Civil War, many Ohio Butternuts served the Union cause, but some lay among the "Copperheads," who favored the Confederate cause and resisted Emancipation. With many more such social and economic elements rattling through the state politics of the late 19th and into the 20th century, the cultural sentiments and politics among Ohioans continued to display a quite conscious North/South divide. The line here could be hazy at times. Undeniably, some reform sentiments did take root in Southern Ohio. Furthermore, and yet more strikingly, racial prejudice and keen resistance to reforms seeking to improve the status of African Americans readily came forth in Northern Ohio through many newspaper editorials as well as in various institutional arrangements in such areas as housing and education.[5]

By the early 20th century, when Walter Alston was born, many race-based patterns of law and social custom remained in place throughout Ohio, customs and norms which had indeed implanted themselves as strongly in the arrangements of Yankee-rooted Northern Ohio communities as in the South. Some of the Southern Butternuts may have lain among the Democrats and "Copperheads" (the derisive term for pro–South activists in Northern states), but they had also voted to keep slavery out of the region and served the Union cause. By the early 20th century, a simple and key point about the politics of Ohio's small towns, including Alston's Darrtown, was that virtually all racial matters were abstractions. In these years, racial issues did not arise over such specific topics as land ownership or schooling, simply because there were virtually no African Americans living in the rural regions of Southern Ohio.

In tiny Darrtown, Walter Alston grew up without African Americans or other minorities in his community or in the schools he attended. In the day-to-day life of the town and the nearby farms, the various social and political legacies in the region regarding racial matters did not appear in any practical issues or concerns among the common people of the day. Racial issues occupied no space in local newspaper articles or editorials, nor did they come forth in ministers' sermons or community gatherings. Had any such issues ever presented themselves in a tiny community like Darrtown, some families may have been surprised at the views a few of their friends expressed, Here it is not difficult to imagine such a dynamic then occurring in such a community as Darrtown, circa 1910, in which the majority, preoccupied with community harmony, could readily "capitulate" to any strident expressions, however surprising they may have been, from friends and neighbors.[6] Ideas about any such potential political churnings remain speculative, however; the fact was that in most rural communities of the early 20th-century Midwest, the issue of race did not arise in any practical way. Alston himself never revealed any traces of racial prejudice in any of the thoughts and deeds of his childhood. The issue never really intruded into his early life. Later, in his professional career, he would show few if any strains over the issue and be very much part of the forces of progressive change.

All such backdrop involving race in the vagaries of politics of 19th and early 20th-century Ohio is significant, not just because it was part of the culture in which Alston was raised, but, even more, because of key events that would later enter Alston's career. In his various post–World War II managing posts, Alston would find himself managing teams in an organization, the Brooklyn Dodgers, involved in the first efforts of the 20th century at racial integration in professional baseball. In his usual quiet ways, Alston found himself part of professional baseball's avant-garde in the cause of racial integration and progress.

Later, when a preponderance of the politics regarding race in America, including, indeed especially, the world of professional sports, modulated away from straightforward matters of equality of opportunity and turned towards often more complex matters of racially-driven identity, Alston would appear far less at the forefront. All these elements would surround his career as it evolved. At the time Alston was growing up in rural Ohio, such matters were utterly distant from any aspect of his life or his community's daily frames of reference. In certain ways, Alston's "blank slate" in regard to such important issues would prove both useful and render him quite receptive amidst the unfolding innovations in which he played a role.

Walter's father, Emmons Alston, was a simple farmer. He raised his son as Midwestern farmers typically did, teaching him the basic farming and home skills, all with the unquestioned assumption that such a life and the skills it required would pass on to his son, as well as to subsequent generations. Vastly more than anything about politics, young Walter Alston learned a lot about planting, harvesting, and handling horses, cows, and pigs. He also learned quite a bit about carpentry, a skill he would hone and enjoy for the rest of his life. Like most small-town Ohioans, the Alstons, senior and junior, never bought a house. Rather they bought land and built their houses on it. Throughout most of his years in Ohio, Walter Alston and his family lived in a house he had built himself. His daughter lived in a house he built for her. He also made virtually every piece of furniture in both houses. By any measure, Alston was thoroughly proficient in all matters of woodworking, as well as with a hunting rifle. These were life skills assumed by virtually all who lived in rural Ohio in the early 20th century. Later, Alston would develop keen skills with a pool cue. If the need ever arose, as with many farm boys, Alston could also be quite competent with his fists.[7] This all underscored notions about the positive legacy of the self-reliance and the hard work commonly attributed to the values and sensibilities of Middle America (Alston's finely-honed skills at the pool table notwithstanding).

When farm chores were not pressing, Emmons Alston also taught his son to pitch. Horseshoes were one thing at which the elder Mr. Alston could pitch quite well. He won several Butler County horseshoe-pitching contests.[8] Young Walter was a pretty fair pitcher of horseshoes himself, but he was an even better pitcher with a baseball. His father often threw with him. He had Walter aim his throws at a section of a barn door that was about the size of a strike zone. "We wore out many a barn door," Alston recalled. When his son was hurling, Alston's father always urged him to "put some smoke on it." Young Walter did, and his growing ballfield prowess came to be such that he soon gained a nickname—"Smokey." 'Til the day he died in 1984, no matter his fame, "Smokey" was always the name by which folks in Darrtown, Ohio, affectionately referred to Walter Alston. He would not have had it any other way.[9]

Emmons Alston lost his farm and livelihood to the Depression of 1921–1922, when plunging marketplace prices for pork yielded Ohio farmers insufficient income to cover the costs of raising the animals. Many others lost their livelihoods and land too. Alston had to sell all his land, his animals, and his farm equipment. He moved the family to a bungalow in Darrtown. There they survived on the wages he made at a factory job in the nearby town of Hamilton at a Ford Motor Company plant that manufactured wheels and running boards. The wages enabled him to keep a little income and pay off his debts. He would work at the Ford plant for 29 years. In those harsh times, many debtors ducked their creditors by declaring bankruptcy. Alston never did this. He made a point of paying off his creditors. Walter Alston quoted his father thus: "I didn't have a dime to my name and I owed the bank twenty-nine hundred dollars. ... Farmers all over the country were taking bankruptcy. But I'm not built that way. If I owed I was going to pay, and I wasn't going to look for an out."[10] One can draw a legacy here about Alston's decision revealing Butternut traditions, which contrasted markedly with the financially slicker uses of bankruptcy for which many opted in these hard times. The latter was more clearly a legacy of Northern Ohio Yankee origins. Jeffersonianism versus Hamiltonianism, "Wet" versus Temperance, many of the Southern Ohio roots of the Alston family are clear. Amidst their spartan lives in the 1920s, they made do with what they had, never complained or made excuses, and rejoiced in their family and community ties.

For the Alston family, their patriarch's decision to pay off his debts yielded them a rather meager existence, but in the 1920s few families in Butler County, Ohio, ever had much anyway. America's 1920s economy may have "roared" in some areas, but such rural regions as those of southwest Ohio remained quite poor. Low food prices in the 1920s played a significant part in what made life more prosperous and financially easy for many urban and suburban Americans. These same low prices aggrieved many rural Americans, however. For America's farmers, the 1920s were indeed a very different, often rather impoverished era. Alston never reflected upon the economic conditions in his background with any hints of bitterness, however. He regarded his community and family life as blessed.

In the 1920s, life for young Walter Alston involved a great deal of hard work, but there was no sense of oppression or depravity. He tended to chores, took odd jobs, and went about his schoolwork, as did virtually all the young people in the community. Alston attended local schools, weaving his domestic chores and small jobs around his studies and activities. He would regularly be up at 4:00 a.m., spend several hours at home at chores or local jobs, then be off to school, with more work in the late afternoon.

The school Alston attended in Darrtown was small. His high school graduating class consisted of only 12 people. Graduating in 1929, Alston ranked fourth.[11] In such a small environment, up and down the ranks from seniors to freshmen, all the students were expected to pitch in their share of time and effort to make various school enterprises succeed. Alston thus took part in school plays, even though he showed absolutely no skills at acting or music. One can search forever for any character flaws or mishaps in the early life of Walter Alston, but a researcher will find nothing significant. The only "crooked" thing that ever appeared to arise with regard to young Walter Alston concerned his acting in a school play in the fall of 1927, when he was in the 11th grade. The play was entitled *Why Not Jerry?* and Alston played the part of "Burke, a crooked sales manager."[12] With such a tiny group of students in each small-town high school in that era, participation in such things as a school play was always expected. Non-participation was the only choice that would invite any sort of sanction. Within reasonable bounds, all results were acceptable. The only stricture was that everyone was simply to do her/his best. Alston lived in a world with that sort of ethical clarity with respect to social obligations. This carried over to his unwavering sense of teamwork onto which he held for the rest of his life. As with stage efforts, when any sports team was formed, everyone in the school was also expected to take some part. In this area, Alston happened to show considerable talent. By the time Alston was in his junior year in high school, he was already over six feet tall. His father's early urgings about throwing hard paid off, as he could hurl a baseball better than anyone else in the school. He was also a star in basketball. By 1929, Alston was such a standout on the court that he was named to the first team of the All-County Boys Basketball Team.[13]

As Alston gained some note in local circles for his baseball and basketball prowess, several teams in such nearby towns as Millville, Oxford, and Hamilton engaged him in various semi-professional and community summer leagues. At one time, Alston played on a semi-pro team in Oxford with his father and two of his uncles.[14] Playing well here extended his family's notoriety as well as his own, so much so that he gained the notice of the baseball and basketball coaches at nearby Miami University, in the town of Oxford, only a half-hour away from home.

Upon finishing high school, Alston gained acceptance and would attend as a commuter. This saved a lot of money.[15] Enrolled at Miami, Alston studied an education curriculum with a focus on sciences, ultimately obtaining state certification to teach the various sciences and wood shop at the secondary level, something he would do for many years. While a Miami student, Alston did not take part in much of the University's social scene of fraternities and general campus frolicking. Part of this extended from the simple fact that he did not live on the campus. He could afford neither the extra time nor the money necessary for such social amenities.

Alston's matriculation at Miami University also coincided with the onset of the Great Depression. While a student, Alston had to take on extra work, driving a laundry truck in the early morning hours and working in a pool hall during lunchtime and in the early afternoon. This was where he first developed his mastery of the pool cue. Despite these part-time jobs, financial pressures amidst the worst years of the Great Depression forced Alston to drop out of Miami for two years. A local Methodist minister, the Rev. Ralph Jones, raised a bit of money ($50) for Alston, enabling him to return to school and finish. In 1932, $50 amounted to a great deal, and Alston never forgot the kindness: "If it hadn't been for Rev. Jones's timely gift," Alston recalled with sincere gratitude, "I'd probably be a [mere] farmer somewhere near Darrtown." He would have never played ball for Miami University, and major league scouts would have never taken note of him. To Alston it was part of the sustaining community strength to which he was so fondly attached. Later, when Alston was doing well as a major league manager, that little Methodist church in Darrtown would find itself very well endowed.[16]

At Miami, Alston was a standout in both baseball and basketball. As late as 1963, *The Sporting News* declared, "He is still regarded as one of the finest basketball guards in Miami's history."[17] Alston was a fair (B–/C+) student. He had actually flunked the first semester of freshman English and had to repeat it, but he completed the curriculum and earned a Bachelor of Science degree in education in 1935. With the credentials to teach in the sciences, Alston accepted a position at a local high school in the town of New Madison. There he would teach various sciences and wood shop, and coach both the basketball and baseball teams.[18]

While obviously a matter of coincidence, Miami University certainly produced a string of subsequently outstanding coaches in these years. First came Earl "Red" Blaik (class of '18), who would later be an outstanding football coach at Dartmouth College and, most famously, at West Point. In 1928, Wilbur "Weeb" Eubank graduated from Miami and subsequently coached National Football League championship teams in Baltimore in 1958 and 1959 and with the New York Jets in 1969. (Eubank was one of the few head coaches to win NFL championships with two different teams.) Paul Brown, many times a professional football championship coach, graduated from Miami in 1930. And then there was Walter Alston, class of '35. In 1960, the *Cincinnati Enquirer* noted this string of successes with a clear note of beaming regional pride. Soon thereafter, Miami U. would send out a string of other outstanding football coaches. Among them were Sid Gillman of the Rams and the Chargers, Ara Parseghian of Notre Dame, Paul Dietzel of Army, Stuart Holcomb of Purdue, Johnny Pont of Indiana, and Bo Schembechler of Michigan. Alston's career lasted the longest, and, as a baseball manager of course, he would win the most games.[19]

After graduating from Miami, Alston continued to play for some baseball teams in the local county leagues of Southwest Ohio, usually with his father and brother-in-law. During his student days at Miami in 1930, Alston had also married his high school girlfriend, Lela Alexander. The marriage would last a lifetime. They would have one daughter, Doris LaVerne, born on Wednesday morning, December 31, 1930.[20] Alston knew his teaching post was critical for him in establishing a stable livelihood and support for his new family. He stuck with the high school teaching and would not give it up until 1947, only then because his managing duties in baseball had grown too time-consuming for him to do the high school teaching and coaching well enough to suit him.

While Alston had a thoroughly settled, stable world for himself and his family in rural Ohio, the world of professional baseball loomed for him, albeit faintly. Scouts in the St. Louis Cardinals' organization had taken notice of Alston's playing, both at Miami and on various Butler County teams. In 1935, Frank Rickey, brother of Cardinals general manager Branch Rickey, offered him a contract to play in their burgeoning farm system.[21] The administrators of the various school systems where Alston would teach and coach would always be generously flexible with him. They allowed him to leave his teaching and coaching duties several weeks before the end of the school year to begin the baseball season with a professional ball club, as well as to return late in the summer in case any end-of-season games ran into the start of fall classes. With this fortunate flexibility available to him, Alston kept his teaching job and signed to play ball with the Cardinals' organization in 1935.

2

Mr. Rickey Had an Eye
for Talent

When Alston signed with the Cardinals, he boarded a bus in Richmond, Indiana (not too far from Darrtown) and headed to St. Louis. When he reported to the Cardinals' main office, they were not sure where to place him. He spent a full week in St. Louis nervously awaiting his assignment. Finally, he was sent to play in Greenwood, Mississippi, in the East Dixie League, Class C. The pay was all of $125 a month. Upon signing Alston, Frank Rickey firmly told him that the monthly figure was $25 more than average. Alston recalled, "I didn't ask anything else; I just reached for the pen."[1]

Greenwood, Mississippi, was hardly a big-time venue, but Alston knew that virtually anyone who dreamt of making it to the big leagues had to start at such a lowly station. His attitude in going to play ball in Mississippi was anything but begrudging. Naturally, he missed his home life in Ohio. (He wrote his wife regularly, of course, but with his wife then living in Oxford, Ohio, he naively addressed his letters to "Oxford," unaware there was also an Oxford, Mississippi. In an era long before zip codes, this was more than a bit confusing to the postal service. Nonetheless, his letters ultimately found their location.) Baseball was in young Alston's dreams, and his family and friends were all in favor of him seeing how well he could perform. The little extra money beyond his teacher's salary, which usually ran about $1,350 a year, was also quite helpful to his family.[2]

In the 1935 season in Greenwood, Alston mainly played third base. His manager there was Clay Hopper. Hopper was a native of Greenwood. Long after the 1935 season in Mississippi had passed, Alston would cross paths with Hopper in the Brooklyn Dodgers' organization. In the late 1940s, Hopper and Alston would each manage triple-A clubs in Montreal and in St. Paul, Minnesota, under Branch Rickey's Dodgers. (In Montreal, Hopper would famously be the Royals' manager when

Rickey sent Jackie Robinson to play there in 1946.) Down in Greenwood, Alston played well. Reporters noted a few miscues at third base, but his hitting was strong. His batting average was an impressive .326. The Greenwood Chiefs finished only in fifth place (of eight teams), but some of the players showed promise. Besides Alston, three other players on the team would crack the majors. Two had very brief stints. Pitcher Carlos Moore had appeared in four games with the Washington Senators back in 1930. Tom Sunkel, also a pitcher, put in a few appearances with the Cardinals, Giants, and Dodgers, mainly during major league baseball's talent-lean World War II years. Catcher/first baseman Bob Scheffing later played eight seasons in the National League, mainly with the Cubs (in 1948 he batted .300). In Greenwood, Alston's .326 led the team.[3] That was good enough for the Cardinals to keep him for the following season. In addition to sticking with the Cardinals' system, Alston was happy to find the site of his new club, while still Class C, much closer to home. His new team, the Red Birds, was in Huntington, West Virginia, in the Mid-Atlantic League.[4]

In Huntington in 1936, two things of significance would come forth for Alston. One involved a specific game event, the other a seasonal matter. On May 27, in a long game against Portsmouth, Ohio, Alston struck out in each of his first five times at bat. One would naturally think that various officials in the Cardinals organization would take the news of such a performance as a signal that this young player was not worthy of further attention. What gained notice, however, was something quite different. In his next at-bat in the 16th inning, Alston stepped up and stroked a triple, touching off a four-hit, four-run rally that won the game. Local reporters noted the positive point that, despite the successive strikeouts, this young lad never let himself get down and simply resign himself to the fact that he was just having a bad day. Indeed, Alston quickly gained that sort of reputation—always upbeat, never alibiing and genuinely encouraging of himself and his teammates. Back in St. Louis, club president Branch Rickey liked to read and hear reports of this sort of character. At the time, Alston knew nothing about how any such knowledge could work its way "upstairs," but Rickey was keeping up with all the details within his vast organization. Young Alston's strengths and weaknesses were among the many things he noted.[5]

In the 1936 season in West Virginia, and of much more immediate significance for Alston, now playing first base, was the fact that he batted .326 and cracked 35 home runs. Many of his doubles and home runs were also timely game-winners for the Red Birds. In one game on June 2, he hit two singles, a double, and two triples. His home run mark of 35 led not only the team but the entire Mid-Atlantic League. He had started the season batting sixth; by mid-season he was a fixture at clean-up.[6] With this strong record at the plate, after the minor league season was over, the Cardinals brought young Alston all the way up to St. Louis. Along with several other minor leaguers who showed some promise, Alston spent the last three weeks of the 1936 season with the Cardinals. "Darrtown is justly proud," proclaimed one Ohio paper. "His many friends here wish him continued success."[7]

The famous 1930s "Gas House Gang" St. Louis Cardinals were a power in the National League. They had most recently won the World Series in 1934, and they were always contenders. Fresh out of the minors from West Virginia, young Alston found himself up with the big boys, taking batting and fielding practice with the likes of Frankie Frisch, Dizzy Dean, Leo Durocher, Pepper Martin, and Joe Medwick. It was heady stuff for a young man in only his second professional season. He would room with another rookie, Don Gutteridge, who, as it turned out, would stick in the majors, lasting a full 12 seasons with the Cardinals, Browns, and Red Sox.[8]

Back in his school days in Ohio, Alston had played a variety of positions, including a lot of shortstop and third base. But in the faster company of professional players, and with his 6'2", 210-pound frame, he had settled into playing first base, despite being right-handed. With the 1936 St. Louis Cardinals, unfortunately, the position of first base was a little crowded. The Cardinals had started the season with Jimmy "Ripper" Collins at first base. Collins had hit .313 in 1935. But in May of 1936, he fell into a batting slump, and manager Frankie Frisch decided to bench him in favor of a highly prized rookie named Johnny Mize. Mize played well and remained a fixture in the Cards' lineup for the rest of the season, with Collins doing a lot of pinch-hitting and remaining ready to come off the bench. The presence of Mize and Collins left little room for a youngster like Alston, and for those three weeks of September, he simply rode the bench and took practice with the gang; sometimes he even pitched batting practice. As Alston would recall: "I sat, and sat, and sat." Once, while playing third base in practice with Joe Medwick up, Alston recalled: "Medwick tied into one. I leaped up over my head and back-handed the ball." Afterwards, Medwick trotted past him and snarled: "What are you trying to do? Show me up?" Alston said he "loved every minute of that September. ... You remember the good guys, the good things that happened to you. You also remember the blasts you've taken from the stars."[9] Medwick was the source of one verbal strafing. (Dizzy Dean would later provide another.)

Beyond the presence of Collins and Mize, what kept Alston further tied to the St. Louis bench that September concerned that year's

National League pennant race, more specifically, the first division race. By mid–September of 1936, the New York Giants had a reasonably good lock on the pennant (they would win it by five games). Still, even with the Giants all but mathematically out of reach, the question of who would finish second, third, or fourth place was still up for grabs, and to the players that was extremely important. It meant not just a matter of pride but money. In the World Series, it was not only the winning and losing teams that shared in the game receipts. The players of the second-, third-, and fourth-place teams in each league received some World Series money too. This was the basis of the old baseball term: "finishing in the money." (In order not to encourage any hint of corruption and money padding, the players would share only in the receipts from the Series' first four games; the rest stayed with the teams' owners.) The amounts of cash at stake may not have been too large. Indeed, back then the individual player's share for the fourth-place team of the losing league was often under $75. For Depression-era players, however, still often making such paltry sums as $2,500 a season (sometimes even less), any post-season bonus of even 80 bucks meant a great deal, especially as it usually came in late October/early November just as the Christmas season was approaching. (Even as late as 1940, in the season after his rookie year in Boston in which he led the AL in RBI, Ted Williams made all of $25,000, and among the team owners, the Red Sox' Tom Yawkey had a reputation for generosity!)

In September of 1936, the Cardinals were in a fight for first-division shares of that fall's World Series money with Chicago and Pittsburgh. As a second-place finish would garner more money than a third, and a third more than fourth, there was every practical reason, as well as the simple principle of athletic pride, for the teams to play every game hard and not give away a thing, such as may occur by giving playing opportunities to some untested rookies late in the season. Had Alston come up with such a lowly NL team of that era as the Phillies or the Braves, he may have been given more opportunities. But with the Cardinals fighting hard for extra cash, Alston spent every game that September sitting on the bench, merely hoping some opportunity would come.

Then came a *Field of Dreams* moment for Alston. In the famous 1989 film, Archibald Wright "Moonlight" Graham (played by Burt Lancaster) began his famous reminiscence: "It was the last game of the season...." That was the very situation for young Alston. The Cardinals' last game of 1936 was against the Cubs, and it had real financial meaning for all the players. As the two Western-most teams in the old eight-team NL circuit, the Cardinals and Cubs had always maintained a keen rivalry. Even when one club was weak, the rivalry was still present, and when they were both pennant contenders, as was often the case throughout the 1930s and 1940s, the clashes could be quite heated. From 1926 to 1946, indeed, the Cardinals would win the pennant nine times, the Cubs five, and throughout those years, the two were regularly among the top teams in the league. This was certainly the case in 1936, all the way down to the final game of the season. In the final week, with the Giants having clinched the pennant, the second-place Cardinals were three games up on the Cubs, and the last three games pitted them against one another. The Cubs took the first two games, so on the final day a Cubs win would tie them with the Cardinals for second place, five games behind the Giants. A tie versus a second/third place standing would definitely affect the players' shares of World Series money. Thus, on that late September afternoon, both teams were very much in earnest. It was about pride, about rivalry, *and* about money.

As usual, Johnny Mize started the game for the Cardinals at first base. By the bottom of the sixth inning, the Cubs had taken a commanding lead. Dizzy Dean was pitching for the Cardinals. Dean had won 24 games that season, but this was not his day, and it would be his 13th loss in his last good season of pitching. (It was in the All-Star Game of the next season when Dean sustained the toe injury that ruined his career.) In the bottom of the sixth inning, the Cards were down. Johnny Mize was batting, and from the batter's box he apparently made some "undiplomatic" comments to the plate umpire about the accuracy of his ball and strike calls. No reporter recorded for posterity what exactly Mize proclaimed to the umpire. It was likely unprintable. Whatever the specifics, and after a few more comments, the umpire angrily tossed him out of the game. As it happened, a few innings earlier, Manager Frisch had already used Rip Collins as a pinch-hitter, so he was unavailable. Frisch inserted himself to complete Mize's at-bat. At the bottom of the inning, Frisch had no choice but to send in young Alston to play first base. Excited, but nervous, young Alston ran out, took his position, and promptly botched catching a pop-up. An already frustrated Dizzy Dean let him have it in front of everyone. From there, Alston steadied in the field and made no more errors. In the 9th inning, he actually came up to bat. Lon Warneke was pitching for the Cubs. So, just like the fictional "Moonlight" Graham of *Field of Dreams*, young Alston played only on the last game of the season, but he also lived out the dream "Moonlight" Graham had of actually getting "to bat in the major leagues—just once." Alston stood in against Warneke; the first pitch was a called strike. On the next pitch, Alston connected with a hard liner. The ball flew towards the right field bleachers but faded just outside the foul pole. Next pitch: called strike three. Alston was out. The

Alston, pictured here in 1955, graduated from Miami University in 1935, where he was a standout on both the baseball and basketball teams and gained the notice of scouts in the St. Louis Cardinals' organization. He was signed in 1935. His quickly rising prominence led the Cardinals to bring Alston up to St. Louis for the last three weeks of the 1936 season. Under manager Frankie Frisch, Alston practiced every day with the boys of the famous "Gashouse Gang." Still, he never played an actual game until the last day of the season, against the Cubs. Alston promptly botched an infield pop fly. He got up to bat once and struck out. It would be his only appearance as a Major League ballplayer. He went back to the minors, not returning to the majors until 1954, as manager of the Brooklyn Dodgers (National Baseball Hall of Fame and Museum, Cooperstown, NY).

Cubs won and shared second place (and the second–third place money) with the Cardinals.[10]

Dizzy Dean's anger notwithstanding, no one on the Cardinals team or in the press affixed any blame on young Alston for the Cards' 6–3 final game loss to Chicago, especially since the Cubs had swept all three games to draw even with the Cardinals that final week in St. Louis. There certainly was anger in St. Louis, but the anger had many points of focus, the least of which was young Walter Alston. For Alston, nevertheless, one game, one error, and a strikeout hardly provided much of a basis for any future big-league hopes. Still, the following spring, Alston did receive an invitation to the St. Louis Cardinals' training camp.

(Each season, the Ohio high schools where Alston taught and coached gave him permission to leave his teaching early, a matter for which he always expressed sincere gratitude; later he always saw to it that many of the local sports programs in the various Ohio counties where he'd taught were well funded.) Alston had some hopes with the Cardinals in 1937, as they had traded Rip Collins to the Cubs in the off-season—for pitcher Lon Warneke, as it happened. (Cardinals pitcher Paul Dean, Dizzy's brother, was having arm troubles after an injury. That was why they gave up Collins, plus a journeyman pitcher named LeRoy Parmelee, for Warneke.) Meanwhile, they held onto Johnny Mize, of course. While dealing away Collins, St. Louis did trade for Dick Siebert, a young first baseman from the Brooklyn Dodgers. The first base position with the Cardinals thus remained crowded, and young Alston did not stick. One local paper also reported that Alston had come to camp "very much overweight," but the *avoirdupois* was not the central issue.[11] Frankie Frisch and Branch Rickey believed Alston needed more seasoning in the minors. Only years later Alston would learn that "the die was cast early insofar as my playing career was concerned." Branch Rickey had pretty much made up his mind that Alston would never make it to the majors as a player.[12]

While St. Louis did not keep him, the organization did promote Alston to a higher-level farm club than Huntington, West Virginia. They assigned Alston to the Rochester Red Wings of the International League, the Cardinals' top farm team. There, unfortunately, he did not make quite the splash for which he had hoped. As pre-season training was ending and the Red Wings' lineup was emerging, Alston did secure the starting position at first base. As one reporter declared: "Walter Alston, first sacker, and Martin Marion, shortstop, are the youngsters with the Red Wings in the field." Marion would do well, Alston less so. The same reporter described Alston as "an untrained rookie from Huntington in the Mid-Atlantic League … [who] lacks fielding polish and is puzzled by class AAA pitching."[13] Alston's ability to handle higher-level pitching would indeed always prove problematic, just as Rickey had reckoned. While he had hit .326 in both Greenwood and in Huntington, his average with Rochester fell to a mediocre .246. He could get around on most fastballs he saw, but a good curveball would usually get the better of him.

In mid-season, Alston found himself switched to the Houston Buffaloes of the Texas League, still a high level in the minors, but slightly down from Rochester. (On the same team were Johnny Keane and Herman Franks, two future National League managers with whom he would later compete.) When Alston arrived in early July, the Houston Buffaloes were mired in last place. Amidst such a demoralized state, Houston's player/manager, first baseman Johnny Watwood, had asked club president Fred Ankerman to release him from managerial duties. They obliged Watwood and, with St. Louis's cooperation, sent him to Rochester. Houston, in turn, picked up Alston to fill in at first base, and they signed a new manager, Ira Smith, who had been pitching in Rochester but who had previously managed Houston in 1936.

In Houston, Alston played no managerial role, of course, but he was filling the conspicuous spot in the lineup where the manager had been. A local reporter immediately noted how the "new Houston player had a rough introduction to the Texas League.... He went down swinging on his first appearance at the plate, hit into a double play the next time up, and fanned again his third and last time up." In the second game of a doubleheader that July evening, "he walked once ... and was safe on an error ... but still did not pick up a hit." With but a slight hint of encouragement, the reporter added, "however, he is a big boy with a good record behind him and will probably make Houston a fair performance. He hardly can be expected to fill John Watwood's shoes."[14]

In both Rochester and Houston, Alston held onto the belief that if he could do well, he could possibly get back to St. Louis. This would not happen. While Alston's .246 average in Rochester did not help his cause, his mere mark of .212 in Houston served him even less. Texas papers noted a few good days, including one in early September in which he set a Texas League mark with three sacrifices in one game. In Texas, Alston proved to be, as one reporter panned, but "a fair juvenile first baseman."[15] All of Alston's hopes which had risen after leading the Mid-Atlantic League in home runs in 1936, and after the proverbial "cup of coffee" with the Cardinals, now faded. All prospects for the majors now looked dim. Rickey had already determined so, but Alston did not quit. The extra cash was an important addition to his $1,350 annual teacher's salary. More than that, baseball was in his blood.

In 1938 Alston found himself sent back down to the same Mid-Atlantic League where he had played in 1936. St. Louis had actually first assigned him a team in Asheville, North Carolina, in the Piedmont League. But the Cardinals switched the assignment back to the Mid-Atlantic. Since 1937, the Cards' Huntington Red Birds had left West Virginia. Their new home was in Portsmouth, Ohio, straight south of Columbus on the Ohio River. This was nice for Alston as it was even closer to his Butler County home. He finished his teaching and coaching duties in New Madison and reported to Portsmouth in April.[16] As in 1936, Alston played well. So did the Portsmouth team, paced especially by a 20-year-old named George "Whitey" Kurowski, who led the league in hitting with a mark of .386. Alston hit .311 and pounded out 28 home runs. By one game, Portsmouth edged the Canton Terriers (a Red Sox club) and took the regular season pennant, despite the effective pitching (22–7) of Canton's young star and future Boston hurler, Tex Hughson. Then came a four-team league playoff series. Portsmouth won the first round, and, after falling behind three games to one, Portsmouth beat the New York Yankees' team in Akron to win the league's post-season playoffs. In the seventh game, Alston himself hit a walk-off home run to win the title. With the victory and the championship, the Portsmouth players earned extra cash. As in the majors, playoffs yielded some bonus money in minor leagues. For the Portsmouth Red Birds, their take amounted to a whopping $700 (and this was for the whole team)![17]

While the cash per player was minimal, the fans of Portsmouth was ecstatic about their championship season. One local reporter held that "Walter Alston looked just as good on first base as Johnny Mize if you want our word for it." (No one did.) Alston received some votes for the league's Most Valuable Player award; the award went to C. Frank Silvanic of the Akron Yankees, Canton's Tex Hughson placing second in the voting. Reviewing the town's 1938 championship season, Portsmouth Manager Benny Borgmann wrote a glowing article in the local newspaper, praising both the team and the fans in the community. Whitey Kurowski, Borgmann predicted, was definitely going to the majors "unless his arm proves to be his downfall." (Kurowski would indeed end up with St. Louis and do well.) Borgmann noted further: "I'd like also to say something about Walter Alston. His fielding and batting records speak for themselves. But what is not generally known is the fine influence Walter has on the men who play with him. I have yet to hear an alibi from him. He makes no excuses, asks no quarter and gives his best at all times." Borgmann used Alston in many positions that season. He even pitched in one game. Throughout, Alston displayed unflagging good spirit, and it rubbed off on the rest of the team. Although Alston did not know it at the time, Branch Rickey received all such reports. Benny Borgmann would himself remain a big fan of Alston all through the years after Alston rose to the majors and managed the Dodgers. The one exception came in 1965, when Borgmann greeted Alston at Metropolitan Stadium in Minneapolis just before the first game of the Dodgers–Twins World Series. (This was the famous game when Sandy Koufax would not pitch on *Yom Kippur*.) There Borgmann happily admitted to Alston that, for the first time, he'd be rooting against him. (The 66-year-old Borgmann then worked as a scout for the Twins.)[18]

Beyond Borgmann's praise, the mark Alston made on Portsmouth in 1938 would reveal itself in other ways too. After the 1940 season, the Portsmouth team would relocate to Springfield, Ohio, and during World War II the entire Mid-Atlantic League would fold. By 1948, organized baseball had thus long departed from Portsmouth, but in 1948 a new Ohio-Indiana League (Class D) would form, with Portsmouth again securing a team, this time in the Philadelphia A's organization. This was still many years before Alston had achieved fame among the general baseball public, yet here, trying to promote the new team and induce ticket sales among local fans, a Portsmouth sportswriter named Pete Minego urged that people "should be remindful of the days when Walter Alston, Whitey Kurowski [by then a well-known player with the Cardinals] and others won the Mid-Atlantic pennant in 1938. Remember those happy days?" he asked; "they're back again. [So come out to the ball park, ...]" The new team would last in Portsmouth but three seasons (the League for but one more season after that), but the fact that the still unknown Walter Alston served a touchstone of happy memories for a promotion-minded Ohio sportswriter speaks to the appeal that young Alston's qualities and character had made on a team and a community.[19]

After the successful 1938 season, Alston quickly returned to New Madison for another year of coaching, wood shop, and science teaching. (Manager Borgmann needed a job too, as did everyone in the minors. Borgmann moved to Hawthorne, New Jersey, to work in a plant that made fountain pens; this had at least one link to baseball, as the company made pens that looked like mini-baseball bats, manufacturing them to celebrate the game's 100th anniversary in 1939.) In the spring of 1939, Alston was again to report to Portsmouth, but he did not arrive until late in April. He had his teaching and coaching duties to which to attend. Additionally, that month his family home in New Madison, Ohio, had been quarantined for scarlet fever! Even the postman would not go there, so Alston could not receive or mail in his contract.[20] Those problems would work themselves out, and Alston eventually reported.

He started the season at Portsmouth, but after two games the Cardinals organization decided once more to shift Alston up a bit in the minor league ranks. He played the season in Columbus, Georgia. There he hit .323. In one game he drove in drove in four runs, and at various junctures in the season he was leading the league in hitting. Branch Rickey wanted to keep Alston at the higher-level team in Georgia for the 1940 season, but having always appreciated the Board of Education in his Ohio school district letting him leave his teaching/coaching duties a few weeks earlier than the end of school, Alston did not want to impose upon them any further. Hoping to place Alston in Georgia, Rickey wanted him to head down to spring training much earlier in the year. At Portsmouth, Alston would make less money, but he preferred to hold onto his teaching and coaching job in Ohio. Alston's wife, Leila, also had relatives in Portsmouth. As the Cardinals did not outright own their affiliated minor league teams, Rickey often had to negotiate such personnel matters. Had Rickey held stronger hopes for Alston rising to the level of major league play, he may have insisted more strongly on the "move up" to Columbus, Georgia. As it was, he acceded to Alston's preference to stay in Portsmouth, and the club and the fans were happy to have him back. The decision to stay in Portsmouth seemed a minor decision at the time, but as the 1940 season unfolded, it would prove highly significant.[21]

In 1940, Alston again played well for Portsmouth, but that spring the team proved rather weak. By mid–June, the Red Birds' record stood at a paltry 17–27 (.386), and they floundered in last place. Amidst the dismal times, the local paper still praised Alston; "the genial first baseman," they called him. On June 11, Alston hit for the cycle, his home run being a grand slam, to boot. The next day's sports headline simply read: "It's that man again."

As it happened, Branch Rickey came to town that very week amidst a mid-season inspection of his farm clubs (with their terrible salaries, some preferred to call the string of clubs "Branch Rickey's chain gang"). Whether it was the immediate news about Alston's prowess, the otherwise lackluster play of the team under second baseman/manager Fred "Dutch" Dorman, or remembered bits from Alston's prior seasons, Rickey made a move, one that would be of major significance in the life of Walter Alston. On June 23, Rickey fired Dorman and the next day named Walter Alston player/manager of the Portsmouth Red Birds. A newspaper in Dayton, Ohio, noted, "When Rickey started to help Portsmouth, he wasn't fooling." By the end of June, Portsmouth reporters noted how "Alston helps give the boys renewed hustle" and how the team looked "revamped and revived [as it] continues to ramble along victory highway." While some of the praise in the Portsmouth papers can be discounted as mere hometown hype, reporters from other cities in the league were also enthusiastically noting much the same about the leadership of young Manager Alston. When Alston came through with a single with the bases loaded in the bottom of the ninth to beat Youngstown, a Massillon, Ohio, reporter praised: "As usual, Manager Alston of the ... Red Birds had what it took in the pinches."[22]

Branch Rickey appeared to have found someone who could run a team and create an atmosphere in which everyone wanted to do his very best. Alston was always good to his players, and as player/manager he immediately showed this in Portsmouth. Knowing how low everyone's salaries were, he and his wife let two young players—Joe Schmidt and Hank Zajae—board at the house they rented on Sunshine Avenue. Alston conceded that he would be happy to let more of his men stay with him, but there was simply no more room. On the ballfield, Alston's own hustle was always in evidence too. "We'll have to admit," enthused a Portsmouth reporter, "that Wally Alston's our favorite player. He's a real gentleman, a fine player, and what a slugger! ... The secret of Alston's success," the reporter added, "is to be found in the little things, such as his eagerness to run out on a field with a jacket for the pitcher who gets on base. Spirit like that makes ball players, but, more importantly, it makes men!"

On July 22, Alston and several of his players volunteered to run a clinic for boys in the town of Massillon, instructing them in pitching, fielding, and batting. Alston brought a genuine spirit to the team and to many local communities, with the results buoying everyone involved. He was accustomed to this sort of community spirit of pulling together. He grew up with it in Darrtown, so it manifested in him in a completely natural way without any sense of mere posturing. As Don Drysdale would later comment: "If you can't play for Walter Alston, you can't play for anybody." Signs of that spirit were in evidence in his very first months at the helm in Portsmouth.[23]

While Alston's calm, upbeat nature worked its ways with his players, Alston's own play was strong as well and further helped lift the team. In August, he was hitting .325. He led the league in home runs with 29 and had 113 RBI. In June, he hit two winning home runs to sweep a doubleheader over Dayton. In August, Alston "cinched the game by slamming ... a home run far over the center field wall, and his boys mobbed him." In late July, Alston was pitching batting practice and was hit in the neck by a line drive. He badly bruised a muscle, and no one would have begrudged him taking the day off. He insisted on playing anyway. In another July game, Alston conned a Youngstown pitcher into balking in a run for Portsmouth. From his third base coaching box, with a runner on third, Alston yelled, "Wait a minute!" just as the pitcher was in his wind-up. Not the best sportsmanship, some may have said, but it worked; Portsmouth won the game. (Alston recalled the incident to have occurred against Canton, and he said the pitcher was Cliff Alexander, his own brother-in-law! Alexander was indeed the pitcher, but, as the reporters of the day affirmed, the game was with Youngstown.) In a bad loss to Dayton one day (Dayton scored 11 runs in one inning), Alston showed another level of managerial wisdom, as he took much of the pressure and shame off the rest of the team by inserting himself as pitcher for the last two innings. Dayton cruised to a 17 to 2 win, but the Portsmouth players felt more of a chuckle than shame from it.[24]

Many injuries plagued Portsmouth that summer. "Pitchers [were] in the outfield, outfielders in the infield, and infielders pitching and catching." One reporter noted that the "team got plenty of breaks—all bad." Throughout the struggles, no one could fault the unflagging spirit in Portsmouth's play under Alston. In August one weekend, they swept the first-place Akron Yankees, and the whole town rejoiced. Throughout the minor league baseball world of the late 1930s, New York Yankees farm clubs were hated nearly as much as the parent club. The rich and powerful Bronx Bombers aroused such emotions everywhere. Akron would win the pennant, but under Alston, Portsmouth, their many injuries notwithstanding, would play just above .500 ball that summer.[25] Branch Rickey had spotted a bit of managerial talent in his system.

In 1941, the Portsmouth team moved to the larger community of Springfield, Ohio, just west of Columbus. There they maintained ties with Rickey and the Cardinals. The owners of the new Springfield team made some inquiries about Alston. Executive Secretary Robert M. Ireland wrote to Mid-Atlantic League President Elmer Daily: "Rickey ... has secured Walter Alston as a playing manager for us. No contract has yet been signed, but he [Rickey] told me that everything has been arranged. What do you know about this fellow?" Daily wrote back: "I am of the opinion that Mr. Rickey sent you a good man in Walter Alston. He is a long-distance hitter, and he is a grand type of fellow. He should fit into your picture fine."[26]

Alston was able to switch his teaching position from New Madison to Lewiston, in Logan County, near the town of Springfield. In New Madison, Alston had enjoyed a good relationship with the local school superintendent. Alston admitted taking up golf to help maintain good relations with the superintendent. Alston and he would partner against various other pairs of players at the local club. They were regular winners in various "Nassau" wagers. Years later, he admitted to a gathering in Middletown, Ohio, with a nod and a smile: "That made for a nice situation."[27] He did not need to play golf in Lewiston; the school administrators there would also be cooperative with Alston's need to leave a bit earlier than the end of the spring term for his professional baseball duties. With the Springfield owners' approval, Rickey fully contracted Alston to manage, and in his first full season of managing Alston pulled the Red Birds out of the cellar into fourth place and led them to a winning season, 69–57. Alston himself led the league in runs scored with 88, and a consensus of league reporters selected him as the Mid-Atlantic

League All-Star first baseman. The owners in Springfield were pleased. Mr. and Mrs. Alston were pleased too; for the first time in his baseball career, Alston made $2,000![28] Rickey was content too, but, of course, in the fall of 1941 bigger events were beginning to preoccupy baseball, as well as the whole country.

In 1942, Alston would have another season managing in Springfield, but the league cut itself from eight to six teams; Akron and Youngstown folded. The War's employment pressures mounted, and the six teams limped through the season. Alston led the league in home runs and RBI. One of his home runs was one of the few that ever cleared the center field barrier in Springfield's Norton Street Stadium. He hit .310 and compiled a pitching record of 1–0, hurling 21 innings. When a newspaper in Charleston, West Virginia, one of the six sites remaining in the league, "failed to put Walt Alston on their all-star team," a Portsmouth writer, still reflecting the community's enthusiasm for Alston, chided: "How cum, boys?"[29] The local popularity of Alston was still in evidence, but in the summer of 1942, bigger issues loomed. With the conclusion of the 1942 season, the entire Mid-Atlantic League folded.

Back in St. Louis, meanwhile, Branch Rickey had struck a deal that involved Larry MacPhail, the occasionally brilliant, always zany, bi-polar, alcoholic general manager of the Brooklyn Dodgers. With the cooperation of the Dodgers' board of directors, Rickey agreed to take over the running of the organization while MacPhail enlisted in the Army. With Rickey gone from St. Louis, Alston's ties to him appeared to be over. That would change a few years later. With the war, Alston himself sought enlistment but failed the Army physical. Science teachers were exempt from the draft, but Alston attempted to enlist nonetheless. A knee injury in college had left him unable to execute the Army's required squats, the successful completion of which was necessary for the service.[30] Meanwhile, President Roosevelt wanted "a little baseball" to continue for the sake of domestic spirits and morale during the war and everyone's longer work hours. Always needing a little extra money for his family, Alston thus had the opportunity to continue to play professional baseball as good players were in very short supply. (Only with a slight degree of facetiousness, Ty Cobb, then age 57, went on record in early 1944, saying he would play if any team in the majors felt they needed him.[31]) Alston maintained his school teaching and coaching, and he continued to play ball.

With the level of talented ball players so greatly thinned by 1943, the Cardinals again moved Alston to a higher league. They first had him set to go to Columbus, Ohio, in the American Association. Then, just before the season began, they dealt him back to their top farm club in

Rochester, New York, where he had played in 1937. As a coincidence, Rochester (and Columbus) took their pre-season training in Portsmouth, Ohio. (The parent St. Louis Cardinals trained in Cairo, Illinois, with wartime restrictions disallowing any lengthy travel. Even the great New York Yankees had to train in the cold of New Jersey.) Moving to a higher league as a player, however, Alston's career as a manager appeared to be over. With Rochester in the International League, Alston would play under former Cardinals star John Leonard "Pepper" Martin. Like Rickey, Pepper Martin came quickly to appreciate Alston's usefulness, and he had Alston do some of the first and third base coaching.[32]

In Rochester, Alston played reasonably well for Martin. He was part of what one reporter called the Red Wings' "potent punch." Only one player on the Red Wings had more home runs that Alston that year. As in prior seasons at the higher minor league levels, Alston's batting average would drop significantly. He was facing a better brand of pitching and could not handle it very well. Curve balls were still a puzzle. At one point in June, Alston was hitting .250. That was his highest mark of the season. His final average was .240. (A 20-year-old shortstop named Al "Red" Schoendienst would lead Rochester, and the entire league that season, with a mark of .337.) While Alston's play was merely adequate, Pepper Martin nonetheless noted Alston's general usefulness to the team. In addition to doing some coaching at first and third, amidst injuries to several teammates, Martin asked Alston to fill in at third base, making a point of noting to the local papers how "He [Alston] is taking an unmerciful riding out there, and he is doing it all as a favor to me. ... He's playing out of position, not because he wants to but because I asked him to take the rap and play there for me." Martin went on to extol Alston: "He belongs on our club if for nothing more than his ability to get up off the bench cold and get a hit when it is sadly needed. ... He's one of the best pinch hitters in our league."[33]

Again, Alston showed his selfless willingness to do all he could for his team, but now, at the age of 31, there appeared no possibility of him going too terribly far as a player once the Spartan context of wartime play was over. Meanwhile, managerial posts also appeared unavailable. Alston finished the 1943 season. The Toronto Maple Leafs (a Pittsburgh Pirates club) won the IL pennant. Rochester finished a distant fifth, out of post-season play.[34] Alston went back home to teach in Ohio, and in April 1944 he reported to Rochester again.

Early in the 1944 season, after playing in only 13 games, and getting but three hits in 19 at-bats (.158), Alston hurt his back while sliding. Manager Pepper Martin, now 40, had been called back to play for St. Louis. Rochester's new manager was Ken Penner, a journeyman minor league pitcher who had played in the majors but a few games with the Indians and the Cubs. In his previous year of managing in Sacramento, California, his team's record was 41–114. A Rochester reporter sarcastically noted that Penner had "lost ONLY 114 games [emphasis his]" in 1943 and had never won a pennant in his seven years of managing. Amidst the pressures and long hours of wartime work, baseball was supposed to be an upbeat break for the fans, but some sports reporters could still be caustic in their coverage. Penner would do only a little better in Rochester: 71–82. In May, young Red Schoendienst was drafted into the Army. That proved a huge loss. With Schoendienst, Rochester had been in second place; without him they quickly fell to seventh. Amidst this dismal season in Rochester, Penner showed little appreciation or concern for Alston, and with Alston's back injury, Penner and Rochester released him.[35]

With his release from Rochester in July, Alston's ten-year association with the Cardinals organization was over, and his professional baseball career, such as it was, appeared to be over as well. It was, Alston recalled, "the nadir of my whole career—the very darkest day of my life. ... I must believe that the big-league ballplayers ... couldn't possibly get as low spiritually as I was the day I got the word in Rochester. I was sure I had blown my whole baseball career." It had been a good run, but Alston had no choice but to go back to Ohio. He prepared for a new school year of teaching science, shop, coaching baseball and basketball, and living the small-town Ohio life with his friends and family.

One week later came a phone call; more specifically a verbal message came from a friend about a series of calls that had come into the local general store in Darrtown (Vic Wycoff's grocery). Alston did not have a phone. The message via the general store was for him to call Mr. Branch Rickey in Brooklyn. Rickey had indeed taken note of Alston's work managing in Portsmouth and Springfield. He had long written Alston off as a possible big-league player, but Rickey saw managerial talent, and he decided to offer Alston a chance—to manage one of his low-level Brooklyn farm clubs in Trenton, New Jersey, the Trenton Packers. His baseball career had come back to life. Rickey told Alston to report to Trenton straight away, adding emphatically: "Get a _____ telephone!" Alston took the advice. The next time Alston received such a phone call from Brooklyn was in October of 1953, when he was called up from Montreal to manage the Dodgers. By this time, he had installed a phone in every room in his house. Mrs. Alston thought it a bit excessive, but Alston knew it was usually best to pay full heed to any dictum from Branch Rickey.[36]

In Trenton, Alston found the Packers club mired deep in the cellar of the six-team Interstate League. (The six teams were in Allentown, York, and Lancaster, Pennsylvania, Wilmington, Delaware, Hagerstown, Maryland, and Trenton.) Late that July, a local newspaper sarcastically scowled that the "Punchless Packers Continue [their] Furious Grip on [the] Cellar Seat." When Alston took over managing, Trenton's record stood at 30–56.[37] Alston had a major task of revitalization on his hands. He had an added personal incentive, as Dutch Dorman, the man he'd displaced as manager in Portsmouth, Ohio, back in 1940, was now managing the Wilmington Blue Rocks. At Trenton, Alston would manage and play first base, but aside from the removal of the previous first baseman, Jack Schotike, who was optioned to Olean, Pennsylvania, of the Pony League, the Trenton team remained the same. (No one on that Trenton squad ever rose to any major league significance.) With the same sad personnel at whom the local reporters had been scoffing through July, Alston took them to six wins in their first eight games. Suddenly these same sarcastic scribes were writing of the "revitalized Packers."[38]

Alston certainly seemed to make a huge difference. His bat was impressive. In his first two weeks, he hit .667. In the short season he had with Trenton, Alston would hit .350. Twice in August he belted two home runs. Most noteworthy to Rickey, with Alston in charge in those last weeks of the 1944 season, this same lousy Trenton team compiled a record of 31–18 (.633). At the end of August, the Trenton community and various local businesses expressed their delight. Trenton papers noted, "the superlative manner in which they have been playing lately." On September 1, the city happily hosted a "Walter Alston Night" at Trenton's Dunn Field, "to give Alston a night of felicitation and gifts." Alston received vouchers from local stores and several payments, in the form of War Bonds of course. "Manager Alston," wrote one Trenton scribe, "is one of the leading hitters of the league and has brought the Packers from a losing streak to one of the most feared clubs in the league." He "transformed the club," wrote another, "from a doormat to a serious threat to any and all opponents." He "has won the respect and admiration of Trenton fans. Those fans," a reporter concluded, "are unanimous in their hope that the husky first baseman will return."[39] He would.

The Trenton team would remain within the Brooklyn system, but in 1945, new local ownership took over. The principal figure here was Bill McKechnie, Jr., son of the famous Cincinnati Reds manager. McKechnie and his friends renamed the team the "Spartans." Wisely, they kept Alston at the helm, and there were certainly no objections here from Branch Rickey. Alston was able to make a similar arrangement with the Spartans as he had previously made with clubs in Ohio. He continued with his high school teaching through March and came to the Trenton team's training site in April. In Alston's absence, none other than former major league star George Sisler ran the team's training, which, given wartime travel restrictions, took place in New Jersey. As in 1943, the major league teams could not travel far that spring either. War restrictions had again kept the mighty New York Yankees training in Atlantic City, and with a desire to practice against anyone handy, the Yankees played lowly Trenton in an exhibition game that spring. In his major league career, managing against the touted Yankees in several World Series, Alston would famously face, and beat, both Casey Stengel and Ralph Houk. Beyond these two Yankees skippers, Alston squared off once against the great Joe McCarthy too, albeit in the pre- and not the post-season. In that spring game of 1945, McCarthy's Yanks would defeat Alston's Trenton squad, 15–2.[40]

Branch Rickey, pictured here in 1946, first signed Alston to the Cardinals in 1935. He soon realized Alston did not possess the requisite talents for the big leagues, but he also saw in Alston some of those elusive qualities needed for the successful managing of a ball club. In 1940, Rickey made young Alston player-manager of one of his Cardinals' minor league teams in Ohio. Alston took a team which had been floundering and quickly turned it into a contender. In 1944–1945, Alston again turned around a poorly performing club, managing a team in Trenton, New Jersey (National Baseball Hall of Fame and Museum, Cooperstown, NY).

As the 1945 season unfolded, the Spartans thrived under Alston. The team and the city endured the passing of President Roosevelt—his "death," wrote a Trenton reporter, "costs big league baseball its No. 1

fan." Three thousand gathered at Trenton's rail station as Roosevelt's train passed on its way from Washington, D.C., to Hyde Park, New York. Alston was there among them.[41] Soon thereafter, the winning of the war in Europe would elate everyone, and in Trenton the success of Alston's Spartans added a little extra merriment to the general euphoria. Under Alston, Trenton stayed above .500 all season and vied for second place with rival Wilmington. (Dutch Dorman was still in the league, but he was now managing in Hagerstown, Maryland.) The best team in the league that season was the Lancaster Red Roses. Led by a 17-year-old (hence not yet of draft age) leadoff hitting and second base fielding whiz named Nellie Fox, Lancaster was the class of the league that year. Young Fox was a sensation. He hit .314. (Alston hit .313.) Meanwhile, Alston held the Trenton team in contention all season. He played first base and led the league in fielding percentage. (Nellie Fox came in second to Alston on that score.[42])

Building on what he'd done in Portsmouth and Springfield, Alston learned all the details of management in Trenton. With war conditions, there was no room or money for any hiring of assistants, either on-field or administrative. Everything fell to Alston—field manager, traveling secretary, physical trainer, groundskeeper, batting practice pitcher, scout, sometimes bus driver, surrogate father/big brother, as well as playing first base and batting cleanup every day. Alston did it all, as he had in Portsmouth and Springfield. During the war, when Rickey wanted to have a camp/clinic for interested youngsters in New Jersey, hoping he could nudge some talented young players to keep baseball and Brooklyn in mind after their wartime duties were over, Alston supervised this clinic too.[43] Rickey was pleased. Trenton made the league playoffs that year, but they lost to Nellie Fox and the Lancaster Red Roses. Alston would win one back from Fox, but it would take 14 years for him to do it—in the 1959 World Series. In September 1945, Rickey sent Alston a nice telegram, congratulating him on the fine work he had done for him that year.[44]

At the end of the 1945 season, the Trenton Spartans were bought by the New York Giants organization.[45] Questions of what players they would keep and who would run the team in the next season were then out of the hands of Branch Rickey and the Brooklyn organization. The Trenton team had no players whom Rickey and the Dodgers felt possessed any potential talent for Brooklyn. But Rickey had a keen eye for talent in managers as well as in players, and there was certainly one member of the Trenton team he wanted to keep. This he would do. Rickey had big plans for 1946, and young Walter Alston would play a role in them. With his usual modest tone, Alston would later reflect:

"I have to say that the late Mr. Branch Rickey had quite an effect on my career."[46] In 1935, Rickey's Cardinals signed Alston to his first professional baseball contract. In 1940, Rickey gave Alston his first job as a manager. In 1944, he brought Alston, his baseball career seemingly over, back into the game. As a manager, Alston had confirmed Mr. Rickey's confidence every time. Alston would do this many more times as well.

3

Quiet Integration
in New Hampshire

With the war over, Branch Rickey had some major innovations in mind for his Dodgers, for baseball, and for the whole nation in 1946. As is well known, Rickey had signed Jackie Robinson, beginning "the Great Experiment" of racially integrating the National Pastime. For the 1946 season, Rickey placed Robinson with the Brooklyn organization's top farm club in Montreal. Rickey chose this site and community because he felt, as did others in the Dodgers' organization, that a Canadian city would be less resistant to racial integration than most sites in the U.S. The plan worked. Robinson played superbly in Montreal, and he and his wife found the city to be a most congenial environment. The baseball fans loved Robinson's stellar play, and the people of the city accepted the Robinsons warmly. Although Robinson's situation grabbed most of the press coverage, Rickey's pursuit of racial integration in 1946 did not stop with Robinson and Montreal, however, and Walter Alston would play a significant role in some of the less heralded but nonetheless important parts of Rickey's plans.

After Alston's success in Trenton, Rickey assigned him to manage a new club in the Dodgers' system. Alston was sent to manage the Dodgers of Nashua, New Hampshire, in the newly revived New England League.[1] There he would have two players on his roster whose signing made the Nashua Dodgers the United States' first integrated professional baseball team of the modern era. (Back in the 1880s, several African American players, notably Moses and Weldy Walker, played with Toledo of the American Association, then considered a "major" league roughly equivalent to the National League. By 1901, with the formation of the modern American and National Leagues, major league baseball club owners had fallen into complete accord, maintaining a ban on all players of African descent. All their affiliated minor league clubs were in lockstep here as well.) The two African American players who came to Nashua, New Hampshire, in 1946 were Don Newcombe and Roy Campanella.

42

Many have recognized the cagy wisdom in Rickey first assigning Jackie Robinson to Montreal, as racial prejudice indeed appeared to run far less strongly in Canada. Most certainly, Robinson would have encountered sheer hell had Rickey sent him to any such Dodgers farm clubs as he had in Fort Worth, Texas, or Mobile, Alabama. Rickey believed that, in addition to Canada, New England was also a good locale for integration at the minor league level. One of his young office managers, Emil Joseph Bavasi, advised him in this regard. "Buzzie" Bavasi raised the idea to Mr. Rickey that Nashua, New Hampshire, would be a good town in which to establish a Dodger team in the emerging New England League. While relatively small in size (population just under 35,000) even for the New England League, Nashua appeared to have an amenable population. They also had a new stadium they eagerly wanted to start generating revenue. As Bavasi knew, close to half of Nashua's citizens were of French-Canadian ethnicity. (On his father's side, Bavasi was himself of French-Canadian descent, hence his Christian

Emil "Buzzie" Bavasi (above) and Walter Alston had a long-time working relationship and friendship that lasted from 1946 until Alston's passing in 1984. The two first met in the spring of 1946, when Branch Rickey assigned Alston to manage a Dodgers farm club in Nashua, New Hampshire. Rickey sent Bavasi to Nashua to run the club's office and business affairs. The two worked very well together. In New Hampshire, they made a concerted effort to stand firmly against grumblings from players, fans, and other elements within the little New England baseball circuit over the fact that the 1946 Nashua Dodgers were the first racially integrated professional baseball club of the 20th century (National Baseball Hall of Fame and Museum, Cooperstown, NY).

name "Emil.") As with the people of Montreal *vis-à-vis* Jackie Robinson, Bavasi and Rickey both felt African American players would encounter less prejudice in such a community. They proved to be correct.

Further evidence of the relative lack of racial prejudice and resistance in New England came forth when the Dodgers signed Jackie Robinson, as some New England journalists and editors, in contrast to many of their Southern colleagues, went out of their way to comment favorably on the move. In Rhode Island, for example, the *Providence Journal*, which, back during the World War I years, had been stingingly vehement in its anti–German vitriol, editorialized openly, apropos of the opening of baseball's new season in April of 1946:

> Striking a more serious note, the Brooklyn Dodgers acted with discretion when they selected Nashua of the New England League as a farm team to which they are going to send two Negro prospects. We in New England are not letter perfect in the matter of racial tolerance. But we are a few jumps ahead of most other sections of the country—and many miles ahead of Jacksonville, Florida, where, a short while ago, the use of a ball park was denied the Dodgers because of two Negro players on their exhibition roster.[2]

That same week, similar sentiments came forth in New Hampshire's *Manchester Union-Leader*: "As parting gesture," the sports editor noted in an April essay covering his thoughts on the upcoming new baseball season, "may we doff the chapeau to the Nashua Dodgers not only for accepting the two Negro players assigned by the parent club, but also for collaborating with the Gate City [Nashua] school authorities in organizing the Knot-Hole Club."[3] The Knot-Hole Club was a little organization that allowed children to join and, with their membership card, come to ball games, if any seats were open, for a minimal fee of 30 cents. The hope here was to form the habits of local youngsters attending town ball games, habits that would presumably roll into future years.

The plan to promote attendance by young people did not work terribly well, not because the club made any mistakes in the encouragement of children attending games, but because of the spread of television. In New England, no matter the rivalries between the towns in the New England Baseball League, virtually everyone, save a few Yankee-fan perverts, rooted for the Red Sox, who, as it happened, were an especially good club in the late 1940s. The emergence of television gave people in the small towns of New England, as well as in other parts of the country, the opportunity to watch their favorite Major League Baseball teams. And this they would often elect to do rather than go out to the local park to watch minor leaguers. Indeed, in the region of the Midwest where Walter Alston had played and managed in the Mid-Atlantic League from 1937 to 1942, much the same thing occurred. The Mid-Atlantic League had folded during the War, but in 1947 a new "Ohio-Indiana League" formed, locating teams in many of the same towns, like Portsmouth, Ohio, which had had ball clubs in the old Mid-Atlantic. This new league would only last five years. Similar failures and the general decline in attendance of minor league baseball occurred all over the country in these years. The growth of television was the major factor here.

In regard to the racial integration coming to the newly reformed New England League, the sports editors in Providence (Earl Lofquist) and Manchester (Lee Cloutier) were clearly going out of their way to make an explicit point to their respective communities, one they sensed would resonate positively among many of their readers. Each was a town with a ball club in the newly re-established New England League, and the newspapermen wanted to do all they could to nurture success. Praising such innovation in racial matters was an effective way of speaking to the better angels of peoples' natures, thereby minimizing any shrugging ambivalence and capitulation that may have arisen in regard to the actions of any retrograde racists in their midst. Had any such outspoken writings appeared in a paper in any such contemporaneous Southern towns of similar size as Macon, Georgia, or Petersburg, Virginia, the community outrage would have been overwhelming. There the sports editors would have been run out of town, or worse. But in 1946, many New England towns, by no means all, had become more enlightened. A striking irony with regard to the *Manchester Union-Leader* also lies in the fact that the notoriously conservative editor William Loeb III would buy the paper but a few months later. For many decades with the *Union-Leader*, Loeb would be notoriously reactionary in much of his editorial work, but the apparently acceptable editorializing of the paper's sports editor showed a decidedly more liberal bent to thrive in regard to racial issues, at least among some in the community of the day.

Besides Manchester and Providence, Portland, Maine's *Press-Herald* also displayed some enlightened sensibilities. Portland would also have a New England League team in 1946, albeit the worst one. In April, the paper gave markedly positive coverage to Jackie Robinson's outstanding play in the Montreal Royals' opening games of the International League season. In addition to their coverage of Robinson's play, the Portland paper happily noted how many fans were seeking Robinson's autograph and giving him great encouragement. In regard to the New England League, Portland's team (the Gulls) would prove quite weak. They had the lowest payroll. With less financial backing, they were the only team in the League that did not travel South to train before the season. In their pre-season training that cold April in Maine, however, the Gulls did play some practice games against a Boston team—the Boston Giants, a "Colored" team. The *Press-Herald* gave these games coverage conveying no hint of any perceived controversy.[4]

Rickey and Bavasi were wise in selecting New England as part of their great experiment. Rickey was also cagy in the way he presented his intentions to integrate, both in regard to the unfolding of the revived New England League and to the establishment of the team in Nashua. Concerning the coming of racial integration for the first time in the 20th century to an American professional baseball team, an often-repeated story was one first recounted by Roy Campanella in his 1959 memoir/autobiography, *It's Good to Be Alive*. Campanella told of his meeting to discuss contract matters in March of 1946 with one of Rickey's assistants, Bob Finch. With Robinson already assigned to Montreal, Finch said Rickey wanted to place Campanella on another Dodgers team. Here, according to Campanella, Finch first brought up the possibility of Campanella going to a club in Danville, Illinois. In Campanella's presence, Finch phoned Danville and, after a brief conversation, he told Campanella, "they don't want you." Apparently, the Danville management clearly expected hostile reactions among their rural Illinois fans to the idea of racial integration. Then Finch supposedly phoned Buzzie Bavasi in Nashua, where Bavasi had already been assigned to run the team's office, in turn reporting to Campanella: "It's all set. Bavasi will take you." These two phone calls supposedly set the integration of the Nashua Dodgers into motion.[5]

Campanella's story already had cogency, and it would gain greater and greater cogency through repetition in various sources. Even earlier, in 1950, the *Saturday Evening Post* published a piece about pitcher Don Newcombe in which they mentioned that in Danville, Illinois, people would not be at all welcoming to any African American players. In what is likely the most renowned book on the whole saga of Jackie Robinson and baseball's integration, author Jules Tygiel repeated and galvanized the story of the entrenched, resistance-prone folks in Danville. Campanella's phrase, "They don't want me," were the very words Tygiel employed as the title of the chapter in *Baseball's Great Experiment*, where he covered the part of the story involving the 1946 signings of Campanella and Newcombe. In 1997, a *Boston Globe* piece covered the story similarly, quoting the then much older Buzzie Bavasi, who declared that "racism in Florida and Illinois led the Dodgers to assign Don Newcombe and Roy Campanella to Nashua."

One historian/chronicler of the various incarnations of the New England League, Charlie Bevis, holds that the two-phone-call, Nashua-by-default story may not be entirely accurate, however. Doubtlessly, resistance to integration would have spewed forth from any Southern town, and such prejudice may as well have existed in such a small, rural Midwestern community as Danville, Illinois, but Bevis raised the point that Campanella heard only one side of the March 1946 telephone conversations that Finch held both with the Danville people and with Bavasi. Bevis conjectured that Rickey planned on Nashua as the site for integration long before Campanella's meeting with Finch. Back in December of 1945, Rickey had sent Bavasi to Danville, and from Bavasi's talks there, the opposition in Danville was already quite clear. "Rickey did not want to arouse suspicion," Bevis noted, adding: "He had a plan for minimizing the distractions so that black players could develop within the all–Caucasian system of Organized Baseball." In the *Boston Globe* piece, Bavasi did emphasize how he and Rickey did go to lengths to ensure support from people in Nashua. This included the hiring of Fred Dobens, editor of the local *Nashua Telegraph*, to be president of the new team. This hiring, like Bavasi's visit to Danville, occurred in December of 1945, several months before the signing of Campanella and Newcombe. Of course, winning the support of the local newspaper editor provided many benefits for Rickey, well beyond the one matter of minimizing resistance to integration.[6]

Securing support in Nashua, Bevis held, was also a matter that readily linked to New England League President Claude Davidson's desire to elevate the quality of play in his new league to as high a level as possible. In this spirit, Davidson met with Rickey in December of 1945 in Columbus, Ohio. There Davidson emphasized to Rickey the accommodativeness that New England towns, with their large French-Canadian populations, would present with regard to black players. Lynn, Massachusetts, he underscored, had hosted several Negro League exhibition games during the War, all without incident. Rickey was looking for safe locales for his noble experiment. Davidson was looking for the best quality of baseball to attract fans, to win respect among baseball insiders, and, of course, to maximize incomes. It was a mutually beneficial arrangement.[7] (Lynn, Massachusetts, would not prove as accommodating as hoped, however, but their resistance and hostility would not spew forth until the season was underway.)

The sense that the Dodgers organization chose Nashua as an improvised response to the resistance from locales like Danville stemmed from Roy Campanella's sense of a phone call he witnessed. Rickey was quite content to leave that impression in order to minimize the sense and resulting suspicions over how carefully he had actually laid his plans. Where outrage grew over integration among the baseball public, a sense of careful planning versus improvisation may have made little difference, however. Racists prone to resistance were not going to be mollified by any scenario that showed any sort of last-minute improvisations. Those less racist but prone, out of apathy or fear, to capitulate to racists in various communities were also not likely to be affected by any sense of planning versus improvisation. Separating the potential capitulators from the unreachable, obdurate Klan-types was usually an intelligent strategy. Rickey and Bavasi were certainly setting up plans to install a club and pursue integration in Nashua well before the Dodgers organization signed Campanella and Newcombe. One can only speculate as to whether levels of racism-driven resistance would have risen to greater degrees had there been, in November and December of 1945, any full, open airing of plans to install a racially integrated ball club in Nashua when the New England League was being organized. The announcement of integration did come forth in March of 1946, just before the season was to open, and the Nashua newspaper was indeed enthusiastically "all-in," ready to go with positive spins on any related stories.

Rickey may have calculated the whole matter. It was certainly well within his ability and character to manipulate matters so skillfully. It is also possible that the stories of Danville's and other locales' discomfort with the "great experiment" may have been fully expected and simply been a matter that Rickey and the rest of the Dodgers management exploited to convey to such players as Campanella and Newcombe that the situation into which they were stepping was indeed a delicate one, hence one in which their full cooperation was both appreciated and absolutely necessary. The two would have known all this quite well anyway. Just as Rickey had asked/demanded that Jack Robinson not fight back and quietly endure any racial slurs and insults hurled at him, both on the field and off, in this first year of integration in Nashua, much the same was expected of Campanella and Newcombe. In the carrying out of all these delicate plans, much of the day-to-day responsibility for Campanella's and Newcombe's success rested with the Nashua Dodgers' manager, Walter Alston.

By any purely baseball/athletic standard, it was, of course, anything but an imposition for a manager in Alston's position to have two such players as Don Newcombe and Roy Campanella placed on his squad. Like any good baseball man, Alston quickly saw the talents each possessed. In addition to their considerable talents, Alston was especially impressed with Campanella's basic love of the game and enthusiasm for playing. There would be some strong player/umpire/fan reactions in New England, "plenty of razzberries," as Alston recalled. Rickey relied on Alston to navigate the waters here. Alston did so in several intelligent ways. Just as Rickey had advised Robinson, Newcombe and Campanella were indeed to ignore the many taunts and play their best. This would prove harder on Newcombe, as he did not have the internal psychological "shock absorbers" that Campanella possessed. "Roy was a steadying influence," Alston recalled. "Both," he felt, were able to "shrug off the nasty comments and made no effort to retaliate," but it would prove difficult for Newcombe.[8] Age and maturity were part of the picture here. At the opening of the season in 1946, Campanella was 24 years old and had already played several seasons in the Mexican and Negro Leagues. Newcombe, meanwhile, was only 19. While Campanella possessed a gentle, friendly nature to which so many fans warmed, Newcombe could be more aloof as well as fiery. This contrasting aspect of his nature may have been a significant component in Newcombe's eventual turn to and problems with alcohol.

As the season unfolded, when some fans hurled verbal taunts, Alston himself stepped forth and tossed some coarse language back at the abusive folks. Bavasi did too. Despite the gentlemanly image that posterity has assigned him, Alston (as well as Bavasi) could apparently hold his own quite well with the insults here, both with his mouth as well as with his fists when necessary. Matters were especially tense along racial lines in games between Nashua and the Lynn (Massachusetts) Red Sox. Lynn was part of the Boston Red Sox system. Their management under racist South Carolinian Tom Yawkey contrasted starkly with that of Brooklyn and Branch Rickey. It is doubtful if, and no evidence has ever shown that, Yawkey took time explicitly to convey to anyone connected with his little New England League team in Lynn his umbrage at baseball's integration, but his deeply Southern sensibilities were well known, and they may have given an added touch of entitlement to some in towns under his organizational umbrella. No matter its New England location, Lynn was also a traditional blue-collar working town, and many of the area's factory workers held onto racist outlooks that were typical of the uneducated white working classes of the day. Subsequent popular culture images, based on such famous TV characters as "Archie Bunker," may have lent such blue-collar classes tinges of softness and humor, but in the post-war era, such working-class folks could be quite harsh in their racial sensibilities. Race riots had occurred throughout the North during World War II, most notably in Detroit. Factory workers could be as hard-bitten and retrograde in their sensibilities as Southern racists. Klan membership in Northern cities and towns had often been as pronounced as in the South, as would the subsequent popularity of such political figures as George Wallace.[9]

When such folks in various minor league towns vented their hatred at Campanella and Newcombe, Alston was ready to give it back to them in full measure, and he could be rather harsh when the situation called for it. "I used to coach third base," Alston later remembered, and this guy kept firing one question at me at the top of his lungs. "Are you still sleeping with Campanella? Are you sleeping with that _____?" And he used that despicable six-letter word. I tried to ignore his taunts, figuring I'd find a favorable time and place to answer him. Just before the final game of the series, I managed to forget my lineup cards and had to go back to the clubhouse for them. Let me admit that the oversight wasn't purely accidental. Coming out of the visitors' clubhouse to the field in this park, you had to go past the home team bench through a run-way. The [opposing] manager ... was standing in the runway with one of his players when I came through, and that's exactly where I thought he would be. Now I had a chance to shut this loudmouth up. "All through the series," I said, pointing a finger at him, "you've been trying to find out whether I share my bed with Roy Campan-ella. I'm going to tell you something right now. It so happens I haven't been sleep-ing with him, or with any other player. ... But I want you to know that if I ever had a choice between sleeping with a man like Campanella or a blankety-blank vulgarism like you, I'd dam[n]sight rather sleep with Campy every time." ... The message got through, and that was the last problem on the racial bit I ever had with him.[10]

In addition to confronting any racial taunts directly, another thing Alston did in Nashua that both made good baseball sense and helped set a positive tone with the players and fans, was to give great latitude to Campanella. Obviously, Campy was more than good enough as a player to earn this level of trust, so from a purely baseball standpoint the tac-tic was easy to justify and institute, but Alston also made a definite show of the trust he had in Campanella. In the handling of the Nashua Dodg-ers pitchers, for example, Alston left much to Campanella's discretion. Campy called most of the pitches, and Alston set great store by Cam-panella's sense of who was or was not effective when decisions were at hand as to who should start or who should be relieved. Alston also established a major contingency plan for the whole team: if he was ever tossed out of a game (and that happened several times that summer), or if he was absent for any other such reason as sickness, Campanella was to manage the club. Just a few days after he announced this plan, Alston was tossed from a game in Lynn, Massachusetts. In this case, he was not even allowed to stay in the ballpark. Alston had to go to the parking lot and sat on top of the team bus to watch the game. Campy was in charge. With two out in the ninth inning and a man on second, Campanella inserted Newcombe as a pinch-hitter. Newcombe promptly hit a home run, and Nashua won. When Newcombe hit the homer, Campanella recalled: "Walt was so excited that he almost fell off [the roof of the bus] where he'd perched himself to watch the rest of the game."[11] Campanel-la's obvious quality as a player and as a man made this managerial tactic of Alston undeniably sensible. It also preempted any "concerns" that any Nashua players may have privately harbored. No one on the team took exception, and there were no racial incidents among the players on the

Nashua squad that summer. If any of the white players held any racial hostilities, Alston's (and Bavasi's) actions made it quite clear that they had best keep any such thoughts to themselves. They did.[12]

While Alston had had to learn to be a jack-of-all-trades back in Trenton, in Nashua he was first exposed to a very different situation—management within an organization. This is an important aspect of modern baseball management which not all field managers can handle (e.g., Billy Martin). It was in Nashua that Alston first met and worked with Buzzie Bavasi, whom Rickey had assigned to manage the Nashua team's administrative matters. Alston and Bavasi got along extremely well and would continue to for another 30 years. With Nashua's significant French-Canadian population, Bavasi had actually made some attempts to hire former major league journeyman Stanley George "Frenchy" Bordagaray to be the manager, as "Frenchy" was French-Canadian. But when that effort did not pan out, he made a concerted effort with Rickey to get Alston. Back in Trenton, Alston showed he could handle, whenever needed, all the grounds keeping, scouting, physical training, batting practice pitching, hotel and transportation services along with field/game management on top of playing every day. In Nashua, he showed he could also work well with others on the same management team.

A related element here, something at which Alston had always been good beforehand, concerned relations with the press. Alston, Bavasi, and the rest of the Dodgers organization in Nashua, and elsewhere, maintained strong press cordiality. Rickey and Bavasi had brought *Nashua Telegraph* editor Fred Dobens into the management circle of the team. In New Hampshire, Bavasi persuaded Alston (with little trouble) to take up the sport of golf. Alston had played golf earlier in his days as a high school teacher in New Madison, Ohio, when he regularly partnered with the local school superintendent (and helped him win quite handily in many "cut" and "Nassau" outings).[13] Alston saw no need to tell Bavasi that he had played golf before. As a result of staying mum here, he likely garnered a half a stroke a hole or so when it came time to set up the wagers on the first tee. Alston had played golf, and here he played Bavasi. At the course in Nashua, several sports reporters were among Alston's and Bavasi's regular golfing partners. It was another little element of a picture that could easily turn ugly if handled poorly. It turned out to be another tidbit Alston proved to more than able to handle and do so with but a shrug and a chuckle.

When he wasn't partnering with Alston against Bavasi and a fourth player in golf matches, the *Nashua Telegraph* writer Frank Stawasz was strongly singing the praises of Alston and the work he did in Nashua.

"There isn't a better pilot pulling the reins in the league today than our Wally Alston," he wrote. A year later he remembered: "There wasn't a team in the New England baseball league we visited last season that someone didn't pipe out with the thought: 'Boy if we had Wally Alston managing our ball club we'd be right out there....' The big Ohioan gained a host of admirers simply through the ability to get the most out of the boys who played for him."

Don Newcombe, pictured here in 1955, first played for Alston in Nashua, New Hampshire in 1946. Along with Roy Campanella, the two future stars were the first African American players on the nation's first racially-integrated professional baseball club of the 20th century. (Jackie Robinson played that season in Montreal.) Newcombe was still a teenager when the season began, and he felt many of the great pressures that came with baseball's integration, even in the small circuit of the New England League. The town of Nashua treated him well, but elsewhere in New England many fans and players proved hostile. Newcombe persevered yet as he developed as a player, he grew frustrated at how long the Dodgers' organization kept him in the minors. He cracked the majors in 1949, earning Rookie of the Year honors. In 1955, the year Brooklyn won the World Series, "Big Newk" won 20 games, *and* hit .359 (National Baseball Hall of Fame and Museum, Cooperstown, NY).

Frank Stawasz and Alston's friendship was such that they pulled a nasty little trick on Bavasi that summer on the golf course. One day Bavasi actually scored the golfer's dream of a hole-in-one. When they got back in the clubhouse, however, Stawasz and Alston feigned "not recalling" the ace, telling Bavasi he was a bit delusional. Briefly, they balked at attesting the scorecard, with their signatures needed to make the hole-in-one official. (Alston's stage acting from his high school days may have paid off here.) Alston and Stawasz ended up attesting Bavasi's ace, of course, but their hesitation certainly raised Bavasi's blood pressure for a few moments. Bavasi phoned his wife and told her to bring some contract "release" forms to the golf club. Alston was not as shaken by Bavasi's "threat" as was Bavasi by Alston's feigned memory lapse.[14] Amidst such good-natured jousts, the positive press coverage in Nashua was obviously good for community relations, and it appeared to help ticket sales. This was an important matter in general financial terms for the Dodgers system, even more for the community of Nashua as they had just built and were then paying for a new ballpark, Holman Stadium. Bavasi had said that he would have been satisfied with a season attendance of 50,000. The 1946 Nashua Dodgers drew over 70,000.[15]

In that season in Nashua, Alston also ended his regular playing days. This was by no means a happy choice. Up in the majors, the long-standing rivalry/hatred between the Brooklyn Dodgers and the New York Giants was especially intense in those years, and the rivalry echoed into various minor league circuits where the two organizations each had farm clubs. In the Midwest's old American Association, for example, the Dodgers/Giants rivalry was extra-bitter, as the two franchises sat in Minnesota's forever-clashing twin cities of St. Paul and Minneapolis. Minneapolis was a Giants' franchise; St. Paul was a Dodgers' club. In the New England League, the Dodgers played in Nashua, while the Giants played in Manchester, just 19 miles apart, north/south on Route 3 in New Hampshire, much the same distance, and pretty much the same direction as from the Polo Grounds to Ebbets Field. Against the hated Manchester Giants one day in July, Alston was playing first base as usual. He called for a pop-up hit by the Giants' Sal Yvars, a journeyman catcher who would have a few "cups of coffee" with the Giants and the Cardinals. As Alston was camping under the ball along the first base line, Yvars ran towards first, lowered his shoulder and rammed into him. That was illegal, of course, as the fielder has the right of way. Yvars had also run well off the base line to accomplish his little ice hockey maneuver. Alston landed on his neck. He came up swinging. The benches emptied. Buzzie Bavasi later said that in all the years he knew Alston, he never saw him so mad as he was that day when Yvars rammed him. Yvars was anything but apologetic.

Later in the season, Yvars appeared to spark another incident with Nashua when he allegedly threw dirt in Campanella's face. (In 1950, playing for the Jersey City Giants, Yvars would be fined $100 for getting physical in an altercation with an umpire.) From the collision with Yvars, Alston's neck was never the same. He took treatment for it two to three times a week for the rest of his life. From that point, Alston never again played regularly. He did a little pinch-hitting but nothing more, and whenever he got a hit, he would take himself out for a pinch-runner. Back in Ohio a few months later, just before the 1947 season began, Alston also injured his knee during a workout with his high school basketball team. He badly strained a tendon and underwent surgery to have pins inserted to reconnect tendons to bones. This underscored the need to end his playing days in baseball.[16]

Three years later, when Alston was managing in St. Paul, Yvars was playing for the Giants' club in Minneapolis in the American Association. One day, Alston was coaching third base with the Minneapolis dugout right behind him. From the dugout, Yvars began to "give it" to Alston. After a few minutes of this, Alston turned from his coaching box and, in total red-faced earnest, proceeded to challenge Yvars to any sort of fight he would like: "Just because you've got all your teammates with you," Alston yelled, "don't let that stop you from coming out of the dugout on your own if you want to." Yvars promptly shut up, and Alston never heard a word from him again. Alston once noted about himself that he rarely lost his temper, but when he did, it was hard to hold him back: "Now I don't easily get mad, but when I do I'm usually beyond the point of control." (One afternoon on the streets of St. Paul, Alston encountered a "big redhead" who had been heckling him at the ballpark. Alston "moved right in front of him [and] grabbed him by the shirt collar." Alston would see the big clod at several more games in St. Paul that summer, but he never heard another word from him.[17])

Among adolescent boys, almost any sort of "pecking order" is based to a great degree on the matter of who can take whom in a fight. It may be a sad fact, but it is nonetheless real. (The German philosopher Otto Schopenhauer once wrote, very much with this point in mind, that "there can be no democracy before the age of eighteen.") While Alston always had a reputation among his players for being an altogether calm leader, that element of potential physical prowess was, and likely had to be, always present, however faintly, as many professional baseball players, some indeed still in their teens, hold onto to some adolescent sensibilities. Alston's occasional willingness to make or accept challenges at this adolescent level, while not the most mature area of his behavior, was actually a small but necessary part of what made him an effective skipper.

Into September, the 1946 New England League season went down to the last game for Alston and the Nashua Dodgers. They were in a battle for the pennant chiefly with the rival Lynn Red Sox. The competitiveness of it all was part of the reason that attendance in Nashua that season was so much better than expected. Throughout, Alston's role in

Nashua's success in the league was noted, even by rivals. Five months after the season was over, an official with the Boston Red Sox, Eddie Doherty, conceded to a New Hampshire scribe: "Had Alston been managing Lynn, he would have won the pennant by twenty games."[18] As it was, the pennant would not be decided until the final day of the season.

On the last day, Nashua was in second place, but just one game behind Lynn, with the two teams slated for a doubleheader. The Dodgers needed to sweep the doubleheader from Lynn to win the flag. Alas, they split the two games. Lynn won the regular season crown, but in the playoffs between the top four teams of the league, Nashua first beat Pawtucket with three straight wins. Then they squared off against Lynn (who had defeated Manchester). Nashua beat Lynn four games to two to win the league's post-season Governor's Cup. "There isn't a better pilot pulling the reins in the league today than our Wally Alston," concluded the *Nashua Telegraph*. The only criticism the *Telegraph* could find came later from an umpire, Bill Jackowski of the American Association: "'Wally was fine,' reported Bill [to a NH reporter], 'but he sure couldn't argue very well with me.'"[19] (Some umpires can be intimidated, but Alston was neither willing or nor temperamentally equipped to adopt such a fearsome style.) Alston had won the New England League title. He helped guide a franchise to attendance and profit levels which far exceeded all management expectations. He maintained excellent relations with both the team's community and the local press. He worked extremely well with the rest of the administration of the Dodgers organization. Most of all, he had calmly and successfully led the nation's first professional baseball team of the 20th century (indeed America's first professional sports team of any sort) into the enlightened realm of racial integration. Once again, Mr. Rickey was very happy with his talented young field manager.

4

A Corking Good Manager

After their successes in Nashua, the NH club's three principals—
Alston, Newcombe, and Canpanella—went their separate ways, for a
time. Roy Campanella moved up the ranks in the Dodgers' system. He
had hit .290 in Nashua and would be up with Brooklyn by 1948. Meanwhile, Don Newcombe remained in Nashua, and he was not at all happy
about it. He had actually hit .311 (Newcombe would indeed be one of the
best-hitting pitchers in the game), but his pitching record was merely
14–4. Bavasi felt he needed more time in the minors.[1] Newcombe's
unhappiness here was not the least bit focused on the community of
Nashua. He simply believed he should have moved up toward the majors
more rapidly. At one point, amidst his frustrations, Newcombe contemplated leaving baseball and put in an application to become a local
policeman in *Nashua*. Testimony to the sense of the Dodgers' organization, especially Bavasi's sense of Nashua, Newcombe was quite happy
with the community, but he was not at all content with the level of baseball to which he felt he was being relegated. Newcombe would have to
wait until 1949 to make it up to Brooklyn, and then he would indeed be
the National League's Rookie of the Year.

As for Alston, in 1947 Rickey promoted him from Nashua to pilot
a team in the newly reestablished Western League. The team was in
Pueblo, Colorado. Another young figure in Rickey's organization, Al
Campanis, succeeded Alston in Nashua. (Over the next 40 years in the
Dodgers' organization, Campanis would prove quite positive and helpful in regard to matters concerning racial issues. It was only many years
later, in April of 1987, on the 40th anniversary of Jackie Robinson's break
into the National League, that Campanis made some unforgivable comments on national television in response to the question as to why so
few African Americans had, to that point, ever risen to become major
league managers. Here Campanis clumsily mused: "I truly believe that
they [African Americans] may not have some of the necessities to be,
let's say, a field manager, or perhaps a general manager." There could be

no candy-coating of that statement, and Campanis' legacy was then forever shredded. Alston was long gone by that time, but he would likely have scratched his head as to how anyone, especially Campanis, could say something like that.[2]) In Alston's view, if anyone ever showed the skills and "necessities" that it took to be a good baseball manager, it was Roy Campanella

In 1947, the very spring he brought Jackie Robinson up to Brooklyn, Rickey had just established Pueblo as part of his Dodgers system. Having negotiated the partnership, Rickey made a point of writing to the local Pueblo paper, promising the fans that they would be very happy being part of the Dodgers' organization. To the team officials and fans in Colorado, Rickey proudly proclaimed: "There is good news today for Pueblo fandom. ... Pueblo will be proud of their team of Dodgers in the Western League. ... Pueblo [now] has a corking good manager and some of the players [from the Dodgers] now named for the team are very good men."[3] Alston proved, indeed, to be "corking good." He would fulfill all of the promises Rickey made to the good people of Pueblo.

In Pueblo, Alston worked the team hard, getting them and keeping them in good shape. They contended for the league lead all season long. The fans were ecstatic. Game attendance was strong, and the public readily welcomed the players into their community. One Pueblo pitcher, Omar Joseph "Turk" Lown, who would later play for the Cubs and the White Sox, remembered in 1978: "It was the most fun I ever had playing here. The fans were great to us. You'd walk down the street and people would come up to you and ask you over to the house for dinner. It was the same way with the newspapermen and the broadcasters. This was really a great place to play ball."

With Alston at the helm, the Pueblo Dodgers played winning baseball, and enthusiasm was everywhere. Pitcher Turk Lown could also thank Alston in another special way. One afternoon, with Lown pitching ineffectively, Alston took him out of the game. Lown left the mound, of course, but from there he also left the dugout altogether. He wandered into the stands, found a buddy, and glumly sat down with him. Lown's friend thought he'd do something to help Lown in his dispirited mood and introduced him to a woman he knew. The young pitcher's glum countenance suddenly changed. Lown liked the young lady. He asked her out, and they soon started dating regularly. Early the next summer they were married! After Turk Lown's pitching days in the majors were over, he and Mrs. Lown would resettle and raise a family back in her native Pueblo. When a manager relieves a pitcher, comments often arise to the effect: no telling what would have happened had the manager not put in a reliever. Here with Turk Lown, the more appropriate comment would be: no telling what would *not* have happened had Alston left him in. The Brooklyn-born Lown and his wife would live out their later years in Pueblo. Lown passed away there in 2016 at age 92. Like most pitchers, Turk Lown never liked being taken out of a game, but he certainly came to accept and appreciate the wisdom of Alston's judgment of 1947.[4]

In September 1947, Alston and the Pueblo Dodgers went to the Western League playoffs. They beat Des Moines and then edged Sioux City to take the championship. Adding a nice bit of spice to the victory here was that Sioux City was another New York Giants club! None less than the Governor of Colorado, William Lee Knous, presented Alston with the League Championship Governor's Cup.[5] Still proud of their boy "Wally" from the previous summer, a paper back in New Hampshire, noting Alston's continuing success, wrote at the end of 1947: "One of the brightest rising stars in the Brooklyn Dodger farm system is Walter Alston. ... Don't be a great deal surprised if he manages the Brooklyn club before too long."[6]

In early 1947, when Rickey first offered Alston the job in Pueblo, he slyly told Alston that there would be no difference in salary but that it was a higher-level league, class A not B. Alston quickly responded: "If it's a Class A league, I'll take it." "In that case," smiled Rickey, "there'll be a little more money. Not much more," he quickly added, "but a little more." Alston was sure that Rickey had indeed been testing him to see whether money or baseball came first, so he behaved as he knew Rickey desired. This was another good trait that Alston always exhibited, especially with Rickey—be as sharp as the boss but do so without letting him know you're that much his equal. The story also underscored another key point with Alston. It was not merely that baseball came first, which it certainly did, it was also that he truly did not worry terribly much about financial matters. He could make career calculations with a completely clear head. By no means was Alston independently wealthy. The key was that the roots he had in his Ohio family and community were such that if he was ever in a position which compelled him to leave everything and go back home, it would not bother or impinge upon him in the slightest. "There's something about going home to Darrtown," he noted, "that spells peace, security, and solitude."[7] The famous series of one-year contracts Alston would have with Brooklyn and Los Angeles, which certainly became ceremonial after a time, could leave many other managers feeling insecure and affect their work. Alston never worried about this. It was no mere contrived posture; it was truly part of his nature. He could carry out all his work, all with the deep conviction that if he suddenly had to leave everything and move back to Darrtown, Ohio, he would be a very content and happy man. It was another key, utterly natural, uncontrived component of Alston's makeup and success.

Rickey had still more in mind for Alston. After the successes in Trenton, Nashua, and Pueblo, Rickey moved Alston a major step upward in 1948, naming him to manage the St. Paul Saints of the American Association. The Saints had a long history in Minnesota. Alston was moving into a town with strong baseball traditions, but one where he and some of the Dodgers' management team were relative newcomers. The Saints' ties to Brooklyn had only begun in 1944, and full involvement of the Dodgers' management in the team did not come until 1948. A proper diplomatic touch would secure the support of local press and the fans, along with the winning of a fair number of ball games, of course. Here Alston again proved deft.

As the opening of the season approached, sports reporters from the eight American Association cities revealed that no one expected much from Alston and the Saints. In 1947 the team had finished in seventh place (69–85), a distant 24.5 games behind leading Kansas City, a club owned by the hated Yankees. In 1948, pre-season prognostications of sports reporters from each of the Association's cities had the Saints likely finishing seventh again. Wrote one: "So bad are the Saints' chances, despite the new Brooklyn Dodger regime taking over, that they received two votes for the cellar." During pre-season, the Saints appeared to meet these low expectations, as they lost four of their first five exhibition games.[8] Under Alston, things would change.

From the season's outset in late April, the Saints were in the thick of the race. Steadily they held a place among the leaders and were actually in first place from time to time. The Indianapolis Indians (of the Pittsburgh Pirates' organization), led by new manager Al Lopez, were St. Paul's chief rival that season. One St. Paul reporter, Mark Tierney, opined about the Saints and their surprisingly strong play. Among his accountings, Tierney asked rhetorically:

> What part is a fellow by the name of Walter Alston playing in the Saints' success story? Alston admittedly doesn't pitch, hit, or field but he has the job of planning the strategy and keeping the team working in unison—something lacking last year. Reporters in Texas [where the Saints had trained, and in the AA cities of], Toledo, and Columbus say the Saints are in complete harmony. ... Veterans and rookies alike pull together like a good team of horses, and the man responsible for that pull is Alston. He's quiet—on the schoolteacher side. But like a school master he can bark loud. But like a good teacher he knows where words can do the most good.

Reporter Tierney went on: "One of Alston's formulas for success is HARMONY." An unnamed veteran player in St. Paul confided to Tierney: "The team this year is behind Alston. It's got the best spirit of any

team I have played on. ... There just aren't any CLIQUES this year"
[emphases his]. Under such guidance, at the end of April, the Saints
were indeed the "surprise of the American Association race."[9]

As the surprising success of the Saints continued into the summer, Branch Rickey and the Brooklyn organization added to St. Paul's
morale by feeding them some good talent. Mel Himes, Danny Ozark,
and Roy Campanella each put in some time with Alston and St. Paul in
1948. Campanella proved especially valuable. As in Nashua in 1946, the
local papers in St. Paul were full of applause regarding the integration
of teams in the American Association. When Campanella joined the
Saints, a reporter happily noted, "the players have taken Campanella in
and are pulling for him to make good." Like Robinson in Brooklyn, Campanella also made a conscious effort never to argue with umpires or to
direct any remarks at a hitter, as catchers often will. Meanwhile, reporters regarded his handling of the pitching staff as "flawless." In addition to
Campanella, an African American pitcher, Don Bankhead, also played
some of the 1948 season in St. Paul. He received great support as well.
Bankhead appeared in six games, compiling a record of 4–0; he also hit
.500.[10]

With such quality players, the Saints' contending for the league
lead continued into July. Alston won praise for a "strategy [that] clicks."
He appeared to have a good "knack for when to pull a pitcher." Trying to capture the intangible qualities of the leadership at hand, a St.
Paul reporter noted how Alston "won't stop fighting for what he thinks
the team has coming." As a result, he smiled, the Saints "are hustling,
and Alston's leadership is credited [for it]."[11] An incident in early May
showed something of the intense camaraderie quickly established
between Alston, the Saints, and their fans. In a home game against Indianapolis, the bench jockeying from the Saints was intense, so much so
that the umpire turned toward the St. Paul dugout and issued Alston a
warning about the verbal abuse. Unable to hear the actual words, the
fans were a trifle unsure about the specifics regarding the various ges-
tures and exchanges here. With that confusion as backdrop, an inning
later Alston came out of the dugout to relieve his pitcher. Along with
Alston, the pitcher had been yelling a lot at the umpire about his ball/
strike calls. As Alston called for a reliever, this same umpire also signaled to the bullpen. The fans then perceived that the umpire was actually ejecting Alston, and they erupted, showering the field with soda
bottles. Alston and St. Paul were compelled to forfeit the game. American Association President Frank Lane fined Alston $100 for his failure
to control his own players and for his own demonstrations against the
umpires that led to such a ruckus from the fans.[12] Despite explanations

and appeals from Alston and the Saints, the forfeit stuck and the fine had to be paid, but the fans' solidarity with Alston and the Saints was clearly showing its strength.

By June 5, including the bottle-throwing night, St. Paul's total home game attendance had reached 74,957. In the same number of games in the previous season, they had drawn but 64,319. In 1947, home game attendance had averaged 3,307; as of June 21, 1948, the new season average was 4,700. In July, the team began fading a bit in the standings. The fans remained loyal, however. Alston called for extra workouts, sometimes in the mornings before games. He was vehement in his efforts to combat any loafing or mental lapses. Alston's intensity was genuine, so much so that in early August it personally got the better of him when he vigorously protested an umpire's call. He was not only ejected but was fined $25 by Association President Lane for a "prolific use of profanity." Such behavior was unusual for Alston, but his occasional flares of anger did not hurt team morale. Quite the contrary, they strengthened it, as did his occasional confrontations of obnoxious fans and opposing players. Personal slips of profanity notwithstanding, Alston kept his Saints battling. His insistence against mental errors was manifest in the Saints boasting the best fielding percentage in the league.[13] He had demanded and achieved this from himself while playing first base for Trenton. Such seemingly little things as consistent defense are often a mark of a good manager, one who keeps his players' mental focus at a keen level. Attention to detail results in fewer little mishaps that can often be the difference between a win and a loss.

While some could ascribe the enthusiasm of St. Paul's newspapers' coverage of Alston and the Saints' success as standard "home-town rah-rah," it was not just local reporters who were noting the Saints' exceptional play that season. A reporter in Indiana effused: "With a new owner Branch Rickey and a new manager Walter Alston, the Saints are confounding the Association baseball writers who predicted a second division finish, by hovering around the top rung since the start of the season." After the season, papers in Atchison, Kansas, and in rural Brainerd, Minnesota, called Alston "the brains behind St. Paul's American Association playoff title." Toward the end of the season, an Ohio paper remarked how "St. Paul is literally 'baseball mad.'" The city's all-time season attendance record of 288,000 had been set in 1946; Alston's 1948 Saints passed that mark on August 16.[14] Alston was receiving praise from all corners of the Association.

A slip in the standings remained a problem for the Saints from July into August. At one point they had fallen to fifth place. With the slide, a St. Paul writer, tongue-in-cheek, actually added to the volume of praise for Alston, all in hopes of stirring the squad. "If they haven't got what it takes to win, then it isn't your [Alston's] fault. ... All in all, Walt, the fans are satisfied with your handling of the club. ... The fans hope you'll be back next year with better material."[15] Whether or not the reporter's goading played a role here, St. Paul came back in late August and began to regain ground. By September 1, they were back in third place, just two games behind second-place Milwaukee. In their last 23 games, the Saints won 20. They made the AA playoffs and beat Indianapolis in the finals for the Association Championship. Indianapolis manager Al Lopez conceded, however begrudgingly, "The hottest team in baseball beat us out of the playoffs." Praise continued for Alston: "He kept the team together when it easily could have folded." He was "respected and admired by every member of the club." Earning even more praise was the noted fact that "Alston refuses to take the credit. He feels the fellows hung together and had a spirit that he hasn't seen matched in his years in baseball."[16]

A long-standing minor league baseball tradition involved the champion of the American Association facing the champion of the International League, the other top minor league in the game. This match was always called "The Little World Series." In 1948, the Saints lost the Little World Series to the Montreal Royals. The loss may have saddened Alston, the Saints, and their fans, but it did not bother Branch Rickey, for Montreal was a Dodgers club too. Montreal's manager was Clay Hopper, the very person for whom Alston had first played back in 1935 in Greenwood, Mississippi. Hopper had scoffed at the 1948 Saints when he compared them to his Royals: "There isn't a ballplayer on the St. Paul club that I could use or want in my Montreal lineup."[17] While such a statement may have angered some St. Paul scribes and fans, Hopper's words actually underscored a matter that Saints' followers had been voicing, especially during St. Paul's slide in late July and August—that Branch Rickey was not delivering sufficient talent to St. Paul and was helping his clubs in Montreal, Ft. Worth, Texas, and Mobile, Alabama, more. Whether or not that point was factual, Saints followers expressed that much more praise of Alston for doing so well despite the allegedly mediocre support from Rickey. Meantime, while Hopper had sniffed at the Saints, Alston never raised any complaints to anyone about any alleged insufficient support from Branch Rickey and Brooklyn. He never would. Rickey appreciated such decorum.

Rickey certainly grasped the contrast between the less and the more outspoken of the managers of his two top farm clubs. Rickey had always preferred cooperative team players within his organization. In 1948, that outlook was especially poignant to him, as in July up in

Brooklyn, he had grown thoroughly exasperated with his outspoken manager, Leo Durocher. Rickey negotiated a termination of Durocher's contract, a transaction which freed Durocher to sign with the hated Giants, a move that enraged Brooklyn fandom even more. The mature behavior of Alston looked rather good in comparison—so intensely getting the most out of the players he had been given, never alibiing, and never raising any intra-organizational "support" issues with the press or the public. Any such complaints during the season would have risked blunting the spirit of the team's ability to pull together, and it would not have sat well with Rickey either.

Rickey kept Alston in St. Paul for the 1949 season. In the off-season, Alston would continue to teach and coach in Lewiston, Ohio. The school district allowed him to go to the Dodgers' training camp in Vero Beach, Florida.[18] The strains of high school teaching and coaching amidst higher-level minor league managing were growing, however. After 1949, Alston gave up his career of high school teaching and coaching. He was always grateful to the officials in Lewiston and New Madison for hiring him, and even more for their flexibility in allowing him to leave in the spring to manage and play ball. Now he had bigger issues with which to contend, but he never forgot the kindnesses.[19]

In the 1949 season, Alston and the Saints started superbly, running off an opening mark of 16–1. With a slight lapse in late July, Alston and the Saints proceeded to win the American Association's regular season crown. It was St. Paul's ninth American Association pennant, the most of any team in the AA to that point. When the Saints went through a little dip in July, Alston was buoyant: "The club isn't through. It won't quit.... We'll bounce back with a bang." Later, with the pennant secured, he conceded: "I won't say we weren't worried, but I felt all along we'd come through." The team had been up by six games on September 4. Then they lost several games in succession, finally winning the pennant on September 11 by a single game. Even here Alston was upbeat: "I'm prouder of the boys for doing it as they did with their backs to the wall than if they had sewn it up five days ago."[20] As with other teams, Alston always spoke in terms of what the players did. He never put his own ego into the mix, and the players always responded. He made it easier for them. Unlike some clubs, Alston's teams never won in spite of their manager. As in 1948, criticisms had arisen in 1949 about the less-than-fulsome support St. Paul was receiving from Brooklyn and Branch Rickey. Brooklyn appeared to be keeping all the best pitchers.[21] Throughout all such griping, Alston uttered not a word. Alston would only later confide that in the last week of the 1949 season, some meddling from Rickey had contributed to the slide of the team and the near loss of the pennant. In that last week, Rickey told Alston he wanted to see how one player, Wayne Belardi, would perform at first base and how another, Jim Pendleton, would handle center field. Reluctantly, Alston abided Rickey's directive, and with those two in the lineup, the team began to lose. After five successive losses, Indianapolis nearly overtook St. Paul. With St. Paul's lead having dwindled to one-half game, Alston quietly contacted Rickey. Rickey phoned Alston (at 3:00 a.m.!) and told him, "Go ahead, use your own judgment from here."[22] Alston did so. He benched Belardi and Pendleton, and the Saints clinched the pennant on the final day.

With his pennant in St. Paul in 1949, Alston's place as a manager of bona fide credentials seemed well set. He had spent six seasons in Trenton, Nashua, Pueblo, and St. Paul and had been a winner wherever he went. Reporters praised his "knack for handling players." Alston, noted one, "will come in for his share of 'minor league manager of the year' honors." Knocks at Branch Rickey not helping St. Paul too much continued to appear in the papers in 1949. As one scribe noted: "For some reason, Hopper [of Montreal] seems to be able to gain the most valuable excess timber from Rickey." Again, Alston offered no comments, and he did have such players passing through his ranks that season as Danny Ozark, Mel Himes, and Clem Labine. Labine would pitch in 20 of St. Paul's first 48 games. Clyde King and Gil Hodges also played a bit under Alston in 1949, albeit only in the pre-season, so any complaints at Rickey may have been a trifle dubious as well as impolitic.[23]

As the Saints led the league throughout much of the 1949 season, Alston continued to win praise from the fans and reporters. One evening, St. Paul's Mayor Joseph Kesler presented Alston with a gift of a ham; the team responded with a barrage of 21 hits and 23 runs against the Toledo Mud Hens. Beating any opponent like that was always fun, and the lengthy existence of the eight teams in the American Association gave each of these pairings a lot of history and rivalry. Each team had roots going back to the late 19th century, so each pair had stories of infamous games from seasons past. Among the rivalries in the American Association, Toledo-Columbus was strong given its intra-state nature. The Louisville–Indianapolis rivalry was also keen. But without question, the Minneapolis–St. Paul rivalry was the most intense. St. Paul fans had always been especially edgy about their standing against the cross-town Minneapolis Millers. The rivalry actually took many forms, although in baseball it was the most intense. In many winter seasons, the two cities had competing minor league ice hockey franchises, also named "Millers" and "Saints." In 1949, Saints baseball fans were most pleased with their Saints' regular drubbing of Minneapolis. "The Millers get jittery when facing the Saints," taunted one scribe. Our "Saints hypnotize the Millers," laughed another.[24] As the smaller of the two towns, fans in St. Paul may have felt the rivalry more pugnaciously, so when the Saints could triumph under such a steady guiding hand as that of Alston, the feelings of admiration and gratitude were that much stronger.

For Saints fans, the ongoing rivalry with their Minneapolis neighbors, and all its psychic and historic meaning to the community, developed an extra element of urgency in the late 1940s amidst Alston's tenure there. Rumors were starting about a major league baseball team moving to Minneapolis. The New York Giants were indeed contemplating a move there. The Millers were their farm club, and New York's links with Minneapolis here had always been cordial and profitable. Rumors and conversations about this move would continue over the next decade. Any such move could easily wipe out the viability of two ongoing minor league franchises in the region, with the larger of the two cities likely gaining more of the benefits from the arrival of a major league team. The NY Giants' move to Minneapolis actually came quite close to occurring, but in 1958 New York ultimately opted for San Francisco. When the Washington Senators did move to Minneapolis in 1961 to become the Twins, they tried tactfully to eclipse the many complexities of the historic two-city rivalry with their genial employment of the regional name, "Minnesota Twins." In the same decade, both the National Football League Vikings and the National Hockey League North Stars would also diplomatically adopt the "state" title; so would the NHL's "Wild" when they later began in 1997, as did the National Basketball Association's Timberwolves when they opened in 1989. (The NBA's previous team in the region had not done this—the powerful basketball team of 1947 to 1961 was the Minneapolis Lakers.)

The "Minnesota" diplomacy worked to some degree, especially so for the Twins when they became a baseball power in the mid and late 1960s. The arrival of the Twins did indeed diminish the baseball part of the twin cities' rivalry. The Minneapolis Millers had moved to Seattle, and took the name "Rainiers." The Saints shifted to Nebraska to become the Omaha Dodgers. In 1993, however, St. Paul would reestablish a minor league team in the "Northern Division" of the evolving American Association, with no affiliation to any major league team. Once again, the team was called the Saints. The intense local pride of the smaller of the "twins" never fully abated. Indeed, the fact that the NHL's Wild actually play in St. Paul is a matter in which St. Paul fans take great pride. St. Paul's strong community feelings run deep, and the memories of Walter Alston's highly successful leadership there in the late 1940s was part of the legacy that has kept this pride alive.[25]

After Alston's winning seasons in 1948 and 1949, Branch Rickey engaged in an unusual front office gambit. While Alston was doing so well in St. Paul, Clay Hopper was also quite successful in Montreal. Whether Hopper's more outspoken ways with the press were a negative in Rickey's mind when comparing his two managers, Rickey never said. He did, however, come up with an unusual way of testing his two top minor league managers. Hopper and Alston were each being touted as major league managerial timber. Given Alston's Southwest Ohio roots, several local sports reporters there were pointing to him as a good candidate to take over the Cincinnati Reds who, after World War II, had failed to resume the winning ways they had boasted in the late 1930s and early 1940s. "Alston would be extra popular in Southern Ohio as manager of the Reds," predicted one scribe. "Alston has proven himself a first-class manager. ... He has aided in the development of most of the youngsters who have made a power of Brooklyn in the National League."[26] The Reds never made any overtures to Alston, however, and their losing ways would continue for several more seasons. Meanwhile, Clay Hopper enjoyed a solid reputation for the play of the Montreal Royals. In 1950, Rickey tried a little ploy within his organization, one that was not altogether popular in either of his two top minor league cities—he switched his managers.[27] In the first week of March 1950, just as spring training was commencing, Rickey announced that Hopper would now manage St. Paul, and Alston would take over Montreal.

Alston did not speak a word of French; neither did Mrs. Alston. While in school growing up in Ohio, the only foreign language to which Alston had had any exposure was Latin. Alston and Lela would come to fit in nicely in Quebec, however. The landlady where they boarded spoke only French, but fortunately she had a daughter who was fluent in both English and French. At first, though, the sports networks of Montreal were a trifle edgy, not at Alston, per se, but at Rickey's managerial switch. Clay Hopper had been both successful and personally popular in Montreal. In 1949, Rickey took pitcher Don Newcombe from Montreal. It proved a good move for Brooklyn, as that season Newcombe went 17–8 and earned National League Rookie of the Year honors. Royals fans and press felt slighted, however. They felt their Royals, with Newcombe, could have won the International League pennant in 1949. Indeed, in that year, Montreal writers noted, other Dodgers clubs like St. Paul and Hollywood (of the Pacific Coast League) had won pennants. To Montreal fans and press, Rickey's seemingly off-handed switching of managers but a few months later appeared yet another arrogant slight.[28]

People speculated about the meaning of Rickey's move. A widely held view had it that Hopper or Alston was being groomed for the top job of managing Brooklyn. Sources at the *New York Daily News* dismissed such talk. Quoted in the *Montreal Gazette*, the *Daily News* sniffed, "Montreal President Hector Racine had to tell the populace something to justify the transfer of the successful Hopper to St. Paul." The New York sources affirmed that neither Hopper nor Alston but the great Brooklyn shortstop Pee Wee Reese, then 32, was likely the next Dodgers manager. The "real motive," in Rickey's move, said the unnamed New York source, "still remains to be disclosed." Rickey never spoke here.[29]

Alston faced Montreal newspapermen and fans who had high expectations, ready to blame any less than excellent result on whoever succeeded Hopper. Al Parsley of the *Montreal Herald* sneeringly referred to Rickey as "the meddling Mahatma." He went on: "Beyond Mr. Rickey's policy for tampering, and never allowing his underlings a sense of security [which never bothered Alston], fans could find no rhyme or reason in the sudden and startling move." Buzzie O'Meara of the *Montreal Star* suggested that Rickey was penalizing Hopper for "having the temerity to ask for a pay raise and making it stick." Alston, O'Meara opined, "is heading for Montreal with two strikes against him. As it stands now, it [Rickey's switch] does not rate as a very bright move." Dink Carroll of the *Montreal Gazette* sentimentalized a point Hopper had made to him: "if I can't manage in the big leagues then I want to stay in Montreal." Implying that Rickey showed no feel or concern for the good rapport Hopper had with the Montreal sports world, Carroll criticized Rickey's switching managers in "a casual manner," adding: "Branch Rickey has never shown any hesitation in dropping pilots even when they won pennants. But if he does not put a top-notch club in Montreal this season this move should boomerang."[30] All such grumblings in the press raised no ire specifically at Alston, but it was clear that the city's rabid sports fans had their proverbial knives out and were ready to pounce if Hopper's successor showed any managerial flaws or if the team did not perform splendidly. Still, one Montreal writer conceded that Montreal's "fans will forget Hopper fast enough if Wally Alston has a winner." The scribe added, however, "if he hasn't, then the next season could be a rough one."[31]

While Alston and Rickey were very much on notice, Alston did encounter a general tone of good wishes. *La Presse* wrote: "*Même si la direction du Montréal souhaite la plus chaleureuse bienvenue à Alston à Montreal elle voit partir Hopper à regret et souhaite que l'homme de Greenwood* [Mississippi] *continue sa serie de succès dans le baseball.*" ("Even if the directors of Montreal wish a warm welcome to Alston in Montreal, they see the parting of Hopper with regret and wish that man from Greenwood [Mississippi] continued success in baseball."[32]) *La Presse* may have been more interested in wishing Hopper well than in welcoming Alston, but they were open to the prospect of the new manager doing a good job. They would simply wait and see. Meanwhile, of course, a much bigger issue loomed before Montreal's sports fans that April—hockey! Montreal would fare well, but the Detroit Red Wings won the Stanley Cup that spring.

During the pre-season, Alston and the Royals had one success of note: they beat Hopper and the St. Paul Saints in two straight games, the first by a margin of 15 to 4.[33] Then they began the regular season with six straight victories. Fans were obviously pleased. Alston was circumspect, however. He said he was not yet satisfied with the team's play, adding that the team had yet to play such stronger clubs as Toronto, Rochester, and Baltimore. *La Presse* noted: "*Le gérant Walter Alston est beaucoup plus pessimiste que son prédécesseur Clay Hopper.*" (Manager Walter Alston is much more a pessimist than his predecessor Clay Hopper.) Some fans may have felt a trifle non-plussed here. Hopper was always boisterous after any good streak. A bit more head-scratching ensued when Dink Carroll of the *Gazette* pronounced Alston "A huge muscular balding man with a quick smile and not much to say."[34] Alston did go on the record about one player early that season, declaring he especially liked the look of the curveball of one of the team's young pitchers. The pitcher was Tom Lasorda.[35]

Feeling proud of Montreal's role in the success of Jackie Robinson in the racial integration of baseball, Montreal papers made a point of giving coverage of how some African American players like Sam Jethroe and Don Bankhead were faring, especially because each, like Robinson, had passed through Montreal. In this same context, they gave some coverage to the altogether positive way that Alston had managed in Nashua in 1946 when his team had Roy Campanella and Don Newcombe. As a widely circulated article on the Jackie Robinson story of integration appeared in the *Saturday Evening Post* that very May 1, the issue was that much more underscored to Montreal fans. (Indeed, in 1946, as the *Post* article noted, when Montreal won the Little World Series, the jubilant Quebec crowd carried Robinson off the field on their shoulders. Robinson was so touched that he openly wept.[36]) Montreal fans were genuinely proud of their role in baseball's integration. This served Alston well, as he had played a positive role too. In August 1950, the 44-year-old Satchel Paige arrived in town and asked to pitch an exhibition game in Montreal. Alston readily approved, and, despite the short notice about the game, 10,151 Montreal fans turned out to watch Satch pitch.[37]

Beyond Alston's supportive role in the pride that Montreal felt in their support of racial integration in baseball, the wider issue in Alston's good reception in Montreal that spring was simply that the Royals were winning. By May 20, their record stood at 16–5, and they were four games ahead of second-place Jersey City, the NY Giants' IL club. A few slips occurred in late May and June, but the Royals remained in contention. The 1950 race was very tight. On June 26, for example, Baltimore was in fifth place in the IL, and they were only 1½ games out of first.[38]

A number of Alston's pitchers, including Carl Erskine, Clyde King, and Tom Lasorda, had some trouble with sore arms that spring and summer. Here reactions in the papers focused mostly on the old theme of how the team needed more support from Branch Rickey in Brooklyn. "The Mahatma" was the object of much suspicion and derision. Carl Erskine recovered and was soon pitching so well in Montreal that on August 8, Rickey called him up to Brooklyn.[39] Fans in Montreal understood that, but they were not happy. Meanwhile, Alston appeared to have won most everyone's confidence, and he always made a point of saying nothing when any player went up to Brooklyn. His quiet, calm demeanor impressed. "Up here," he noted to the press, "the fellows are a little older and a little smarter than they are in the lower leagues. You don't have to spend time teaching them the fundamentals." Alston was being factual here, but he was also imparting a calm maturity he wanted in his players. It seemed to be effective. One player that summer did not feel sufficient influence from Alston's calm manner, however. In Syracuse, on June 22, first baseman Chuck Connors, later of television fame, responded to a razzing from a fan by jumping into the stands and punching him. (At least he did not shoot him with a repeating rifle.) Alston benched him for three games.[40]

For the season, the Royals finished in second place. (Rochester, still a Cardinals team, came in first.) In the playoffs, Montreal faced the Baltimore Orioles, then the top farm club of the St. Louis Browns. Alston actually predicted to *La Presse* that his Royals would defeat the Orioles in six games. Despite some good pitching by Turk Lown and Tom Lasorda, the Orioles took the series four games to three, so the Royals' season was over.[41] Assessing the season, Montreal sportswriter Dink Carroll evaluated Branch Rickey's managerial switch of Clay Hopper and Walter Alston.

> Hopper was popular here, and he fitted the town like a glove. This is a bit of a carnival city, and the people like to see a show. Wally Alston is a fine man personally. Hopper is a gambler on the field, and Alston is ultraconservative. Alston invariably plays by the book, whereas Hopper frequently threw it away. You could always tell what Alston was going to do…, but you never knew what Hopper was liable to do.

... Fans like Hopper's hunch playing better than they like Alston's conservatism. The way we hear it, fans in St. Paul liked Alston's book-baseball and didn't fancy Hopper's gambling. The switch didn't do anybody any good.[42]

St. Paul also made the American Association playoffs and lost in their first round. The same thing happened to the Dodgers' Ft. Worth team in the Texas League, and the Brooklyn Dodgers themselves lost the National League pennant on the last weekend of the season to Philadelphia, so there appeared to be a bad strain of luck throughout the Dodgers' system—solid play but painful losses everywhere in the very end. As attendance in Montreal was down 73,000 from the previous season, there may indeed have been a tone of "Ho-Hum" in Montreal with regard to Alston and his conservative tactics, but there was nothing negative. As in subsequent years with the Dodgers, Alston's calm manner would not be altered by any such characterizations and thoughts, be they from reporters, players, or the front office. Indeed, he would patiently wait for success to let attitudes alter themselves in the press, among the players, and within the organization.

Compared to Alston's middling-to-good reception in Montreal, Clay Hopper would not fare terribly well in St. Paul. Early in the 1950 season, he struggled. At one point in May, his Saints were in last place. Reacting to the team's fall, one reporter rhapsodized, *à la* Hamlet: "Alas poor Hopper, he isn't doing well."[43] Hopper and the Saints finished fourth in 1950 and lost in the first round of the Association playoffs. For some St. Paul fans, beyond falling from first to fourth, Hopper's 1950 Saints had also finished behind league-leading Minneapolis, and it was to the hated Millers that the Saints lost in the playoffs.

In 1951, Hopper and St. Paul came in second, but they were still nine full games behind the Milwaukee Brewers, a Boston Braves team with such talented future standouts as Dick Donovan, Johnny Logan, and Eddie Mathews. Hopper again lost in the Association playoffs. It was a respectable but less than outstanding two-season record. With this legacy, Hopper apparently came to recognize that he now had few higher prospects within the Dodgers organization. After the 1951 season, Hopper left the Dodgers altogether, managing five more years in the Pacific Coast League before retiring. Alston, meanwhile, fully settled into Montreal. If Mr. Rickey had had in mind anything to the effect of a contest of records between Alston and Hopper, by the end of the 1951 season the winner was clear. What that would have brought forth in decisions from Rickey will never be known, for, meantime, his own status had changed.

In 1950–1951, the Dodgers' organization went through a bit of upheaval. This involved a rather complicated series of maneuvers and shifts with regard to stock ownership of the Brooklyn club, stadium, and organization. Attorney Walter O'Malley, already a major stockholder, emerged, ever more fully, the principal owner here. O'Malley had already had some disputes with General Manager Branch Rickey. Now with more shares of ownership under his control, O'Malley was able, although not without some difficulties, to buy out Rickey's shares in the club, thereby, in late October of 1950, gaining full executive control of the Dodgers' organization. O'Malley then made Buzzie Bavasi the General Manager of the club. Branch Rickey left and became the General Manager of the Pittsburgh Pirates. Once again, Alston's ties with Branch Rickey were severed. This time it would prove permanent, although no one could be sure of that at the time. During the 1951 season and later, with Alston still managing in Montreal, rumors passed among baseball insiders that Branch Rickey was going to hire Alston away from the Brooklyn organization to manage the Pirates. (Similar rumors had it that Rickey also wanted to hire Clay Hopper or Brooklyn's former manager, Burt Shotton.) Some southwestern Ohioans also continued to push the idea of their lad, Walter Alston, being hired to manage the sagging Cincinnati Reds. As one reporter pressed: "As a Southern Ohio native, he would be a natural for the job."[44] Throughout, Alston remained his outwardly placid self. He maintained good relations with Bavasi, and he and Montreal would have a great season in 1951.

In these years from 1946 to 1951, Brooklyn went through quite a number of managerial shifts—going back and forth among Leo Durocher, Clyde Sukeforth (briefly), Burt Shotton, and Charlie Dressen, who would take the helm in 1951. Amidst these shifts, there is no direct evidence that Rickey, Bavasi, or O'Malley ever contemplated bringing Alston into consideration for the Brooklyn job. Other names did come up; Joe McCarthy, for example, who had left the Yankees in 1946, was actually offered the post once. This came just prior to the opening of the 1947 season when Leo Durocher was suspended. Because the nature of Durocher's highly publicized dismissal/suspension was such that he would very likely be permitted to come back for the 1948 season, McCarthy turned down such a mere interim offer.[45] Clyde Sukeforth, a third base coach, managed in place of Durocher at the time of Opening Day, with Shotton taking over after two games; Durocher did come back in 1948, only to booted again in mid-season and replaced by Shotton, who remained through 1950.

Amidst these somewhat dizzying melodramas, Alston was, of course, still working at slightly lower levels. Whether Bavasi ever brought up the idea of Alston taking the Brooklyn job is not fully known. Ever since Nashua, 1946, Bavasi was solidly behind Alston. When

Shotton left after the 1950 season, Bavasi had just become the team's GM under O'Malley. Even if he harbored any thoughts about advising O'Malley to consider Alston, Bavasi likely knew not to push such a matter with his new boss. He knew, of course, that O'Malley, and many others, could readily point to Alston's inexperience at that point. Besides, Alston's work up in Montreal, so steadily producing and polishing talent for the Brooklyn, was going quite well.

In the 1951 season, the Royals won everything possible. They took the regular season pennant by an 11-game margin over second-place Rochester. They would have been even further ahead had star outfielder/utility man George Shuba not been injured in August. In the International League playoffs, the Royals first swept Buffalo in four straight games. Then they thumped Syracuse (who had beaten Rochester) four games to one, winning the final game with 18 runs. Naturally, the Montreal fans and press were full of praise, but nods of approval for Alston came from other International League cities too. "It seems that Manager Wally Alston is strangely jittery for a pilot whose team has been out in front so long," wondered Syracuse writer Bill Reddy. "Alston fusses whenever his pitcher is in the slightest jam. He spends half his time, it seems, conferring with his moundsmen in the middle of the diamond. He has his bullpen busy at the merest threat. Perhaps this is the reason his team is so far in front."[46] After winning the International League's regular season pennant, as well as the league playoffs, Alston would have loved to face St. Paul in the Little World Series. It was not to be, however, as the Milwaukee Brewers had won the American Association. So Alston and the Royals promptly beat Milwaukee. Branch Rickey may have enjoyed reading of this in his office in Pittsburgh. More importantly, Walter O'Malley and Buzzie Bavasi were very pleased. In that autumn of 1951, the only better news for Alston came with the wedding of his daughter.[47]

One of Alston's effective little managerial ploys in Montreal involved the ways he treated his pitchers. He had concocted no mysterious magic formula as to how to make pitchers throw more effectively or be less susceptible to arm troubles. (No one has ever been able to do that; as the Yankees' Joe McCarthy once sniffed: "Anyone who thinks he understands women or pitchers is a sucker.") Alston did take great pains to attend to every detail he could about the strengths, weaknesses, and tendencies of the hitters around the league, and worked closely with his pitchers so they would be equally up on all such details about each batter they would likely face. Such careful study would enable pitchers to perform with an added edge of informed confidence. Alston would continue to do this with all his pitchers in Brooklyn and Los Angeles.[48]

Beyond such attention to the specifics about hitters that Alston always carefully reviewed with his staff, another matter to which Alston steadily devoted his energies involved demanding that his pitchers work hard on their hitting and fielding, as well as on their general physical conditioning. While he was stating the obvious, Alston did make the point that "it's only reasonable that you have a better chance to win with nine batters in the lineup instead of eight." He held the same attitude about fielding. In the minor leagues, as Alston was generally dealing with young players, even in Montreal. He thus saw no reason why weak hitting in a pitcher had simply to be accepted with a shrug, an attitude many managers took in both the minor leagues and the majors. Back in Nashua in 1946, he had seen how valuable a player Don Newcombe was, beyond his obvious hard throwing, because of his prowess with a bat. Alston wanted to develop habits and abilities in young pitchers before it was too late—habits that would in no way detract from any pitcher's primary functions. To him there was simply no reason to assume that a pitcher would be a weak hitter or an inattentive fielder. Alston had what one writer described as "a pet peeve against hurlers [during batting practice] striding into the batter's box and taking three weak swings before stepping out." In Montreal, Alston set up a system in which, before home games, the pitchers had to report a half-hour earlier than the rest of the squad and spend extra time in the batting cage before the rest of the players arrived for practice. A result here was that in 1951, pitcher Bud Podbielan hit .286, Tom Lasorda hit .290, and Dan Bankhead hit .364. Alston was equally meticulous in his pitchers concentrating on all their base running and fielding responsibilities too.[49] Several of Alston's pitchers from the Montreal years, and before, would help themselves and their teams immeasurably not only with great pitching, but with smart base running as well as with solid fielding and hitting. Later in 1965, for example, while compiling a record of 23–12, Los Angeles Dodgers pitcher Don Drysdale also hit .300 in 58 games. In Brooklyn in 1954 and 1955, Don Newcombe hit .319 in 31 games and .359 in 57 games.[50]

Reporters throughout the International League noted Alston's innovations amidst his successful string of seasons in Montreal. Buzzie Bavasi, Walter O'Malley, and others in the Brooklyn offices noticed such things too. The Dodgers had certainly put together a potent organization. It was winning pennants in Brooklyn, and it had a farm system that steadily supplied the big club with a stream of talented, well-trained youngsters. Alston had established himself as an especially significant part of this "supply system." The great Brooklyn teams which won pennants in 1947, 1949, 1952, and 1953 were chock full of men who had taken some training with Alston. He prepared them well, and these play-ers all respected Alston for his even-handedness, his firmness, his rigor, and his knowledge and savvy. He was a great manager for whom people wanted to play. Alston's roles in the Brooklyn organization would have all been part of a glorious picture in the minds of O'Malley and the rest of the team were it not for one problem, a problem that was not Alston's fault in any way, but one which lurked in the hearts and minds of Dodg-ers faithful everywhere—the team had yet to win a World Series! No matter how perfect any component of the organization appeared, this one ugly fact overrode everything. Amidst such anguish-tinged pride, the question was whether the unfolding of events could ever give Alston an opportunity to help with this problem, as he had already addressed and solved so many others for Brooklyn. The answer would be yes, but it would take a little more time. There would be euphoria, but it would come with some unforeseen edges.

5

Who's He?

When Walter Alston taught high school and coached in New Madison and Lewiston, Ohio, he was always able to maintain a good rapport with the students. Teaching the basic sciences, mechanical drawing, and wood shop, he readily commanded attention as he knew the fields thoroughly. Beyond that, as he recalled, given the practicality of what he was teaching, most of the students "seemed to realize how important what they were learning would be when they had their own farms someday."[1] In his managerial work in minor league baseball, the students/players obviously knew what he was teaching them was going to make them better ball players, and because he knew the game so well, he could readily get his players to perk up. If Alston had any sort of managerial magic touch, it was at least partially rooted in the practicalities on which he harped with all his young players. The turn-around he achieved in Trenton showed that in 1944, as did subsequent successes in Nashua, Pueblo, St. Paul, and Montreal.

With his high school students, Alston also cast quite a figure. Here was one of their teachers/coaches who had actually played in the big leagues with the St. Louis Cardinals and who managed professional baseball when school was out. He was clearly not someone with whom one could trifle, either in class or in the gym. Alston was also a big, imposing man, and in his younger days this had a strong impact in itself. (Back in New Hampshire in 1946, Alston certainly engendered respect from his players when he exploded and had to be physically restrained when catcher Sal Yvars ran over him.)

Along more purely psychological lines, Alston also possessed an innate sense of how any trifling/hazing inklings could manifest themselves in young people, and he knew how to deal with them to great effect. He recalled, for example, one Agriculture teacher at Lewiston High School who "created problems for himself." It seemed the teacher "was always bragging about what a stern disciplinarian he was, that he was a judo expert and [that] none of those big hayseed kids were going to get away with anything with him." Alston innately grasped how any such martinet-like posturings would invariably invite some sort of testing from young people. Indeed, he recalled how, when some Agriculture students had constructed a hog house, they told their pompous Agriculture teacher that they could not fit the final piece of flooring into the house. The teacher went inside to look, and as soon as he was in the pen, the students "closed and locked the door." They "had taken twenty-five-penny nails and closeted him up good and tight." Alston remembered hearing "a big commotion [with] someone yelling and pounding 'Let me out, let me out.'" Alston smirked that "I enjoyed the episode as much as the kids." Hearing the teacher yell, Alston paid no heed—"I went about my work as if I didn't hear a thing." When "the superintendent came by asking if I had seen the ag. teacher," Alston nodded: "'No, I haven't seen him.' [and] I wasn't lying. I hadn't seen him. I just heard him." Alston chuckled, "I had to take a big crowbar to break him out."[2]

As a baseball manager, Alston always maintained the same feel for the instincts that drove his high school students to haze a somewhat highly-strung colleague. As long as there was nothing inherently harmful in what they were doing, such episodes as that of the Ohio hog house were not only good fun, they involved the kind of deflation of pomposities in which some will naturally indulge themselves. Alston would engage in a few mischievous pranks himself. He once wired an Ohio teacher's chair so she would receive a few minor jolts during a faculty meeting. The teacher subsequently complained about a rather shy male colleague of pinching her during the meeting. The truth of this Depression-era incident did not air until 1970.[3]

Alston understood that a teacher, a coach, a manager *has* to wield authority. But he or she best does so with a sense of full command over the subject matter at hand, and with little to no sense of self-gratification. Alston's students never challenged or hazed him. He was too genuine a human being to invite any sniping, and he knew his business so well that respect was all that could come forth. (And being a big muscular man did not hurt his standing here among the young farm boys and girls either, nor did the fact that he could shoot a gun or a pool cue with such dexterity as he did.) Alston knew, without any need to articulate it that gratification should come with the success in the activities at hand, be they in the classroom or on the ball field or the basketball court. Some managers operate like martinets and wield authority like military drill sergeants. Even if their teams succeed, they often do so in spite of themselves. Alston was a manager, and a teacher, who never sought glory for himself. When his teams achieved something, he was quite content to let the players bask in the glory, and this, itself, was no merely coy posture of "retreating into the limelight" either. On the surface, such genuine modesty, combined with utter command over the specific subject matter at hand, appears so simple an issue, yet when quality management questions are at issue in so many businesses and professions, the ideal often proves rather elusive. As far as his own consciousness and training for his work here, Alston did once reflect: "While teaching in the Ohio school system, I learned how to make suggestions tactfully enough so they would be kindly received."[4] Thousands of management manuals and texts may fill the shelves of bookstores and libraries, but so much theorizing usually comes back to the basic elements that go into the handling of the people in one's charge—the requisite knowledge of how to evaluate potential and performance, how to impart lessons to improve work, how to instill a willingness among people to work together. In all such areas, Alston excelled because he so thoroughly knew the business before him, and because he did not muddy any situation with excrescences of personality or ego. Outwardly, it appeared so simple, but it was, and is, quite rare and very successful.

The 1952 and 1953 seasons would both be good ones for Montreal, as well as for Brooklyn. In 1952, Alston and the Royals breezed to the International League regular season title, winning by 8½ games over second-place Syracuse. In 1953, while finishing the regular season in second place behind Rochester, Montreal went on to win the IL playoffs. What proved even more important for Alston was a win that came after the IL championship. The Royals went on to defeat the American Association's champion, Kansas City, in the Little World Series. This post-season victory sat well with the Dodgers' management in Brooklyn, and this would quickly have major significance for Alston.

While such matters as the Little World Series were always important for the Dodgers' organization, the seemingly obscure victory held a special poignancy in 1953. In 1952 and 1953, the Brooklyn Dodgers took the National League pennant. They had clearly established themselves as a truly great team, and with such a record as Alston and Montreal were compiling beneath them, Brooklyn could certainly justify optimistic outlooks about their success continuing into the future. Playing for Alston in Montreal were such future major league standouts as Don Hoak, Jim Gilliam, Rocky Nelson, Gino Cimoli, Sandy Amoros, Dick Williams, Tommy Lasorda, and Johnny Podres. One matter continually chastened any such euphoria about the team's future, however. Brooklyn's pennants in 1952 and 1953, like the prior three in 1941, 1947, and 1949, had each been followed by painful losses in the World Series. For Brooklynites, the even more galling aspect of this string of World

Series defeats was that each came at the hands of the hated New York Yankees.

A sense of borough status was always at issue among competitive New Yorkers. For Brooklyn residents of the era, their standing versus Manhattanites and other New Yorkers was especially significant. Brooklyn was an independent city until 1898. Elite Manhattanites regularly regarded the borough across the East River with a haughty disdain—a poorer, mere working-class community, one where no sane, cultured person would ever choose to reside. The name "Dodgers" had indeed originated from the chuckling disregard that Manhattanites held about Brooklyn residents. The people unfortunate enough to reside "over there" had, by reputation among Manhattanites, to spend their days "dodging" the dangerous horse-drawn, later electric, trollies that whisked through Brooklyn's streets. (There was something to this, as by 1886, Brooklyn pedestrians were being run over by trollies and dying at a rate of one per week.) "Brooklyn Trolley Dodgers" thus became a derisive name that haughty Manhattan residents cast at their neighbors in the late 19th century. Proud Brooklyn residents countered the derision and enmity by rallying around the very words which their neighbors were hurling at them. So notable was the moniker that Brooklyn's ball club would use the name "Trolley Dodgers." Between 1883 and 1932, the team also employed such other names as "Superbas," "Bridegrooms," "Grooms," "Grays," and "Atlantics," but throughout, "Trolley Dodgers" had been a common reference. "Dodgers" simply emerged as a shortened form of the original nickname, and it became official in 1932. (When Wilbert Robinson managed the Dodgers from 1914 to 1931, the team was also nicknamed the "Robins" and sometimes the "Robbies," and throughout the years there was always the informal but popular "Bums," more precisely "dem Bums."[5])

Each baseball season provided another chapter of verbal taunts in the long intra–NYC cross-borough rivalry, as for so many years the Yankees were great and the Dodgers mediocre. Ever since 1920, the regular success of the Yankees had fully reinforced established New Yorkers' proud feelings of superiority over everyone in the baseball world and beyond, including and especially those poor souls across the East River. From 1920 through the 1930s, Dodgers fans could make little use of their baseball team in their search for points of pride against Manhattan and the rest of the city. The Dodgers were usually a terrible team, while the Yankees were a perennial power. Then, at long last, in the early 1940s and into the 1950s, the Dodgers built a most formidable team in which Brooklyn could take great pride. Nonetheless, in these years each of the Dodgers' five pennants had ended with losses to those damned

Yankees. As rabid Brooklyn fan Sid Caesar put it: "It wasn't that we were the second-best team in baseball." That, he felt, may have been acceptable (however begrudgingly). What no one could stand, said Caesar, was that the record clearly meant that "we were not only the second-best team in baseball but the second-best team in New York!" Brooklyn's two consecutive World Series losses to the Yankees in 1952 and 1953, on top of the earlier losses in 1941, 1947, and 1949, thus brought nothing but utter and excruciating anguish all over Brooklyn.

For Dodgers owner/director Walter O'Malley, interested as he was in demonstrating to the team's fans that his leadership would note a decided step of progress even from the impressive legacy of Branch Rickey, the ongoing World Series losses were especially hard to stomach. Under O'Malley's Presidency, the Dodgers had lost the pennant on the last day of the season to Philadelphia in 1950. They tied for the pennant in 1951, (in)famously losing to the Giants in a post-season playoff. Then they handily won the pennants in 1952 and 1953, amassing 201 wins in those two seasons. The team had every reason to feel proud, but no matter the legitimate pride, there stood all those the heart-breaking World Series losses to the ___ _____d Yankees.

In 1951, 1952, and '53, Brooklyn's manager had been Charlie Dressen. The World Series losses notwithstanding, Dressen clearly felt he had done a very good job with his Dodgers squads. His record was certainly laudable. All his players and most of the hard-boiled scribes of the Brooklyn press appeared to agree.

O'Malley had always demanded that his field managers accept year-by-year contracts. After three outstanding seasons, but not very long after the teeth-gnashing 1953 World Series loss to the Yankees, Dressen asked O'Malley for a new, longer-term, three-year agreement. He made his demands known to the press, thus adding a little extra pressure, something for which O'Malley never cared one bit. Alston once noted about the boss in Brooklyn: "I have always found Mr. O'Malley to be a reasonable man, but not one you'd ever want to push around."[6] With the memories of that 1953 World Series defeat still quite fresh, and with his stubborn attachment to one-year managerial agreements, O'Malley was indeed in no mood to be pushed. He had no intentions of acceding to Charlie Dressen's demands and even left him and the issue in limbo for a bit. Dressen's wife wrote O'Malley a most indignant letter, telling him how ungrateful he was![7] Whether O'Malley had already made up his mind or whether Mrs. Dressen's letter marked any sort of Rubicon, O'Malley dismissed Dressen. Reporters and fans throughout Brooklyn's neighborhoods, coffee shops, and (of course) bars began discussing and debating. For over six weeks, the matter dangled unresolved, and Brooklynites argued over whether Dressen or O'Malley was right. Knowing that O'Malley would clearly have his way, they also discussed who would (or should) succeed Dressen.

Throughout October and November of 1953, lots of names were tossed about the baseball world as to who would take the helm in Brooklyn. Some former major league stars who had managerial experience appeared as possible choices. Among them were Frankie Frisch, Lefty O'Doul, Rogers Hornsby, Bill Terry, and Gabby Hartnett. (Bill Terry was a little far-fetched an idea, as he had managed the hated Giants to pennants in the 1930s, when the Dodgers were rather weak; Terry had once sarcastically chuckled about the then cellar-dwelling Dodgers, rhetorically snorting: "Is Brooklyn still in the league?" Brooklynites did not forget.) The names of some recent Dodgers came up too—Billy Herman, Cookie Lavagetto, and Bobby Bragan. Each would eventually manage in the majors, but not in Brooklyn, though each would coach under Alston. A few brought up the idea of Jackie Robinson, now 34 years old, stepping up to run the club. There was certainly some political nobility, as well as good baseball sense, in this thought. How seriously O'Malley, Bavasi, and the team's management ever contemplated such a move in the fall of 1953 cannot be accurately determined. Apparently, the consideration of Robinson was not too deep, if only because, among the active Dodgers, the name that came up most often that autumn was Harold "Pee Wee" Reese, the team's star shortstop. Reese was 35, and he had been with the club since 1940. The idea of Reese as a player-manager appeared to resonate well with Dodgers fans, and many reporters took the idea in earnest.

It was soon after the World Series loss to the Yankees in 1953, and amidst the hubbub in the press concerning Dressen's call for a longer contract and his eventual ouster, that Walter Alston and his Montreal Royals defeated the Yankees' Kansas City club in the Little World Series. They had not only beaten them, but they did it decisively, four games to one. This victory made little impact upon fans in Brooklyn, but it was a point of comfort among some people within the Brooklyn Dodgers organization. Finally, they had at least beaten the Yankees at something! Regarding the significance of the victory over K.C. with respect to the hiring of Alston, the *New York Times* quoted: "O'Malley laughed and said, 'You might call it the clincher.'"[8]

After his Royals defeated Kansas City, Alston went home to Darrtown, as always. He knew about the dismissal of Charlie Dressen. Like anyone concerned with the fate of the Dodgers, Alston anxiously waited to learn to whom O'Malley and Brooklyn would turn. He knew that Dressen had raised O'Malley's ire when he demanded a long-term contract, and that O'Malley was certainly no one to be trifled with along any such lines. Nonetheless, he recalled his thinking: "I had the idea that somehow the problem would be patched up, all would be forgiven, and Chuck still would be invited back."[9]

On November 23, 1953, Alston received a phone call from his old friend Buzzie Bavasi, whom he had known ever since the New Hampshire days of 1946. In trying to call Alston, Bavasi would not be as riled as Branch Rickey had been back in 1944, for Alston now had a telephone in his home. Indeed, as a result of the exchange with Rickey in 1944, Alston now had an extension in each room of his house, something his wife found a bit silly. Still, like Rickey, Bavasi did have to wait a while to get to talk to Alston. Alston had gone out rabbit and pheasant hunting that morning. The Brooklyn job not yet being filled may have been an important matter, but, as far as Walter Alston was concerned, nothing like that was ever going to get in the way of the opening of small-game hunting season in Butler County. Alston bagged a bird and three rabbits that day.

When Alston returned home, his wife relayed the now many messages to telephone Bavasi pronto. "Buzzie's been calling you all day," Mrs. Alston intoned. "He won't say what it's about, but call quick." Alston called back, and Bavasi instructed him to fly to New York City right away. Bavasi further told Alston that he was to fly incognito, using the name Matt Burns. (There was a person of that name working in the Dodgers' front office.) Alston certainly knew that something was in the works, but, as was his genuinely calm nature, he felt no need to ask Bavasi for any further clarifying information. He knew he would find out what he needed to know at whatever time Bavasi and O'Malley wanted to tell him. This was no "lip-biting" act on Alston's part. He was never one to push matters. Here the worst possible scenario could have been that, with a new manager and coaching staff in Brooklyn, he was to be removed as manager of Montreal, in which case he would have happily stayed at home to Darrtown, lived quietly with his pool cues, his hunting rifles, and woodworking equipment, and likely taken up an offer for some local teaching or coaching. With any such worst-case scenarios in mind, Alston calmly, though rapidly, packed some belongings. His brother-in-law chauffeured him to the airport. "We barely made it," Alston recalled, but "Matt Burns" was on his way to New York.[10]

Alston certainly speculated about what he was to face in New York. By his own account, he entertained the thought that someone else was going to be named Brooklyn's manager and that he was to become a coach. His calm sensibilities took his imagination no further. When he arrived amidst the usual hubbub and bustle at New York's LaGuardia Airport, Alston first disregarded the loudspeaker calling "Mr. Matt Burns to the telephone." But he quickly realized who was being paged. Bavasi had sent a driver to pick him up. By the time the driver got Mr. Burns/Alston to the Roosevelt Hotel in New York, it was nearly 11:00 p.m. There he met with Bavasi, with O'Malley's Vice President, Fresco Thompson (a former second baseman who had batted .298 in nine seasons with the Pirates, Phillies, Giants, and Dodgers), and with Al Campanis, now head of the Dodgers' minor league network. There he was offered the job of managing the Brooklyn Dodgers.[11]

Alston's hiring came as a big surprise to Brooklyn fans, as well as to the New York newspapermen. A loud chorus of "Who's He?" came forth from the bars, from the streets, and from the members of the press. One Brooklyn scribe sniffed: "The Dodgers do not need a manager, and that is why they got Alston." A key and contrasting matter here involved no such head scratching, con-

Alston and Walter O'Malley. After the Brooklyn Dodgers lost their fifth World Series to the hated New York Yankees in 1953, Brooklyn fans were in a deep state of mourning. Manager Charlie Dressen nonetheless asked Brooklyn Dodgers President Walter O'Malley for a new, multi-year contract. Dressen had piloted the team to two consecutive National League pennants. He may have felt proud, but the Series losses to the Yankees did anything but sit well with O'Malley (or with Brooklyn's legendary fans). O'Malley not only turned Dressen down, he fired him. A few weeks later, O'Malley named Alston to succeed Dressen. Photograph from 1969, the year O'Malley retired (National Baseball Hall of Fame and Museum, Cooperstown, NY).

sternation, or sarcasm coming from within the Dodgers' organization, especially with Bavasi as GM. There was also no lack of firmness in the support for Alston's appointment among the Dodgers' players. Of the roster of the Dodgers' 1953 squad, 25 had already played under him, some for several seasons, at Nashua, Pueblo, St. Paul, or Montreal. They knew Alston as a fair man, technically capable, sound in all matters of strategy, a tough man when necessary, and, above all, a winner. The incredulity of Brooklyn fans and scribes could be shrugged off. Simple winning would resolve all their qualms.[12]

With the news of the selection of Alston to manage Brooklyn, the initial "Who's He?" shock gave way to more careful probings of his style and character. Fairly soon, a perspective jelled of Alston being somewhat lackluster, even drab. O'Malley himself stepped forth here, and his assertions at the very end of the year made the rounds throughout the New York press, from the city papers to the small-town newspapers upstate and beyond. "It's the team that attracts the crowd to a ball park," O'Malley asserted,

> not the manager. If I picked a colorful personality of the [Leo] Durocher type, many fans would be attracted. At the same time, some fans would stay away. Charlie Dressen was that type. After much thought I made up my mind that the team itself was the main attraction—a good hustling, winning team. And that's what the Dodgers are. Alston, though not an effervescent, colorful man, is intelligent and capable. His record proves that. He can win the National League pennant and finally the World Series. Winning that World Series is our big objective. It's become a fetish with me. We've got to win a Series.[13]

O'Malley's "fetish" was indeed the preoccupation of everyone in any way connected to the Brooklyn Dodgers. Bavasi's friendship and his confidence in Alston were certainly solid, and that meant a lot within the organization. Even with that support, to O'Malley, to the fans of Brooklyn, and for Alston there was then only one real task. He knew it; everyone knew it. Winning a World Series was everything.

6

Welcome to Brooklyn

After getting word of his appointment to manage the Brooklyn Dodgers, Alston went back home to Darrtown. He tried to spend the off-season in his usual quiet way, but newspapermen steadily streamed into Darrtown, peppering him with questions about his plans for the Dodgers in the upcoming season. Buzzie Bavasi had counseled him about the New York press and their incessant probing. Alston would always be cordial but guarded. He never snapped at anyone about any undue prying. He just weathered the pressure, later admitting that he may have been overly cautious, but he knew it was better to err on the side of caution than say something that could create controversy.

With the help of Billy Herman, now one of Alston's coaches, Mr. and Mrs. Alston found an apartment in Brooklyn (in the same building as Herman) at 1809 Albermarle Road. It was convenient, just a few subway stops from Ebbets Field, though riding the subway would take some getting-used-to for friendly small-town Ohioans like the Alstons. They were accustomed to smiling and greeting strangers they encountered in public places, hardly the norm in Brooklyn. More generally, residing in Brooklyn marked a decidedly different way of life for the Alstons. Walter had driven his automobile to Brooklyn, and he quickly realized how pointless it was to keep a car in the city, let alone pay $75 a month to garage it. (In 1954, an entire house would not rent for that much in Darrtown.) He seldom used his car except when he drove back to Ohio, and the first time he tried to leave for Ohio, his car had sat undriven for so long that the battery was dead. In Brooklyn, Alston had to adjust to the fact that he did not know his neighbors, and that his neighbors generally had no interest in trying to get to know him or his wife. On the streets, just as in the subway, people did not only not greet one another, they did not even make eye contact. As Alston recalled, "it took a long time to get used to it," adding: "I can never say that I enjoyed being a city man."[1] Of course, adjusting to life in the city was not his purpose for being there.

When Alston gathered with the Dodgers in Vero Beach, Florida, for spring training in early March 1954, many matters concerning the team's line-up for the coming season seemed well in place. After his appointment in late 1953, Alston had waved off reporters' inquiries about any moves he was considering with the team's lineup. "There is little I can say until I have had time to inspect things at the training camp." Both O'Malley and Bavasi smiled at the news of such calmly muffled style. Even in regard to questions about his general approach to managing, Alston would give little away, and this was no mere posture of stonewalling the press. His answer was sincere: Would he be a strict disciplinarian or an "honor type" manager? His answer: that would depend on future developments.[2]

Alston certainly had a squad that would earn the envy of any other manager—"an all-star at every position," as Alston later reflected. The claim was a slight overstatement, however. Certainly, he had Campanella at catcher, Duke Snider in center field, Pee Wee Reese at shortstop, Carl Furillo in right field, and Gil Hodges at first base.[3] As Alston took up managing the team, other positions on the Dodgers—second base, third base, and left field especially—were a bit in limbo. A major element of the situation here would involve Jackie Robinson.

After being named to succeed Charlie Dressen, Alston had quipped to reporters, with sincere respect, "I'm pretty sure Jackie Robinson will be playing somewhere in our lineup."[4] By 1954, however, Robinson was getting older. Just before the pre-season training, in January, he turned 35, and he was beginning to lose a little of his formidable speed. For any mediocre team of the day like the Chicago Cubs or the Cincinnati Reds (then called the "Redlegs," a conscious capitulation to the McCarthyism-driven anti-communist climate of the era), this would not have been a problem. A man like Robinson would have easily gone on playing every day, with owners and management likely content with the level of both the play and the resulting gate revenues. But Alston was inheriting a team and a situation that required everything to be utilized to its absolute maximum potential. The pressure to win that elusive World Series always loomed. Through 1952, Robinson had usually been the team's second baseman; sometimes he played first base. In 1953, under Charlie Dressen, he had begun to play more outfield, so some adjustments to age had already begun.

Alston began to use Robinson more as a utility player, and in this context, he would give Robinson a bit more rest. In 1954, Robinson played in 124 games, down from prior years. Naturally, Robinson did not like or agree with this slight relegation; it stuck with him. "When I'm fit," Robinson exclaimed to a reporter towards the end of spring training in 1955, "I've got a right to be playing and Alston knows it. Or maybe he doesn't know it." Later, in the pre-season of that spring in 1955, when the club had stopped in Louisville for some exhibitions, Alston would have a meeting with Robinson. Robinson later described the meeting as "a humdinger." The two did come to an understanding. Some players came to believe that the settled nature of Robinson-Alston relationship helped solidify the squad emotionally. Some went so far as to say that the Dodgers' 1955 pennant was won at that meeting. Alston understood and certainly respected Robinson here, not in spite of the resistance but indeed because of it. To Alston, a truly great athlete could react no other way. Alston noted: "this was Jackie's eighth year with the Dodgers. ... He was recognized as the kind of player whose performance had inspirational qualities. He was a born leader, who had survived the greatest challenge [integrating the game] ever faced by a big league player. ... His whole career provided one solid example after another that challenges were his meat; he literally thrived on them."[5]

Alston certainly understood the need for tact and diplomacy. He always held to the point that "there was never a feud" between himself and Robinson. One bit of tension did come forth in 1954 during their first spring training in Vero Beach. Like all managers, Alston started every daily practice with calisthenics. Robinson would arrive late for the exercises and usually found a reporter with whom he would converse. Alston waited a few days, and then spoke with Robinson privately. Robinson, Alston recalled, "didn't like being called on it," but thereafter he began arriving on time and exercised with the rest of the team. Another time that spring during an exhibition game, Robinson was not playing. He was supposed to remain in the dugout for possible pinch-hitting, but Robinson chose to go out to the bullpen and chat with a reporter. Alston and the Dodgers had a spring training rule—reporters could speak to players before or after exhibition games, but not during them. With Robinson electing to defy this rule, Alston called a pre-game meeting. He raised the fact of the rule to the whole team. While Alston was speaking, Robinson chose to converse with a teammate. Alston decided to challenge him on his behavior.

> When I called him on it in front of everybody, he talked back a little. The conversation got a little rough. But it never really got out of control. I told Robinson right then and there that he, as well as any other player, could talk to me any time, any place, about anything. This was interpreted by some of those present as a physical challenge. It could have been. I inferred that if Robinson wanted to test me, the man-to-man way, that was all right with me, too. Roy Campanella, one of my all-time favorites as a man and player, helped to calm the situation. We did not fight. I was glad it happened that way. It was good for the whole club. ... I was in the habit of treating everyone alike. This was the way it had to be with Jackie Robinson, and if we were to continue on the same team this was the way he had to understand it.[6]

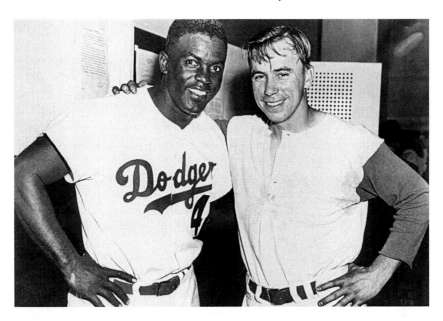

Jackie Robinson (left) and Pee Wee Reese in 1955. Appointed manager of the Brooklyn Dodgers, Alston inherited a fabulous team. As Alston acknowledged: "an all-star at every position." It was, indeed, a most impressive lineup, with the likes of Roy Campanella catching, Gil Hodges playing first base, Duke Snider in center field, Carl Furillo in right field, and such pitchers as Sal Maglie, Don Newcombe, and Carl Erskine. The Dodgers' stars had played for Alston as they had come through the minors, except for shortstop Pee Wee Reese and second baseman Jackie Robinson. Alston was effusive in his praise for Robinson, acknowledging both his enormous talents and his fierce competitive spirit. Even more, Alston expressed a respect that bordered on awe regarding the mission Robinson carried out as the point man in the integration of the national pastime (National Baseball Hall of Fame and Museum, Cooperstown, NY).

Alston recognized that a certain amount of testing would naturally come from such a star player with a new manager, one who had indeed played in but one game of major league baseball. In Robinson, Alston saw that while "I caught him on the downgrade, ... he had lost nothing of his pride, the desire, the determination, the dedication, the sheer spirit that made him the ballplayer he was." Alston would yield to some of Robinson's requests. When tired, for example, Robinson would sometimes ask to be taken out of a game in the late innings. Alston would oblige, "but just as often," as Alston mentioned, "if I thought we needed him to win, he would stay in. He always understood." Still, by the outset of the 1955 season, Robinson found himself being used less and less. He had played in 136 games in Dressen's last year in 1953. Under Alston in 1954, he was down to 124, and in 1955 he was further down to 105. Naturally he did not like it, and he would make his feelings known to reporters. Alston grew irate at that. He called a team meeting and denounced players who went to the press with any such thoughts about the team. Robinson reacted here, saying Alston needed to talk to the players, and that players only went to reporters because he did not. Gil Hodges stepped between the two as they approached one another over the matter. Without a hint of masculine bravado, but in a perfectly matter-of-fact manner, Alston would acknowledge: "I held a clubhouse meeting and called him in front of everybody and he talked back. I told him if he wanted to test me physically, man to man, it was all right with me. Perhaps I didn't baby him as much as Dressen and Durocher before me."

On a few occasions during the 1954 season, Robinson found Alston less aggressive in some of his game tactics. This prompted some rumors that Robinson thought his new manager to be lacking in areas of mental agility. In 1954, in an early September loss in Chicago, Duke Snider was awarded a double on a fly ball Robinson and others felt should have been ruled a home run. Noting that Alston did not contest the call, Robinson noted: "The team might be moving somewhere if Alston had not been standing at third base like a wooden Indian." Such stories of player dissatisfaction were repeated, but they did not take too great a hold. Alston's quiet manner would always generate expressions of dissatisfaction, as well as rumors of ineffectiveness. Bavasi and O'Malley always knew better, but with the backdrop of such disputatious skippers as Durocher and Dressen, Alston's manner did not always inspire some already-disgruntled players and uninformed fans.

In regard to Sandy Koufax, some, including Robinson, saw such potential in the youngster that they were frustrated by the infrequency of Alston's early utilization of the fireballer, Robinson and others believing Koufax would grow more consistent with regular starts in the pitching rotation. At the same time, however, other stars like Duke Snider were keenly aware of how many pennants had been lost by a mere game or two. While certainly recognizing Koufax's potential, they felt that too many starts for the wild youngster ran undue risks. Alston simply had to sit through the second-guessing as well as the many contradictions.[7]

Alston anticipated other such testing and pressures as Robinson brought possibly coming from more of the veterans. Pee Wee Reese chose to offer no challenges, however. This was important, as Reese was clearly a team leader and, like Robinson, he was one of the few Dodgers who had never played for Alston in the minors. Gil Hodges, Duke Snider, and Roy Campanella offered no challenges either. Of course, they knew and felt very positively about Alston from their days in Nashua, St.

Paul, and Montreal, so Robinson's actions proved to have little wider significance. This was not only better for Alston, it was better for everyone, including Robinson.

With the positions of second, third, and left a trifle amorphous, Alston had several young players, plus Robinson, to insert in different situations in varying combinations. He had Jim Gilliam, Don Hoak, Sandy Amoros, and Don Zimmer. In prior seasons, Robinson had already played some first base; now he would play second, third, and left, as would Gilliam, Hoak, Amoros, and Zimmer. The shifts were not without difficulties, but few found fault with Alston's thinking and personnel choices here. Generally, Alston employed a basic platooning system here, with left-handed batters used against right-handed pitchers and vice-versa. The collectivity of the play of the five everyday players proved strong. The other four gained valuable experience and never burdened the team with lesser play from the typical learning processes of a rookie/sophomore.

While handling the somewhat delicate Robinson situation, Alston had the ease of his perennial all-stars at the five other starting positions. Center fielder Duke Snider and first baseman Gil Hodges would come through with phenomenal seasons in 1954. Each hit over 40 home runs and batted over .300 (Snider hit .342). Pee Wee Reese also hit .309; Furillo hit .294, and all continued their usual brilliant defensive play in the field. Campanella would have problems in 1954, however. Early in the season he had a bone chip in his left wrist. In early May he had surgery on his wrist and would not return to the line-up until Memorial Day. From the surgery, Campanella had a bit of nerve damage; it left him with a numbness in two fingers of his left hand. Fortunately, this was temporary, but while the problem persisted, Campanella could not handle a bat with his usual dexterity. That season he hit a mere.207, quite a drop from the prior season when he hit .312.[8]

Campanella's injury and surgery left the team a little weaker. Rube Walker replaced Campy for 50 games that season, but he hit just .181. Elsewhere Alston had some problems with his pitchers and being without Campanella to handle the staff made that situation worse. Don Newcombe had won 20 games in 1951 and led the National League in strikeouts. Then he spent two years in the Navy, and when he returned in 1954, he found his skills a trifle rusty. He would bounce back by 1955 and 1956, but in 1954 he won but nine games and struck out only 82 batters. Another former star pitcher, Preacher Roe, was now 38, and in 1954 he won only three games and pitched merely 63 innings. Johnny Podres, age 21, showed great promise, but he came down with appendicitis and missed several weeks of the spring and early summer. He would win only 11 games and strike out 79. Carl Erskine would be the team's ace with 18 wins and 166 strikeouts, but he also lost 15 games. Aside from Erskine, no other pitcher stood out. The pitching staff's collective ERA was a disappointing 4.31. The 1954 Dodgers were certainly a solid team. As of August 29, they were 1½ games out of first place. They would win 92 games, but the New York Giants, led by 23-year-old Willie Mays, just back from a year in the Army, won 97 and took the pennant by five games. They went on to sweep Cleveland in the World Series.[9]

With the end of the 1954 season and the failure to defeat the New York Giants for the pennant, Alston was fully prepared for O'Malley and Bavasi to dismiss him. He had obviously not done as well as Charlie Dressen. The Giants actually clinched the 1954 pennant with a win over Brooklyn on September 21. Giants manager Leo Durocher was certainly happy about beating Brooklyn. After the victory, someone near Durocher chided, "Walter Alston sure lost this one." Durocher took Alston's side here, observing, "He did a great job considering the injuries he had this year. Alston's a real nice guy." When a reporter reminded Durocher of his famous saying, "Nice guys finish last," Durocher smiled: "Well maybe not all the time."[10]

Alston received verbal assurances from Bavasi that his position was safe, but no new contract reached him home in Darrtown. Alston did receive word from Bavasi to come to Vero Beach for the 1955 spring training. When Alston arrived, Bavasi asked him about never mailing back his signed contract. Alston informed him that no contract had arrived. Apparently, it had merely been lost in the mail. Bavasi immediately produced a new one, Alston signed it, and, simple as that, the 1955 season was set.[11] Most other managers would stew unduly over such an ambiguous situation. For Alston, the worst-case scenario in any such hiccough as this contract matter in 1955 would find him moving back to Darrtown, something with which he would always be content. Therein lay much of the solid grounding under which he always worked with Bavasi and O'Malley.

In 1955, all the previous season's little injuries and illnesses to Campanella, Podres, Newcombe, and others had passed. The team was completely healthy, and away they went. Newcombe won 20 games, and he hit .359. Campanella, Snider, and Hodges each had over 100 RBI; Furillo had 95. Furillo, Snider, and Campanella each hit over .300; Hodges hit .289. There were no weaknesses in the lineup. The pitching proved to lack a little depth. Don Newcombe won 20 games, but the next best, Clem Labine, won only 13, and largely in relief. Second to Newcombe among the starters was Carl Erskine, and he won only 11. The offense was spectacular, however, and they could overwhelm any opposing pitching staff in the league. The offense was so strong that the only controversy involved debates as to whether Snider or Campanella should be the league's MVP. The sportswriters' voting yielded a virtual tie between them, with one improperly completed ballot denying a few key points to Snider that would have been decisive in his favor. But no team dissension arose here, and Campanella won his third NL MVP Award. In the pennant race, Brooklyn sprinted the first weeks of the season, going 10–0 at the outset. Six different pitchers won games. By May 10, their record was 22–2. They were well in front in the National League, and from there they were never seriously challenged. Twelve and one-half games up on July 4, Brooklyn clinched the pennant on September 8, the earliest in the history of the National League. They finished the season with 98 wins, 13½ games ahead of the second-place Milwaukee Braves. The pennant was a breeze. Now Brooklyn was going to another World Series, and once again, they were to face those _____ Yankees. It was as though the fates of the game had planned this: with the Giants' pennant of the previous year, Cleveland, not the Yankees, faced them in the Series. Now, once again, the proverbial stars were in proper alignment. The Dodgers and the Yankees were squaring off in October.[12]

After such a great season, Brooklyn reporters and fans were fully enthused about the World Series. Still, all those losses to the Yankees so many times before lingered in the memories of every Brooklynite. The first two games of the Series brought those memories even more fearfully to life, as the Yankees took both games. Even in these losses, however, Alston had enabled the team, and one player in particular, to make a determined statement to all. Throughout the season, Alston had been utilizing Jackie Robinson with a decided measure. Robinson had appeared in 105 games, largely at third base, with Brooklyn's other third baseman, Don Hoak, playing in 94 games. In the first game of the Series, Alston started Robinson at third. The Yankees' Joe Collins hit two home runs and Elston Howard hit one, all off Don Newcombe. The game looked like a breeze for the Yankees as they led, 6–3. In the eighth inning, Robinson reached third base against Whitey Ford. In what became one of the most famous plays in World Series history, the 36-year-old Robinson stole home off Ford. Catcher Yogi Berra screamed at umpire Bill Summers that Robinson was out, a conviction Berra adamantly held for the rest of his life. Alston had always given Robinson the discretion to use his own judgment about stealing in such situations. The daring maneuver helped the Dodgers rally for two runs that inning, drawing to within one run of New York. The Yankees won the game, but, with Alston's approval, Robinson had sent both the Yankees and his own teammates a strong message that the Series was going to be a fight every inch of the way. This outlook maintained itself among Alston's Dodgers, even with the Yankees winning the second game. To some Yankees fans, it may have looked like the beginning of yet another routine New York win over Brooklyn. Some even began to speculate that, by winning the pennant so early, the Dodgers had lost some of their edge. Of further note was the point that, since the very first World Series, no team had come back to win the World Series after losing the first two games. New York scribes and fans raised all such matters with a decided glee.[13]

Down two games to nothing, and with the snarling message and spirit from Jackie Robinson still very much alive among them, the Dodgers went back to Ebbets Field and proceeded to win the next three games. All the Yankees' arrogance and chortling ceased. But back in Yankee Stadium for Game Six, Whitey Ford pitched a great game for New York. This left the Series tied 3–3 with the seventh game in Yankee Stadium to decide everything.

Alston decided to start Johnny Podres in Game Seven. That season, Podres had completed only five of 24 starts. His last complete game was way back on June 12. But Alston had faith in Podres' ability to pitch under pressure. He "really thrived on it," Alston noted. "To me he was at his best with the most at stake." After Podres won the important third game of the Series, Alston had told him, "if there is a seventh game, you're my pitcher." Podres remembered that Alston's words "boosted me up unbelievably." Alston was not one to push psychological buttons often, but when he did, he was usually quite effective. Podres was a quiet person, one who seldom bragged, but here the confidence he had drawn from Alston would be evident, and it would have an impact on the team. When the players gathered in Brooklyn to board a bus for Yankee Stadium for Game Seven, many were nervous. Podres arrived and he cheerfully told everyone, "Just get me one run." The team grew relaxed and arrived at Yankee Stadium in a confident mood. Elsewhere, Alston had his usual line-up with Campanella, Hodges, Reese, Snider, and Furillo. Alston went with Hoak at third base, as Robinson was tiring and hobbling a bit with a sore foot. He had contributed much in earlier parts of the Series anyway. With second base and left field, Alston had done some platooning. Jim Gilliam played left field or second base. When he was in left, Don Zimmer played second. When Gilliam played second, Sandy Amoros played left. This pattern would prove important.[14]

Gil Hodges drove in a run in the fourth inning with a single, and he drove in another run with a sacrifice fly in the sixth. During the Dodgers' sixth-inning rally that produced the second run, Alston pinch-hit for Don Zimmer, who had been playing second base. Up to that point, Gilliam had been playing left field. With Zimmer out for a pinch-hitter, in the bottom of the inning, Alston brought Gilliam in to play second and inserted Sandy Amoros in left field. This set up the situation for the most famous play in the history of Brooklyn baseball.

In bottom half of the sixth inning, Billy Martin led off with a walk. Gil McDougald dropped a surprise bunt that he beat out for a single, moving Martin to second. Yogi Berra was next up, and the clouds of some sort of dreaded inexorable Yankee rally and victory appeared to be gathering. With runners on first and second, Alston was playing the left-handed Berra to pull, shifting both his infielders and outfielders well toward right field. Surprisingly, Berra sliced a Podres offering down the left field line. It would have been a fairly routine out had the outfield been set in a normal array. But Alston had shaded left fielder Amoros well toward center, so Berra's slice appeared to be a sure extra-base hit, one that would likely score both Martin and McDougald, tie the game, and leave Berra on second with none out.

Such offensive plays were often the stuff of Yankee rallies and victories in decisive situations with Brooklyn. It seemed to be yet another Yankee triumph coming forth. But, in one of the classic moments of World Series play, Sandy Amoros, one of the fastest players in the majors, came flying across left field. Unlike Gilliam, Amoros was also left-handed, hence his gloved hand was his right. Amoros' speed was such that he readily got to the ball, even slowing himself a trifle as he approached the railing of the stands down the left field line. Being a lefty, Amoros was able to extend his glove hand, and he made a sensational running catch, while managing as well to avoid crashing into the side railing. Amoros could have banged into the railing and dropped the ball. Even if he had held it, a collision could have prevented any good throw and allowed the two Yankee runners to retreat successfully. But Amoros was able to stop and throw accurately to shortstop Pee Wee Reese. Amoros had indeed made a great play, one that drew much praise, then and since.

Of importance here too was the less noted contribution of Pee Wee Reese. If Berra's slice had landed for a hit, Reese knew he would likely have to relay the ball home. If Amoros caught the ball, he would still have a throw to first or second. In either case, Reese anticipated the difficult throw Amoros could have so close to the railing, so he made the intelligent choice to run over to the third base line, leaving Amoros with a shorter, more easily-sighted throw to make straight down the left-field line, which he did. From there Reese crow-hopped and pegged an accurate one-bounce relay. (One bounce is always the preferred throw from a distance, as a skipping ball gathers a slight bit of speed and hits the receiving glove a split second earlier; Pee Wee did everything perfectly.)

Reese's relay hit Gil Hodges at first. Gil McDougald, the runner on first, had anticipated that Berra's hit would land safely, and he had run just past second base, hoping to score. He did his best to scamper back to first after Amoros' catch, but Reese's perfect throw cut him down. Knowing he could easily score from second, Billy Martin had taken a shorter lead and had but a quick trot back to second base. Martin would be stranded there, however, as the next batter, Hank Bauer, grounded harmlessly to end the inning. What first looked like a game-winning Yankee rally ended with them scoring none. For the next three innings, Podres held New York. The 2–0 lead stood, and the Dodgers had their World Series victory at last. All Brooklyn went nuts.[15]

Alston was as happy as anyone in the Brooklyn clubhouse after the World Series victory. His shift of Amoros to left field appeared clairvoyant. Alston would hear none of that. He simply inserted Amoros as he always did when he put Gilliam at second. (And the earlier use of George Shuba to pinch-hit for Zimmer had not worked anyway.) After the game, Alston expressed great pride in Podres for the shutout he threw: "with three days' rest he had come back to shackle some of the great bats in baseball and win the big one. Twice I had gone out to the mound to talk with him but neither time was I close to taking him out." Alston had Clem Labine ready in the bullpen, "but when John got Berra [in the sixth inning] I decided to leave him in." In regard to the Series victory, Alston was his typical placid self, commenting to reporters how the victory involved "a combined effort not only of one or two players but of the entire squad from the beginning to the end." He spoke of how important the team's great start in April had been, and he praised the value of some replacement players the team had brought up from St. Paul and Montreal.[16] Alston was not being intentionally bland, it was his natural demeanor and his genuine understanding of the value of the contributions of so many to the victory. His consciousness about the value of so many little contributions was part of what made him so effective as a manager.

Folks out in Darrtown whooped it up over Alston and the Dodgers' victory nearly as much as did the people in Brooklyn. In Brooklyn, the night of the victory, Alston could barely make it into his apartment building because of the boisterous crowds, and even once he got home, the noise from the streets made it impossible to sleep. Back in Ohio the rejoicing was huge as well. Over the next months, Alston would remember, "I don't think our phone ever quit ringing or the mailman ever passed our box without stopping."[17] During that off-season he received speaking invitations and awards all over the region. Completely independent of his baseball fame, in that same off-season on February 1,

1956, the Winchester Repeating Arms Company also named Walter Alston the "Winchester Outdoorsman of the Year." Alston was still a top marksman. In one skeet-shooting contest that winter, he hit a perfect 100 of 100! Many of his friends had said: never challenge Alston to any sort of contest involving a pool cue or a gun. Modestly but frankly, Alston admitted that in straight pool he had on several occasions run over 100 balls. The master Willie Mosconi passed through Cincinnati that winter, and he took a side trip up to Alston's home in Darrtown, where they played a game of "straight pool." Alston lost that one, but he always treasured the cue that Mosconi inscribed and gave him. Whether it was pool, skeet, or baseball, in the winter of 1956–1957, Alston was on top of it all.[18]

7

On Top in Brooklyn but Not for Long

After finally winning a World Series, it was difficult for the Dodgers and their fans not to be optimistic about the 1956 season. With the same group of stars back again, optimists throughout Brooklyn saw every reason to expect a repeat. Some of the team's players were getting older, however. Campanella would have more trouble with his hands, but he still played most of the season. Reese continued to play superbly at shortstop even though he had turned 37. Hodges, Snider, and Furillo remained fixtures in the line-up as well. One big issue did intrude upon the team just before the opening of the season. Johnny Podres was called into the Navy. Beyond the loss in the direct value of his actual pitching, given Podres' importance in the World Series victory, this loss dealt the team a psychological blow too. Less than seven weeks into the season, Don Zimmer was also lost for the year. He was hit in the face by a pitch, leaving him with a fractured cheekbone. Reflecting the essential humanity of the man that was always central and foremost in his nature, Alston remembered here: "I'll never forget [Cincinnati pitcher Hal] Jeffcoat screaming on the mound for Don to get out of the way of the pitch, and we all felt pretty sick when we heard the dull thud of that smash, when Zimmer froze in his tracks."[1]

Despite these setbacks, the 1956 Dodgers played solid baseball, but they did not give even a hint of running away from the rest of the league as they had the year before. On April 28, they led the National League but only by a meaningless game and a half. Given the previous year's success, no one could have imagined that this would prove to be Brooklyn's biggest lead of the season. In the summer and through all of September, newly emerging powers in Milwaukee and Cincinnati steadily kept pace with Brooklyn, with no team pulling away from the others. Cincinnati boasted a new star,Frank Robinson, and Milwaukee shone with the likes of Eddie Mathews and Henry Aaron.

When Podres went into the Navy, Alston and Bavasi made an especially smart move to strengthen the pitching. In May, as the deadline approached for major league teams to cut their rosters down to 25 players, the Cleveland Indians placed veteran pitcher Sal Maglie on waivers. The Indians had picked Maglie up from the Giants late in the 1955 season. That following spring in Cleveland, Maglie appeared in only two games, pitched five innings, and gave up six hits. From 1950 through 1954, Maglie had been outstanding with the Giants. He went 23–6 in the Giants' pennant-winning year of 1951. Now he was 39, however, and the Giants and Cleveland had each given up on him, figuring he was well past his prime. Alston nonetheless believed Maglie was worth a risk, noting that his arm still seemed solid, and adding poignantly: "there was no question of his savvy or courage."

Alston's willingness to take a risk proved quite wise. Maglie could not have been happier, given the opportunity to pitch for such a contender as Brooklyn. The old rivalry between Giants and Dodgers involved Maglie but posed no significance to anyone with the Dodgers. (It may have been irritating to some of the Giants, and that was even better as far as Alston was concerned.) Maglie would win 13 games for the Dodgers in 1956, including some big wins in the pressure-packed weeks of September in the heated end of the pennant race, especially a no-hitter he tossed against Philadelphia on September 25. In addition to Maglie's contribution, Don Newcombe had the best year of his career, winning 27 games. Under Alston, the 1956 Dodgers produced the best pitching the team had shown in many years. With his phenomenal 27 wins, Newcombe would be voted a rare double, winning both the Cy Young Award and the NL's Most Valuable Player Award. Of further note here was that second place in the balloting for both awards went to Sal Maglie.[2] In addition to Maglie and Newcombe, Carl Erskine, Clem Labine, and Roger Craig (who had come up from the minors the previous summer) all put in good years for Brooklyn. There were also contributions from two young members of the staff—Don Drysdale and Sandy Koufax, then ages 19 and 20 respectively.

While Brooklyn's pitching was strong, stronger indeed than even the year before, almost to a man the play of those in Alston's regular line-up was down from previous seasons. No one on the team hit over .300. Jim Gilliam did hit .300 on the nose, but otherwise, Alston was frustrated by lesser levels of batting: Duke Snider hit .292, Carl Furillo .289, Gil Hodges .265, Sandy Amoros .260, Pee Wee Reese .257, and Roy Campanella .219. Jackie Robinson, now down to 117 games, hit .275. Only Campanella's hitting could have been called substandard, but no one, save perhaps Gilliam, was outstanding, although Snider did hit 43 home runs.[3] With this less than spectacular hitting, the team never generated a consistent offense and could never put together any great bursts of sustained winning. Brooklyn never slumped disastrously, especially because of their pitching, but they could never pull away from the rest of the league. On September 11, the Dodgers were in a tie for first place with Milwaukee. It was the first time they had led the league since April 28.

Throughout the season, Alston found himself compelled to call team meetings and challenge his players' commitment and courage. It was a very different managerial strategy and demeanor than he had needed or utilized the previous season, when he could seemingly sit back and be the proverbial "push button manager." In 1956 he clearly had to intervene and show much more direct managerial skill. Doubts about his ability had begun in the press with the lack of success in 1954 and continued in 1955 with outlooks which suggested, in effect, that "anyone could be successful with that team." With the Dodgers winning in 1956, Alston's contribution was more apparent, though even here he still had his detractors. Compared to such predecessors as Leo Durocher and Charlie Dressen, Alston's calm, unflappable manner continued to resonate in some as feckless. The players knew better. During the season, Alston recognized the need for more direct intervention, and he responded.[4] So did the players, but it was anything but easy. In the last two days of the season, the Dodgers took the pennant by one game over Milwaukee. Some fans felt as much relief as joy.

Once again, the seventh time since 1941, the Dodgers were to face the Yankees in the World Series. For some provincial New Yorkers, the regularity of these October matchups was an almost spiritual sign of affirmation to the effect that something was somehow right in the universe. For Alston, the message was not so theological; it involved the simple imperative of winning and showing everyone that the previous year's victory over the Yankees had not been a fluke.

The opening of the Series, this time with the first two games in Brooklyn, made Dodgers fans chortle with expectations of a second Series victory. Brooklyn's offense crushed Yankees pitching. In these first two games, the team's batting average was .313, with Brooklyn easily winning, 6–3 and 13–8. Then the offense fell off badly. In the remaining five games, the Dodgers only managed the same number of hits they had put up in the first two. In games three through seven, the Dodgers' batting average was an anemic .142. Game five, of course, contributed strongly to the anemia here, for this was the famous perfect game thrown by Yankee Don Larsen. Opposing Larsen that day was Sal Maglie. Maglie pitched an excellent game himself. He only gave up five hits and two walks, but this yielded two runs, and that was all Larsen, and the Yankees needed that afternoon. Great fielding plays by Gil McDougald and Mickey Mantle certainly helped as well. Alston never relieved Maglie; he never went to the mound to address any matter with him. When a reporter asked Roy Campanella if Maglie made any mistakes that day, Campanella responded: "Sal make mistakes? The only mistake he made today was pitching." Even in the next day's game (#6), which the Dodgers won to knot the series at 3–3, they could collect but four hits. They won 1–0 in ten innings. Any hopes for some seventh-game magic, as happened in 1955, were quickly crushed, as the Yankees breezed to a 9–0 win.[5]

In addition to the Dodgers' hitting going flat, Don Newcombe, despite his phenomenal season, had a disappointing Series too. It was Newcombe who pitched the awful seventh game, and he gave up three home runs. In the third inning, Alston relieved him, and Newcombe took a lot of heat in the press because at that point he not only left the field, he left both the clubhouse and Ebbets Field before the game was over. Members of the press were indeed indignant that Newcombe was unavailable to them when the Series concluded. Alston would be contrastingly generous here. Noting the "heat for not sticking around" to which Newcombe was subjected, Alston wrote "there are two sides to such a situation, and I felt sorry for him. People remembered those home runs in that seventh game. They conveniently forgot about Newk's greatness in winning 27 games to get us into the Series."[6] Only years later, after Alston was gone, Newcombe would admit and come to grips with the fact that alcoholism played a major role both in his pitching and in his reaction to the loss.[7]

After the Yankees' victory, Brooklyn's loyal rooters could find some comfort in the previous year's triumph, and the old Brooklyn refrain of "Wait 'til Next Year" naturally came forth. The team was certainly downcast. Prior to the Series, arrangements had been made for the Dodgers to make a tour of Japan. They were to go the day after the seventh-game loss to the Yankees. No one wanted to go, including Alston. Carl Furillo simply stayed home. The rest of the team went through the motions of it all. Alston noted, "I was so disgusted and ready to go home that if I'd had the money, I would have bought me a ticket and left."[8]

In the rest of the off-season, other issues quickly transcended the on-field matter of whether Alston and the Dodgers could come back in 1957. For over a decade, throughout Brooklyn, thoughts and pressures had been brewing over the clear facts that, in its location, its nature, and its size, old Ebbets Field had grown ever-more inadequate. In Brooklyn, as in other major league cities, many of the ballparks which had been constructed in the early 20th century, such matters as public access to the stadium revealed increasing levels of strain. The Flatbush section of Brooklyn, where Ebbets Field had been built, was no longer a terribly crime-free neighborhood, especially at night. Fans who, in larger and larger numbers, had moved to suburban areas out on Long Island and elsewhere, found transportation and parking for a Dodgers game more troublesome, inconvenient, and even dangerous. Going to Flatbush for a night game did not appeal to many suburbanites as a fun sort of family outing. Like owners of other major league clubs, Walter O'Malley had been calling for municipal authorities in his city to furnish the land, or subsidize the purchase of the land, on which he could construct a larger stadium at a location that could accommodate suburbanites' demands for access and parking. There would be a great deal of wrangling here, with the outcome ultimately being that the Dodgers would move all the way to Los Angeles.

At the time, many reporters placed blame squarely on the shoulders of Walter O'Malley. Words like "piracy" dotted the papers. O'Malley had been making conspicuous arrangements for the Dodgers to play a few of their home games in Jersey City, New Jersey. He wanted New York City to furnish land to build a new stadium, one that had greater attendance, more parking, and ready access to the local subway system as well as to the Long Island Railroad. Setting up his schedule to play a few games in New Jersey was one of many ways O'Malley was applying pressure. (Years later, New York would eventually agree to build a new stadium—what would be Shea Stadium.) Amidst O'Malley's efforts, the New York City Council passed enabling legislation; the State Legislature in Albany passed the bill (by a one-vote margin), and Governor Averill Harriman signed it. Some speculated that New York City officials had supported the bill only out of political expediency *vis-à-vis* local, Dodgers-fanatic voters who would have been furious with any public official who did not help keep the Dodgers in Brooklyn. Such political predictions may have been inaccurate, but at the time the noise of the baseball fans appeared hard to ignore. City politicians may have smugly believed that Albany legislators would down turn any such stadium allocation measures. (Hence their surprise with the one-vote passage in Albany.) How *all* of New York's voters felt cannot be determined; no sort of public plebiscite was ever held, nor did any systematic amassing of subsequent polling data ever occur. Many made noise, of course. The common theme in the noise was simply for the Dodgers to remain in Brooklyn, but among these many people lay differing senses of who should pay for the various items at play in the controversies.

Many New York City politicians simply felt O'Malley himself

should take care of all the costs for any land and new stadium for the Dodgers. He had plenty of money, and he was certainly far better off than the City. After the surprise of the Albany vote and the stadium bill being signed into law, City leaders went to work sabotaging the follow-up details, greatly cutting financial appropriations. O'Malley easily recognized he was "getting the business" here. Other matters bogged down over scores of financial details. O'Malley's primary negotiations here were with New York's Parks Commissioner, Robert Moses. Moses was a notoriously hard bargainer. Instinctively, he appeared to leap to any situation in which he could maximize his political authority and in which he felt he could bend any given opponent to his own will. In regard to all financial details concerning such matters as which party received what percentage of parking fees, ticket sales, and concession and beverage revenues, there would be tiring arguments and impasses. Fundamentally, Moses felt he held the upper hand, as it was beyond his ken to conceive that O'Malley would seriously dream of uprooting the Dodgers and taking them to another city. As long as he believed the Dodgers had to remain in Brooklyn, Moses believed he could act imperiously. Of course, O'Malley would do the unthinkable. At the time, critics in the New York press were vehemently angry, not so much at Moses as at O'Malley. They claimed, correctly, that his team was turning a great profit and was in as sound a financial position as any team in the game. Of course, O'Malley would financially do even better for himself and the team in Los Angeles. Critics in the New York press suffered from much the same sort of provincialism that would be Moses' undoing in the case of the Dodgers.

In 1957, O'Malley had pushed Moses back with pressure of his own. This was the point when he publicized that he had again leased Roosevelt Stadium in Jersey City and announced that the Dodgers would play about eight games a season there. (He had done the same in 1956 but with much less fanfare and notice.) O'Malley also sold Ebbets Field (for $3 million) with a five-year maximum lease-back arrangement, clearly giving him room to leave Brooklyn if he wished but to stay there if it was necessary. O'Malley could (and did) posture here that, with the Ebbets Field sale, he was sincerely trying to raise money to help buy the bonds of the Sports Authority (headed by Moses) that were being sold to finance the city's new stadium for the Dodgers. O'Malley was clearly making maneuvers and postures of his own, both with regard to Robert Moses, as well as with regard to authorities in Los Angeles, where he also bought an old stadium formerly owned by the Chicago Cubs' earlier owner, William Wrigley, Sr. (It too was called Wrigley Field; he had purchased it just after World War I, when he brought the Pacific

Coast League team, the Los Angeles Angels, into his system. Wrigley had his Cubs and Angels do spring training in Southern California, mainly on Catalina Island, a great deal of which he owned as well.) In the end, Robert Moses continued to negotiate with his usual toughness, while Los Angeles officials gave O'Malley virtually everything he desired, including a promise of help and facilitation in his construction of a new baseball stadium in the city (which eventually became Dodger Stadium), with very positive terms ultimately coming, including the control over all such financially important matters as tickets, parking, and concessions.

At the time, the figures from the offices of the major league baseball teams which had moved showed that relocating could bring great success. In 1953, the Boston Braves were the first major league team to move in half a century, and in their new home in Milwaukee, they set league attendance records. The St. Louis Browns fared much better when they moved to Baltimore and became the Orioles in 1954. The following season, the Philadelphia Athletics did well when they relocated to Kansas City. Despite such inviting patterns, Robert Moses arrogantly felt he could stand firmly against O'Malley. At the same time, he and his colleagues also did little to stop the Giants from relocating in San Francisco. The Giants moved, and so did the Dodgers. New York fans were aghast. The city now had but one team! Reflecting further on Moses' failure here, a compelling irony in the Dodgers' departure was that the details of the financial arrangements that Moses later made with the New York Mets when they moved into the new Shea Stadium were more financially favorable to the Mets than was the last (refused) offer O'Malley made to Moses before deciding to move the team to Los Angeles. Moses' infamous arrogance had been his own undoing.

As is well known, the move to Los Angeles hit Brooklyn very hard. Blame and finger pointing (of various sorts) were rampant. At first, the anger was directed largely at O'Malley. The acerbic Dick Young of the *New York Daily News* dubbed O'Malley someone "who leaves Brooklyn a rich man and a despised man." Amidst the rancorous accusations, Alston did not figure terribly much in the shouting, either in the move itself or in the cultural fallout from it. The debate and the rage focused on levels above his station. Alston would reflect, with a kind of shrug: "Four years in Brooklyn were scarcely enough to make a great deal of difference in my way of life when the move to the West Coast occurred." His feelings would not change as he later wrote: "It [Brooklyn or LA] didn't really matter to me one way or the other. Darrtown was still home to me." Alston certainly felt a genuine tenderness in regard to many of Brooklyn's fans. "It was kind of tough," he recalled about the last game in Ebbets Field on September 24, a 2–0 win over Pittsburgh; "when the game was over and Gladys Gooding, our organist, who went all the way back to Larry MacPhail's days, played 'Auld Lang Syne.' Everyone had a tear or two in their eyes. ... [Ebbets Field] held a lot of memories for everyone." While his feelings for the fans were sincere and sympathetic, Alston was far less sentimental in regard to thoughts of some members of the City's press. Some of the goodbye reflections in the newspapers revealed some of the ambivalence about Alston with which he contended for four years. The *Daily News'* Dick Young wrote of the Dodgers' departure, for example:

> The memories of a rich and rollicking history—dating back to Ned Hanlon, the first manager, and skipping delightfully through such characters as Uncle Wilbert Robinson, Casey Stengel, Burleigh Grimes, Leo Durocher, Burt Shotton, Charley Dressen, and now Walter Alston. The noisy ones, the demonstrative ones, the shrewd and cagey ones, and the confused ones. They came they went, but always the incredible happenings remained....

With the last word of description—"confused"—possibly referring to the last manager, and with no such word as "quiet," the little jab here at Alston was there for all to glean, although Young could be nasty about anyone. No matter the sources, Alston was rarely one who answered his critics directly. Such inaction may have confirmed some views that Alston was somehow unaware of the press's alleged "insights." Alston, of course, was at least every bit as astute as any outspoken New York scribe, and he certainly knew what was being said and written. He just evinced a very non–New Yorker sort of personality. The willingness to appreciate such loud-mouthed aggressive sorts as Dressen, Durocher, and MacPhail and to look down on those with quieter natures merely underscored the egos and the provincialisms that were driving some newsmen's angry New York–style projections in the first place. Alston felt no need to respond to media criticisms, and this was something that both Bavasi and O'Malley appreciated very much. Getting along with them was far more significant to Alston, and to the operations of the Dodgers, than any matters of NY-style press relations. (The views of scribes and local readers notwithstanding, the running of a ball team was not akin to sending back a sandwich at a Brooklyn delicatessen.) Now that the team was leaving such a chronically toxic journalistic environment, there was even less press concern for Alston, and maybe even a touch of relief.[9]

Even before the 1957 season began, the team's possible departure for Los Angeles was rumored throughout the press and among the team's fans. It even overshadowed the departure of Jackie Robinson, who was unceremoniously dealt to the Giants, at which point Robinson announced his retirement, something he had already decided. (For many

Brooklyn fans, it was bad enough to trade Robinson, but to the Giants?!)
Alston was fairly off-hand about Robinson's departure: "Whether Jackie
had any particular regard for me as an individual I wouldn't know, or
care...."[10] Without question, Alston harbored no racist sentiments, a
marked contrast to such others of his era in the Dodgers' organization
as Clay Hopper. Alston did, however, appear to have had little feel for
the rage that was driving many African Americans in these years, a rage
which manifested itself in the achievements of many athletes. Managers
of Alston's age felt that most varieties of emotion were best controlled or
cast away. Roy Campanella was an African American athlete who could
do this without any sort of false posture and thrive. Robinson was different, and so was Newcombe.

At the very least, Robinson's rage was partly driven by the stinging
prejudice he had experienced as a black man in a society where racism
continued to thrive. Rather than ignoring it or overcoming it, Robinson utilized it to empower and extend the fierceness with which he went
about his work as an athlete. Subsequently, many other athletes, most
famously Muhammad Ali, would do much the same. The fact that such
professional athletes could achieve what they did implied to any thinking coach or manager that this sort of mentality needed to be rallied and
channeled and not simply ignored. It certainly went against the old dictum that "you can't play baseball with your teeth clenched" (Ty Cobb
notwithstanding). In future years, some managers and coaches would
grasp this and utilize it in the ways they ran their teams and handled
their players. Alston appeared to have not so much any hostility to new
attitudes about race here as a simple lack of feel for what was occurring
among some around him whose life experiences were so utterly different. This would manifest itself in subsequent events in Alston's career.

While Robinson's retirement gave pause to some Dodgers' friends
and to fans, the rumors about the whole team leaving town transcended
all other discussions. During the 1957 spring training in Florida, at
every town in the Grapefruit League circuit that hosted the Dodgers,
local reporters steadily peppered Alston and others with questions
about a move to Los Angeles. Alston remembered: "Every day there
seemed to be a new rumor."[11] After spring training, O'Malley did visit
Los Angeles in both April and May, resulting of course in even more
rumors.

Conspicuously, on May 28, National League President Warren
Giles announced that his office was authorized to grant consent both
to Brooklyn and to New York, should they wish to move to L.A. and San
Francisco. The only stipulation was that any such requests had to come
before October 1. Rumors now turned into expectations, and they ran

rampant. Alston still had to manage the Dodgers through the 1957 season. For Alston and the entire team, trying to play a normal, competitive season of baseball here was a psychologically difficult, if not impossible, challenge. Still, in 1957, the Dodgers would battle credibly for the pennant.

Alston kept Brooklyn on the jump. Into the summer that year, the National League race was tightly packed. As of July 15, the surprisingly strong Philadelphia Phillies were in first place; Cincinnati was in fifth place, but only 2½ games back. Bunched between them were St. Louis, Milwaukee, and Brooklyn. By August 1, Milwaukee had seized first place, with Cincinnati in fifth, at this point still merely four games behind, with St. Louis, Brooklyn, and Philadelphia between them. The key shift came in early August. Milwaukee ran off a streak, winning 11 of 12, while St. Louis, Brooklyn, Cincinnati, and Philadelphia all posted losing records—St. Louis went 4–10, Cincinnati 6–8, Philadelphia 3–9, and Brooklyn went 6–9. From there Milwaukee would not be headed. They won the pennant by eight games over St. Louis, Brooklyn finishing third, 14 games back. Meanwhile, and far more importantly for so many in Brooklyn, on September 18, just as Milwaukee was sewing up its first pennant, O'Malley's office finally made the formal announcement that the team was indeed moving to Los Angeles. Dodgers fans lamented the pennant going to Milwaukee. Many respectfully noted Jackie Robinson's retirement, but, so much more, everyone grieved over the news of the Dodgers (and the Giants) leaving town. The unthinkable had actually occurred.[12]

8

A New Home

While traumatic to many Brooklyn fans, the Dodgers' departure to Los Angeles was simply not a problem as far as Alston was concerned. His home was in Ohio, and that winter he lamented nothing, cherishing the birth of his first granddaughter. Alston clearly understood and empathized with the feelings of Brooklyn fans and such players as Gil Hodges and Roy Campanella, "men," as he noted, "who had deep roots in Brooklyn or on the East Coast." Just as noteworthy to him, however, was the point that the move to LA sat very nicely with players like Duke Snider and Don Drysdale, each a California native. New Yorkers' provincialism and self-entitlement notwithstanding, such West Coast roots were also important, and Alston was sensitive to them too. This outlook lay beyond the ken of many New Yorkers, but sometimes a small-town Ohioan can see things more broadly. Personally, Alston came to enjoy living in Los Angeles, never as nice as life in Darrtown but definitely, as he put it, "more quiet and peaceful than Brooklyn."[1]

While Alston could make the Brooklyn-to-LA adjustment with ease, through the post-season of 1957 and into 1958, Brooklyn fans, the whole baseball world, and some of the nation's wider culture were trying to fathom the meaning of the move to Los Angeles. "Los Angeles Dodgers"—it just did not sound right, and the incongruity of it was, for some reason, so much more striking than was "Milwaukee Braves," "Kansas City A's," or even "San Francisco Giants." The warm familiarity of "dem Bums" and many other Brooklyn legacies had so ensconced themselves, both in baseball's as well as in the nation's culture, and with millions of fans, that this franchise shift proved much more significant than were the others of the day like the Braves, the Browns, the A's, or the Giants. In a myriad of books and movies, and in so many other contexts, New York City, i.e., Manhattan, stood as a bastion of elitism. Brooklyn had been the working-class counterpoint to that elitist world. From such a place, any splendid jab at, or any thorn in the side of Upper East Side pomposity, lent a delightful, nose-tweaking sense of revenge whenever it came forth, be it in a baseball team or in any other cultural genres, like the Marx Brothers or "the Three Stooges." With the Dodgers' departure, one visible element in that identity of anti-pomposity appeared gone. For the devoted fans, the grieving time ranged from a few minutes to a few lifetimes. Meanwhile, of course, though many in Brooklyn may have been impervious to it, other elements contributed to baseball's identity as well as to the nation's culture at large, and one of these elements was the movie/television culture centered greatly in Southern California.

Adding greatly to the post–Brooklyn anguish of this time was a tragedy that struck the baseball world on January 28, 1958, an automobile accident that left Roy Campanella a quadriplegic for the rest of his life. "All of us," remembered Alston, "were shocked at the devastating injury to this fine and remarkable man. ... When he suffered the paralysis that confined him to a wheelchair for the rest of his days ... it was a blow to all. Everybody mourned the terrible fate that befell him." During Campanella's post-accident convalescence, Alston made a point of telephoning him every chance he could. He noted, with no surprise but with genuine respect and admiration, how, despite his fate, "it's a mark of his true character that his spirits [always remained] high, ... 'an inspiration to all who c[a]me into contact with him.' ... He would never ask a friend to share his misery; he would not have it any other way." Even though Campanella never played a game in Los Angeles, LA fandom turned out in droves for him in early May of 1959. The goal was to have a "night" for Campy and raise money to help him with his massive medical bills. (In 1958, Walter O'Malley also paid Campanella the entirety of his $50,000 salary.) Casey Stengel's Yankees came to the Coliseum to play Alston's Dodgers in an exhibition game. Over 93,000 fans came to the game, with an estimated 10–15,000 turned away. "It was a sight to behold," wrote Alston, "when he was introduced. Pee Wee came back to wheel Campy on to the field. The lights were turned off and at a given signal the thousands of fans lit matches. It was a touching scene for a great man."[2]

Of far less gravity than the tragedy that befell Campanella, but nonetheless significant, were some of the actual baseball issues that Alston and the Dodgers faced as they moved to Los Angeles. The construction of the new stadium with which Los Angeles officials promised to help O'Malley would take several years to complete. Temporarily, the team played their home games in the city's gigantic Coliseum, built in 1932 when LA hosted the Summer Olympics. The seating capacity of over 90,000 dwarfed old Ebbets Field, which, Alston smirked, "looked like a toy against the Coliseum."[3] Because the Coliseum was designed as an arena either for track and field events or for football, fitting a major league baseball diamond into it was problematic. Either the right or left field line would be very short. The configuration that Coliseum officials established left very little right-field foul territory and a right-field foul pole but 300 feet from the plate. While that was a short stroke, other stadiums of the era, including the Polo Grounds and Yankee Stadium, had shorter right field lines. Meanwhile, the left field distances were even odder. The left field foul pole was but 251 feet from the plate. No other major league baseball park of the 20th century had so short a dimension. Furthermore, while the right field line was short, the right field area shot outward to enormous dimensions immediately from the foul line. The original right-center field fence point was a mammoth 440 feet from home, longer even than the 420-foot distance to straight center. In left field, unless actual stadium seats and concrete were torn out, as some fancied, the down-the-line distance of 251 feet did not grow much as one shifted toward left-center. The left-center field mark was a mere 320 feet. It was a weird configuration to say the least.[4]

Alston recalled that the left-handed Duke Snider, who had been such an effective power hitter to right-center in every park in the National League, and especially at Ebbets Field, could not believe his eyes when he first saw the right field power alley in the Coliseum. He would quickly be beside himself with frustration. "The dimensions ... were too much even for a talent like Duke," Alston remembered. "I'll never forget coming out one evening during batting practice to find Duke standing out in left field throwing baseballs. He wasn't playing catch with anyone. He was trying to sling one up and over the top of the Coliseum. ... Paul Bunyan might have been cut out for [this] but not Duke Snider."[5]

While the gigantic dimensions of the Coliseum's right field disheartened a star like Duke Snider, Alston grew more sorrowful as he contemplated the implications of the weird left field situation. The Dodgers had Coliseum officials install a 42-foot screen between the left field foul pole and the 320-foot left-center mark, but it was still an easy shot for a home run. This made Alston think yet more sadly about Campanella. "Campy, had he been with us, would have been the one guy on the team that would have appreciated that short fence in left. ... Roy pulled about 95 percent of his pitches, and usually they were long, high fly balls that would have worn the fans out shagging home runs."[6] Alston may have remembered how, back in Nashua, New Hampshire, in 1946, Campanella had been hurt by so many of his high drives to left turning into harmless outs because of the vast size of the no-fence left field in Holman Stadium. It seemed the game's fates were ready to compensate, but then came the tragedy of Campanella's automobile accident.

A healthy Campanella, Alston believed, could have set many home run records hitting high drives over that flimsy screen just 251 feet away.

With the strangeness of the Coliseum's set-up, some speculative discussions actually took place about special adjustments. No less than Commissioner Ford Frick attempted to order the installation of a second fence in the left field stands, making fly balls into the stands landing short of the second barrier counting only as doubles. That would have been an odd local ground rule, unlike any other in the history of the modern game. Commissioner Frick could not have his way, however, as strict California laws, constructed in cognizance of the ever-present danger of earthquakes in the region, would not permit any such major alterations that could affect the physical integrity of such a structure as the

Catcher Roy Campanella, pictured here in 1954, was always one of Alston's favorite players—for his skills as a catcher and a hitter, but even more because of his pure love and infectious enthusiasm for the game. Campanella first played for Alston in 1946 in Nashua, New Hampshire. There, Alston quickly grasped the savvy Campanella possessed, especially at handling pitchers and running a game from behind the plate. In Brooklyn, Campanella won the National League MVP Award three times. Alston was crushed by the news of Campanella's 1958 auto accident that left him a paraplegic (National Baseball Hall of Fame and Museum, Cooperstown, NY).

Coliseum. Those same laws also blocked drilling and cutting down of any part of the existing left field stands to allow the left field area to be expanded.[7] The Coliseum would have to remain intact, and, with its odd dimensions, the intrinsic nature of major league baseball would then undergo some jolts as it was first played in LA. Brooklyn fans may have felt some compensation, as they could now chuckle a bit as they grieved their loss. Meanwhile, as far as Walter O'Malley was concerned, the massive ticket sales in the Los Angeles area compensated for any head-scratching that the Coliseum's dimensions prompted.

For left-handed pitchers on the Dodgers as well, this weird, short "Chinese Wall," as it was dubbed, engendered many headaches as well. The young Sandy Koufax, who had shown promise in Brooklyn, but who still had control problems, now faced another major issue with which to wrestle as he attempted to develop himself. Pop flies to left field that were easy outs in any other park would always present the risk of a home run. Right-handed hitters with any sort of power saw an enormous number of pitches on the outside corner.

Regarding the Dodgers' failure to win a pennant in their final season in Brooklyn, Alston was firm in his conviction that it was not due to any diverting of focus because of the rumors of the imminent move to Los Angeles. "I prefer," he affirmed, "to blame our 1957 drop on natural causes."[8] The team's performance in 1958, however, was another matter to him. The Coliseum's quirks affected many. Duke Snider, who had to that point hit more home runs than any player in the 1950s, found his home run total dropping precipitously. He had hit 40 or more home runs in every season from 1953 to 1957. In 1958 he hit a mere 15. Later admitting his problems with alcohol were catching up with him, Don Newcombe, Alston sadly noted, "appeared to lose everything at once." By June of 1958, his record was 0–6, and Alston and Bavasi dealt him to Cincinnati. Don Drysdale, while happy to be home in LA, had developed as his best pitch a fastball that would sink and fade into a right-handed batter. Many right-handers were indeed fearful of Drysdale's fastball; some were hit by the pitch, many were brushed back, many more broke their bats as they attempted to make contact, and scores of hitters popped harmlessly to left field. Now, with the short left-field dimensions, Drysdale feared that so many of those little pop-ups could turn into home runs. He began using his best pitch with far less frequency and won only one of his first eight decisions. Eventually, in the second half of the season, he went back to his fastball, simply casting the fear of Chinese Wall homers out of his mind. Having gone a mere 1–7 in the first months, Drysdale completed the season 12–13. Other players, such as the aging Pee Wee Reese, were less effective. With Jackie Robinson retired and Don Hoak traded, third base was in a constant state of flux. "As a club," Alston summarized, "we never quite jelled." After winning or at least contending for the pennant in every season since World War II, the 1958 Dodgers finished the season in seventh place, a mere two games ahead of the hapless Philadelphia Phillies in the cellar. Alston put it simply: "1958 was a disaster in almost every respect except for attendance." The team drew 1,845,556 at the Coliseum; no season at Ebbets Field had ever come close to such a figure.[9]

Many folks in Brooklyn may have chortled at the Dodgers' disappointing first season in Los Angeles. Alston himself was obviously not pleased: "my all-time low as a manager," he would later note. Amidst the disappointing season, some sportswriters began once again to predict Alston would be let go. O'Malley and Bavasi actually let everyone know in August that Alston would be back the following season. Bavasi hired former manager Charlie Dressen as a coach as well. This first heightened the speculations that Alston's position was in jeopardy. Bavasi himself stepped in and lectured some reporters here: "I want you guys to realize that Charlie's job depends on you. The first time any of you writes that Dressen would have bunted when Alston hit away or quotes Charlie on anything embarrassing to the manager—then Dressen is fired. It's up to you."[10] Bavasi was being hyperbolic, as he would likely have not let any irresponsible work by a mere sportswriter affect his decisions, but the message was clear: a seventh-place finish notwithstanding, the relationship between O'Malley, Bavasi, and Alston was rock solid.

Prior to the 1959 season, the Coliseum's field dimensions were adjusted a bit—straight center was reduced from 425 feet to 410, and the right field power alley went down from the ridiculous 440 feet to a still-deep 375. Pee Wee Reese also retired. (Alston immediately made him a coach.) A rookie named Maury Wills stepped in, along with Don Zimmer. Wills struggled, especially at the plate, but he hit superbly in the critical last two weeks of the season. Don Drysdale pitched well, winning 17 games. Podres won 14. Roger Craig won 11, all in the second half of the season when he came back from the minors. Sandy Koufax still struggled with control, but in one game against the Giants, he tied a major league record, striking out 18. Duke Snider rebounded a bit, hitting 23 homers. The Dodgers also acquired a veteran outfielder named Wally Moon from St. Louis. Moon contributed much, and he was the first hitter on the Dodgers who was able to use the peculiar Chinese Wall to some advantage. While he was a left-hander, Moon developed an opposite field swing that yielded a slew of pop-ups that sailed down the line, onto or over the Chinese Wall. Fans and reporters dubbed them "Moon Shots." In 1959, Moon led the National League in triples. In St. Louis in 1958, Moon had hit seven home runs. In the three following seasons with LA in the Coliseum he hit 19, 13, and 17 homers; in the three seasons after that, with the club playing in the more normally dimensioned Dodger Stadium, his special Coliseum-based hitting talents held little value; Alston played him less, and his home run totals fell to 4, 8, and 2.[11]

More generally, players simply grew accustomed to the dimensions,

and the increasing comfort was contagious. Alston juggled his pitchers, guided his rookies, and maintained a calm demeanor that kept players from getting too low or too high. The result was that the Dodgers
were the first National League team in the century to go from seventh
to first place. It was no breeze, however; the season involved a frenetic
three-way battle between the Dodgers, Braves, and Giants. San Francisco was in the thick of the race through the last week of the season.
In the end, the Dodgers tied the Braves and faced them in a three-game
playoff. The Dodgers were far from the best team of the era, let alone in
the history of the league, but Alston was especially proud of how they
were able to maximize every ounce of what talent they possessed. "It
was," he remembered, "a manager's dream club."[12]

There had been two playoffs in the history of the National League,
and the Brooklyn Dodgers had lost both—to St. Louis in 1946 and,
infamously, to the Giants in 1951. This time against the Braves, Alston
proved very much in charge in the games. He chose to start game one
with a relatively unknown pitcher named Danny McDevitt. This choice
did raise a few eyebrows, as Alston recalled. McDevitt had posted a mere
10–8 record that season, but Alston remembered how effectively he had
pitched in Milwaukee. McDevitt did not fare too well, however. Milwaukee led 2–1 in the second inning, and Alston immediately relieved him
with Larry Sherry. The move proved wise. Sherry held the Braves, and
the Dodgers came back to win, 3–2, the winning run coming via a home
run by Campanella's successor at catcher, John Roseboro.

The teams flew to Los Angeles for game two. If Milwaukee won
there, the teams would have to fly back to Milwaukee for the final game.
Alston smirked: "There wasn't one of us who wanted to go back to Milwaukee." The game in the Coliseum went 12 innings and took over four
hours. Alston used 20 players, including six of his 11 pitchers. Down
5–2 in the bottom of the ninth inning, the Dodgers rallied with a succession of singles. Milwaukee manager Fred Haney relieved starter Lew
Burdette with Don McMahon. Alston sent up Norm Larker, who sent a
drive to the Chinese Wall, scoring two runs. Haney relieved McMahon
with future Hall of Famer, Warren Spahn. Young John Roseboro was due
up next. Alston called him back and sent up 37-year-old Carl Furillo, who
had played in both the prior Dodgers playoff losses in 1946 and 1951.
Furillo hit a long fly into the deep right-center field alley. Right fielder
Henry Aaron ran down the fly, but the runner on third, Gil Hodges,
scored, tying the game. The game went on for three more innings. In the
11th, each team loaded the bases but did not score. In the 12th, Furillo was
up again, this time with Hodges on second. Furillo hit a hard grounder
just to the right of second base. Milwaukee's shortstop, Felix Mantilla,

was able to glove the grounder. He looked over to third, forcing Hodges to stop there, but then he rushed his throw to first. The throw skipped past first base. Hodges scored, and the Dodgers had the pennant.[13]

With the excitement of the close pennant race and playoff, fans in Los Angeles set attendance records (over 2 million) that no team, including Brooklyn, had ever approached. Some New Yorkers were still lamenting the loss of "The Boys of Summer," but Southern Californians were cheering and laughing in delight. Meanwhile, Chicago had surprised many experts by taking the American League pennant, only the second time the Yankees had not won since 1948. The Dodgers had finished their regular season on the road against the Cubs. From there they went up to Milwaukee for the first game of the playoff. Then they flew back to LA for the exhausting 12-inning victory over the Braves. The very next day, they flew back to Chicago to open the World Series against the White Sox. With the ensuing jetlag, "we played like zombies," Alston recalled. The White Sox clobbered them, 11–0. In the next game, Alston started Johnny Podres, remembering how well he had performed under the pressure of the Game Seven against the Yankees four years before. Podres pitched well, but so did the White Sox' Bob Shaw. Down 2–1 in the seventh inning, Alston relieved Podres for a pinch-hitter, Chuck Essegian, who promptly hit a home run to tie the game. After Jim Gilliam walked, Charlie Neal hit a second home run. Larry Sherry, another Los Angeles boy, pitched the last three innings in relief of Podres, and he held Chicago scoreless, giving the win to Podres and the Dodgers.[14]

Thousands of fans turned out at the LA Airport to greet the Dodgers as they returned from Chicago. The intensity and enthusiasm of the community for the Dodgers made the memories of Brooklyn that much more distant. The next three games at the Coliseum would set attendance records for single games as well as for a World Series home stand that have never been eclipsed, and likely never will be. Each game drew over 92,000. No *four*-game Series home stand, before or since, has surpassed the 277,750 that the Dodgers drew in three games in the Coliseum in 1959. Ticket scalpers were selling tickets for 12 times their face value. Scalped tickets notwithstanding, the official paid revenue for the Coliseum went over a half-million dollars. That marked another first and helped the winning player's share to set another record: $11,231.18. Brooklyn's 1955 victory over New York had not yielded anything close to that.[15]

In the first two games in Los Angeles, the Dodgers came through with key hits, one of the most important coming in the seventh inning of Game Three. The game was scoreless, and the Dodgers had loaded the bases. Alston chose to pinch-hit with Carl Furillo. Many questioned Alston's choice here, as he had Duke Snider on the bench. But Furillo came through with a single that scored two runs. Furillo was the hero, and Alston's second-guessers had to keep silent. After a 5–4 victory in the fourth game, LA fans were anticipating a victory the next day. Here Alston surprised many by choosing to start 23-year-old Sandy Koufax, who had compiled a mere 8–6 record that year. Koufax had pitched well many times in relief that season, and, less than a month before, he had struck out his record 18 in a start against the Giants. Koufax did not disappoint Alston or anyone else that day, but the Dodgers' hitting did. "It wasn't Sandy's fault," Alston said; Koufax gave up but one run, but that was all Chicago would need, as LA could not score. Everyone flew back to Chicago, with the White Sox and their fans optimistic about a rebound from the victory over the vast throngs of the Coliseum and with the memory of the pounding they had inflicted in Game One. Los Angeles native Larry Sherry took care of matters again in relief, however. The Dodgers cruised, 9–3.

In the minds of the game's experts, the 1959 Dodgers have never been considered one of great teams in the history of baseball like the Yankees of 1927, 1939, or 1961, the Philadelphia A's of 1929, *or* indeed the Dodgers of 1955. Drawing with Milwaukee for the pennant, they won only 86 games, then the lowest ever for any pennant winner. But they managed to squeeze every bit of talent out of themselves they could. Fourteen players played in at least 50 games. Ten pitchers each pitched in at least 28 games. No pitcher won 20 games, but four won ten or more. Like the different ways he took teams which had been doing poorly or from whom little was expected, be it in Portsmouth, Ohio, in 1940, in Trenton, New Jersey, in 1944, in Nashua, New Hampshire, in 1946, in Pueblo, Colorado, in 1947, or in St. Paul, Minnesota, in 1948, Alston quietly moved everyone along. There were no factions, there was always strong team spirit, and, as usual, the manager gave all credit elsewhere. His words: "As I've always said about the '59 champions, they played like a championship team all the way."[16]

The old fans in Brooklyn may have remained glum now that their boys had not only left but were winners again, but the in-crowd of Angelinos had a grand time celebrating the first win of any major sports team on the West Coast. The champagne may have flowed, but, as he had been in Brooklyn in 1955, Alston was calm and gently smiled at it all. He was not being arrogantly blasé, nor did he lack any enthusiasm for the team, he simply found other ways to feel his happiness and contentment. "I'm tired," he noted with a smile, "I'm going to go home to Darrtown, take my grandson, Robin, by the hand and go for a walk in the woods. We'll find us a nice log and we'll just sit there for a spell."[17]

9

Leo and the Critics

From the moment Walter O'Malley named him to manage Brooklyn in late 1953, Walter Alston had endured detractors and second-guessers, but at the end of 1959, few of any standing in the baseball world could question Alston's managerial qualifications and savvy. His successes had come with a quiet manner and nature that some, accustomed to the raucous ways of Brooklyn, in baseball or in the hubbub of the streets, found a bit befuddling. The arbitrary conclusions and projections that such a quiet manner as Alston's could not maximize the Dodgers' potential naturally emanated from a city-street culture that saw a wise-cracking aggressiveness and outward quickness of mind and spirit to be essential elements in the seasons of baseball and of life. Without such aggressive proclivities, so the Brooklynesque argument went, one would be easily defeated in any sort of social–Darwinian struggle, be it in life, in business, or in baseball.

Alston's success with the Dodgers confounded the view which held that the best baseball managers were those whose mind and spirit steadily churned, sparked, and created a team atmosphere which enabled it always to get the jump on any rival. Confounding this was both such a person as Alston and the fact that his win of 1959 marked his third pennant in five years. Three more pennants would come in the next seven years. Six pennants in 12 seasons! That was a mark few had ever achieved or would. Those who apotheosized managers of more confrontational fighting spirit would have to square their convictions with the facts of Alston's accomplishments.

While Alston's feats were impressive in themselves, those who looked at the details about the balance of power in baseball in these same years could not but conclude that Alston's success was even more impressive. Both the quality and the balance that lay throughout the National League revealed this. Illustrating the league's balance of that era was the point that, amidst Alston's six-of-12 pennant stretch, there was a seven-season span from 1958 through 1964 in which six different

115

teams won the NL pennant. Besides the Dodgers winning in 1959 and 1963, the Braves won in 1958, the Pirates in 1960, the Reds in 1961, the Giants in 1962, and the Cardinals in 1964 (with the Phillies leading most of the way that year, barely missing the pennant at the end). Aside from the Cubs and the two newcomers (the Mets and the Colt-45's/Astros), every team in the NL was usually a tough opponent.

In contrast to the quality and balance in the National League in these years, the American League was completely dominated by the New York Yankees. From 1949 to 1964, they won every pennant but two. The rest of the league often seemed a clear cut below. Starkly underscoring this point were the results of the All-Star Games. From 1950 through 1982, the National League won 31 of the 37 games played (a few times, two per season); from 1960 to 1982, the NL edge was astounding, 24–2, with one tie. Alston also won more All-Star Games than any other manager in these years as well.[1]

A major point contributing to the NL's superiority, especially in the late 1950s and early 1960s, was the fact that the National League had gained a pronounced edge on the AL in the recruitment of both African American and Latin American talent. The Yankees were slow to integrate; the Red Sox were even worse, and while they could send up such all-stars as Mickey Mantle and Ted Williams, they found themselves facing such pitchers as Bob Gibson and Juan Marichal and confronting an opposition that featured players like Willie Mays, Roberto Clemente, Ernie Banks, Frank Robinson, and Henry Aaron. The Dodgers, of course, had led the way in the integration of baseball. Alston was part of that innovativeness from the outset. He extended the team's proud traditions here. Sometimes, however, even Alston had to gulp when he looked at such foes as Banks, Mays, Clemente, and Aaron. Only half-jokingly, he did once say that "more than anyone else, Hank Aaron made me wish I wasn't a manager."[2]

Alston won against steadily tough National League opposition, and he often did it while making significant adjustments in his own strategies. He was always able to alter his approach to the game depending on the personnel at his disposal. When he first took over in Brooklyn, he won with a powerful, regular line-up of hitters like Reese, Hodges, Campanella, Furillo, Robinson, and Snider. As these stars aged, he adapted with a strategy of platooning various players depending on what pitching he was facing and on what his offensive and defensive needs were. He had first inherited a team which could rely on power. From there he developed teams that relied on speed, and, most famously, he won several times with outstanding pitching. Alston skillfully adapted his strategy and tactics to the composite of players with which he was presented.

Despite the winning, some detractors still sought to raise issues. After the World Series victory in 1959, Alston's Dodgers came back the next year with 82 victories, only four fewer than the 1959 number that had tied them for first with Milwaukee. On August 3, 1960, after a win over Pittsburgh, the Dodgers were but four games out of first place. From there they faded a bit. In September, they once rose to within nine games of the lead, but that proved the closest they would get to the top.[3] With 82 victories, it was certainly a good year, but in 1960, the Pittsburgh Pirates, with especially strong performances from both Dick Groat and Roberto Clemente, and with surprisingly strong pitching, simply breezed past everyone, taking the pennant by seven games over second-place Milwaukee (13 games over LA, who finished fourth). In 1961, the pennant race would be closer. The Dodgers held first place from August 8–15. They held second place every day thereafter, and on September 6, they were but one game out of first. But, led by Frank Robinson, Cincinnati pulled ahead, with the Dodgers finishing second, four games back.[4]

During these two years, Alston again found himself regularly platooning throughout his lineup. In the 1961 season, for example, Ron Fairly and Tommy Davis each played four positions. Four of Alston's outfielders played left, center, and right field. Five different Dodgers played first base. Bavasi, with Alston at first a bit reluctant, employed a statistician, Allan Roth, who kept a myriad of numerical details indicating who played well or poorly against certain pitchers and under various circumstances. Alston felt he had little choice but to juggle lineups and did so continuously. He came to see that detailed statistics could help guide his decisions with precision and intelligence. "I was accused of carrying platooning to extremes. My only answer," he would acknowledge somewhat blandly, "was that if it took a lot of players to win, that's how it had to be. Nobody would have enjoyed playing a regular eight more than the skipper of the Dodgers if he could have found enough consistency in his crew."[5]

In 1961, a dozen Dodgers played in at least 85 games. Tommy Davis was one player reporters found grumbling about the constant switching. Alston never took Davis to task for this. Within limits, he was always one to let his players feel free to express their thoughts. Davis's talents were great, so he was worth some indulgence. Jim Gilliam was one who never complained about the platooning, and Alston always held him in the highest esteem, later indeed making him a coach. In the spring of 1961, Alston heard complaints that Gilliam, nearing age 33, was getting too old. Alston responded, "suggesting to all who would listen that we would find a place for him somehow, and that if I had nine Gilliams on the club, I'd never have to worry."[6]

Because he twice fell short of the pennant in 1960 and 1961, some questioned the wisdom of Alston's incessant changing of his lineup, but the critics of the platooning had short memories, as they had forgotten how he firmly stayed with a set line-up just a few years before in Brooklyn. The Dodgers were facing tough competition in the uniformly strong National League. Virtually every series presented special challenges. The Mets and the Colt .45s were weak when they began, but the rest of the league was not. No matter how strong and balanced the National League may have been, fans and reporters still expected the Dodgers to win. They would almost always contend, and when anything short of a pennant presented itself, Alston would be under scrutiny. He was not surprised, nor did he ever display anger. He expected no less of himself.

Despite disappointments in 1960 and 1961, Alston's pitching grew ever stronger. In 1961 especially, Sandy Koufax appeared finally to have gained control over his phenomenal speed and breaking pitches. Alston noted that, while Koufax's speed equaled that of anyone, one key to his greatness was that his breaking pitches were even better than his fastball. Through an incredibly strict work regimen, and through a comprehension that he did not have to throw quite so hard on every pitch, Koufax grew ever more able to throw his breaking pitches with accuracy. Once he had the confidence that he could put his breaking ball in the strike zone, opposing batters soon realized that they could not bet on a walk and had to take a swing. When the NL batters could no longer wait out Koufax's wildness, he became virtually unhittable. This transformation began in 1961, and the season marked Koufax's first strong year. He posted 18 wins, and his strikeout total of 269 led the National League.[7] The following season, as the Dodgers moved out of the Coliseum, left-hander Koufax no longer had to face happy right-handed hitters peering down a ridiculously short left field line. With the normal dimensions of the new stadium, Koufax's effectiveness grew even more fearsome.

With Koufax rounding into the Hall of Fame–level pitcher so many had dreamt of, as the 1962 season commenced, the Dodgers again found themselves favored by many prognosticators. Koufax would not disappoint. Into mid–July he had already posted 14 wins, including a no-hitter over the Mets. With the season barely half over, he had also compiled over 200 strikeouts and appeared on his way to setting an all-time season mark. Then he suddenly felt a mysterious numbness, primarily in the index finger of his pitching hand. The problem was diagnosed as Raynaud's Condition, sometimes called Raynaud's Phenomenon or Disease. The condition involves the arteries to the fingers (or toes) going into vasospasms due to exposure to cold, stress, or both. The narrowing of the vessels limits blood supply. The arteries can also thicken, which also limits blood flow to the extremities. The limited blood flow lowers the levels of oxygen to the tissues, thus causing the numbness.[8] For Koufax, the numbness in his all-important pitching fingers was critical. He could not grip the ball with any feeling, so he was left with little to no control. In July, he had to leave a game in Cincinnati. He would not pitch again until September, at which point he tried a few times but was completely ineffective.

The loss of Koufax in the rotation was enormous. Nevertheless, the Dodgers stayed in the pennant race, but they could not pull ahead. Near the end of the season their hitting went into a collective slump. From September 8 to 15, they won seven in a row, and the pennant looked secure. Then from September 16 through 30, their record fell to 3–10.[9] Don Drysdale had made up for the loss of Koufax as best he could, posting 25 wins, and Maury Wills set a record of 104 stolen bases. But, Alston sighed, "all of our hitting died at once. With that we faded." The Dodgers did not score a run in the final two games of the regular season. That same final week of September 1962, heavyweight boxing champion Floyd Patterson was crushed by the challenger Charles "Sonny" Liston. Some scribes paralleled the Dodgers' end of season collapse with Patterson's stunning first-round loss and being compared to Patterson conveyed a pitiable vulnerability that was hardly something the Dodgers liked one bit. Alston certainly did not.[10]

With this late September slump, the Dodgers finished the season in a tie with the San Francisco Giants. For the fourth time, the Dodgers found themselves in a three-game NL pennant playoff. "It was one of the most disappointing seasons in my career," Alston recalled. In the playoff with San Francisco, the Giants won the first game. Here Alston took a chance and tried to start Koufax but had to relieve him in the second inning. The Dodgers came back with an 8–7 win to even the series. In the final game, the Dodgers had a 4–2 lead going into the ninth inning. The Giants rallied for four runs, with the go-ahead run coming via a walk with the bases loaded. The players, as well as Alston, were shattered after the loss to San Francisco. Alston did show the grace to trudge over to the Giants locker room and offer congratulations to Giants manager Alvin Dark. Still, as he later reflected, "I'd rather have had my teeth pulled."[11]

Even more than the questioning he endured for the platooning methods he employed throughout 1961 when he lost by four games to Cincinnati, with the 1962 playoff loss to the Giants, Alston faced great criticism. This included sharp words from one of his coaches, Leo Durocher. It was one of the few times that Alston received such open criticism from one of his coaches. Among Alston's coaches, Durocher was certainly different. He had already been a successful manager both with the Brooklyn Dodgers and with the New York Giants, but the Giants had dropped him in 1955. Then married to a film actress, Laraine Day, Durocher moved to the West Coast and tried several stints in various areas of show business, without great success. In 1961, he had hoped to become the manager of the newly formed Los Angeles Angels, but the Angels' General Manager, Fred Haney, would not have him. At this point, Bavasi and Alston hired him as a coach. This move surprised some observers and reporters, given both Durocher's established record as a manager in his own right and, even more, his notoriously abrasive, outspoken ways. In Bavasi's mind, the hiring of Durocher communicated much the same message as he had intended in 1958 when he brought Charlie Dressen back to coach: Alston was his manager, and the hiring of an experienced former manager as a coach merely underscored the security the team's top leadership felt about their skipper.

While the usually outgoing Dressen served well, and generally quietly, as a coach in 1958 and 1959, Durocher's coaching years under Bavasi and Alston proved quite different. There was no surprise about the fact that Alston and Durocher presented markedly contrasting personalities. "Fire and Ice," "Oil and Water," all the clichés were there. Durocher was as brash and outspoken as he ever was. Alston was always the classic "company man," an outlook to which Durocher not only did not give respect but was one he truly did not understand and at which he would often scoff. His famous dictum, "nice guys finish last," appeared to resonate among some fans and reporters whenever the Dodgers appeared to hit any sort of bump. The crash of late September 1962 and the ensuing playoff loss to San Francisco were the worst such bumps imaginable.

Throughout the 1962 season, reporters sensed a rivalry between Durocher and Alston. Once when Tommy Davis ran into his own bunt and Ron Fairly missed a hit-and-run sign, Durocher hollered that they ought to be fined. Alston promptly snapped at him, "You do the coaching, and I'll do the managing." Alston admitted here that he "was mad and plenty loud." He chided Durocher about allegedly needing to be awakened in his third base coaching box to take and relay the signs from Alston. But "the next day," Alston felt, "everything was fine between us. ... I never stay angry at anybody when I know he wants to win as much as I do, which Leo does." Durocher may not have felt the same way, however. In one extra-inning game in Cincinnati, the Dodgers were up a run. In the bottom of the inning, Cincinnati had a man on second with two out. Durocher advised Alston to walk the batter; "and put the winning run on base?" Alston responded. Durocher smirked and asked whether

Alston was afraid. Alston did walk the batter. The next hitter grounded into a force play, so the move worked. In the locker room after the game, when asked about the move, Alston smiled at the reporters, telling them it was a tough decision but the right move. Whether Alston was merely talking in platitudes or whether he was intentionally slighting his coach, Durocher took it personally, and he moved his locker room spot far away from Alston's. Durocher later bragged how he would countermand Alston in many situations. In his own mind, Durocher did not believe he was undermining of his boss. Instead, he felt he was simply making good tactical decisions. When Durocher coached at third base, he said, "Alston would give me the take sign, I'd flash the hit sign. Alston would signal to bunt, I'd call for the hit and run." Puckishly, he held that "I never 'saw' a take sign from Alston [and] with any of the speedsters [like Maury Wills and Willie Davis] ... they loved it. The whole team knew what I was doing, and they were saying, 'Just keep going Leo.'"[12]

As always, Durocher believed he knew best. This would reach a climactic point in the crucial ninth inning of the deciding third game of the 1962 LA–San Francisco playoff. The Dodgers had finished the eighth inning with a two-run lead. When Ed Roebuck came off the mound, and Durocher purportedly asked him how he felt. According to Durocher, Roebuck confessed: "My arm feels like lead." Durocher went to pitching coach Joe Becker, who was sitting within earshot of Alston, and told him he should get another pitcher ready. Durocher said that Becker uttered not a word. Instead, Alston spoke up: "I'm going to win or lose with Roebuck. He stays right there." According to Durocher, Sandy Koufax, Don Drysdale, and Duke Snider were all sitting nearby, urging him to tell Alston not to send Roebuck back out for the ninth inning. Durocher snapped at the three: "What the hell do you want me to do? I'm not managing the club. There's not a goddam thing more I can say than I've said." Alston did not actually have many fresh pitching arms at that point. The bullpen had been used extensively both in the playoff as well as in the final hectic weeks of the season.

Beyond the specifics of the situation at that critical point in the ninth inning of the final playoff game, Durocher seemed to believe he had built a special relationship with various players. He felt they were comfortable coming to him to question Alston, believing he would support them with their complaints. He apparently did this openly, with Alston right there in the dugout with him. It was a hard situation to consider, then or in hindsight, without believing that someone had to be right and someone wrong. There was little room for the notion that people will see the same situation in different lights and react in different manners.

In the fateful ninth inning, with Roebuck pitching, the Giants' Matty Alou led off and singled. Harvey Kuenn hit into a fielder's choice, erasing Alou, but leaving Kuenn on first. Here grew more controversy. Alston had positioned his second baseman, Larry Burright, more towards first base to cover the hole left as his first baseman was holding Alou on base. Some claimed that Alston should have left Burright closer to second base, as Kuenn's grounder could have resulted in a double play that would have changed the whole outcome of the inning, and the season. Of course, the capable Kuenn (he hit .304 that season, .303 lifetime) could quite possibly have smacked a base hit between first and second, leaving runners on first and third and none out. Such a move as Alston made with Burright can always raise questions.

With one on and one out, Roebuck walked Willie McCovey and Felipe Alou to load the bases; then he gave up a single to Willie Mays, which scored one run. At this point, Alston finally did relieve Roebuck with Stan Williams. The next batter hit a sacrifice fly, scoring the tying run. With two outs and runners on first and third, a wild pitch moved Mays to second. The next batter was given an intentional walk to load the bases. Williams then walked the next batter, with the runner on third trotting home to give San Francisco the lead. Alston relieved Williams with Ron Perranoski. The next batter grounded to second, but Burright committed an error, giving the Giants their fourth run of the inning. The next batter struck out, so, finally, the top of the ninth inning was over. Now two runs down, the shell-shocked Dodgers went meekly, 1-2-3 in their half of the ninth, and San Francisco had the pennant.[13] Alston's decision not to relieve Roebuck sooner, and his choice to position Burright as he did with a man on first, stirred up much complaining and second-guessing.

Alston was as sad and angry about the loss as anyone. He even expressed resentment at those who used the word "choke" to describe what the Dodgers did, both in the playoff against San Francisco and at the end of the season.

> There was an unfortunate stigma on the Dodgers. ... To me, the phrase "choke up" is perhaps the most despicable in sports. To call a man "choke-up artist" is a reflection on his competitive courage when the big chips are on the table. Badly as I felt about our late collapse in 1962, the insistence of some writers and broadcasters that we lost because of a lack of competitive heart irritated me even more. Slumps are part of baseball. They attack the great as well as the humble. Absolute consistency over the long haul is an admirable goal but is almost impossible. ... In the eyes of too many, we lost our 1962 lead and then the playoff competitively more than artistically—a view that was both unfair and untrue.

Alston shrugged at most of the specific second-guessing. Of Durocher, he would be terse, even years later: "Leo Durocher was supposed to have second-guessed me in public. A lot was written one way and the other. I've always maintained that if you can't say something good then you shouldn't say anything. I'm sure not going to violate that now [1976], not after all these years."[14]

The controversies that grew out of the Dodgers' loss to the Giants in 1962 ultimately underscore the contrasts that lay between the managerial styles and personalities of Alston and Durocher. Like many managers throughout the history of baseball, Durocher commanded his players much like a marine drill sergeant and sought to be aggressive at all times in regard to opposing teams, umpires, reporters, fans, or even general managers and owners. (When Durocher first managed in Brooklyn, his open fights with the loud, alcoholic GM Larry MacPhail were legendary. They made the later Billy Martin-George Steinbrenner relationship look almost genteel.) An argument can certainly be put forth that such a leadership style can get a great deal out of a team. Contrarily, such a style can just as easily exhaust and decimate a team emotionally. Much depends here on the individual and collective make-up of the team at hand. Alston managed in a completely different manner than Durocher. To some his quiet manner stoked the team with no "fire in the belly." Alston, indeed, was never one to evince outwardly aggressive ways, and when his teams did not win, many raised criticisms which, in effect, extolled the virtues of the well-known aggressive ways of a John McGraw, a Fred Clarke, a Billy Martin, an Earl Weaver, or a Leo Durocher. Durocher had some reason to feel his ways were better. Disdainfully, he referred to Alston as "the farmer." To him, farm boys may have baseball skills, but they needed scrappy, streetwise aggressive managers to maximize their effectiveness. Meanwhile in the 1960s, many of the game's managers were men who had formerly played for Durocher and in whom, albeit in a variety of ways, some of Durocher's inimitable style and personality echoed: Eddie Stanky, Wes Westrum, Charlie Dressen, Billy Herman, Gil Hodges, Phil Rigney, Bobby Bragan, Hermann Franks, and Gene Mauch.[15]

Other managers of the era, such as Billy Martin and Earl Weaver, also appeared to have been cut from the same sort of Durocher mold. When he managed the Orioles, Weaver's nickname was "Mugsy," the same, and not coincidentally, as McGraw's. The writer George Bernard Shaw described McGraw as the most essentially American male he had ever met.[16] That sense of what was truly American underscored the legitimacy of the Durocher style of management for the game that was itself essential to the nation's culture.

In certain respects, O'Malley liked the scrappy, McGraw-style of management. When he was first in charge of the team and hired Dressen to succeed Shotton, his then new GM Bavasi may have liked the idea of considering Alston, but he likely realized that he would have to prove himself to his new boss before overtly intervening in such an important issue as naming a new field manager. By 1962, with O'Malley as disappointed as anyone in the outcome of the season, Bavasi could be more comfortable openly defending Alston against criticisms.

Some fans did grumble about Alston after the 1962 loss. By then, along with Bavasi and O'Malley, Alston felt himself part of an organization that worked with an effectiveness which no other could match over the long term. A sense of the role of the organization, "the total system" as Alston called it, was always central in his mind. It was based on an understanding and on experiences that involved so much more than any mere corporate sloganeering. Back in 1944 and 1945, when he was first managing for Branch Rickey on the Dodgers' team in Trenton, Alston had had to handle all non-baseball administrative and logistical matters while serving as player-manager. To be sure, the scale of such matters back then was rather small in nature, and Spartan wartime labor necessities logically required that a man in Alston's position shoulder all the duties that he performed (and he did it all rather well). Alston knew all this without a hint of acrimony in his heart, and these experiences, as well as such others as he had previously gone through in Portsmouth and Springfield, Ohio, left him with an understanding of the nature of what sound management, at low and mid-levels, as well as the top levels, can do and needs to do for a ball team. He never forgot. He could see how bad work along management lines could hurt a team's performance. As a result, he was sincerely appreciative of the contributions to a team's quality when management saw to all details that a more casual observer or journalist may take for granted or consider extraneous. Alston never took anything for granted because he fully knew the role of all the contributions. Without a hint of sycophancy, he thus wrote: "There are many fine things about managing a major league baseball team. But with the Dodgers they are better, because Mr. O'Malley does everything first class. We never have to wait in an airline terminal for a place. Our plane is there waiting for us. It's comfortable and well-staffed, and that makes baseball travel much easier. It's the same way in spring training."[17]

Within the Dodgers' organization, the nature of the coaching staffs under Alston also illustrated much about the ways the Dodgers of O'Malley, Bavasi, and Alston operated in contrast to other teams. All the coaches that Bavasi and Alston hired fit within the order of the Dodgers' organization. On many teams, some coaches would be hired with a sense that it would be useful to ensure that, in case the manager had to be replaced, the team's on-field functions could readily proceed without any unnecessary stress and jarring. In 1961, Durocher may have felt himself to hold such a position when he was hired to coach in Los Angeles. He never said so, of course. It was clear, however, that under O'Malley, Bavasi, and Alston, no such sense of managerial alternatives, and "in case of …" scenarios, appeared to be part of their thinking. Alston himself wrote:

> Coaches are mighty important to me. … I've never had any particular favorites. … I want them to do their job. I respect them. I try to relay through my coaches as much as possible what I want done. … I like to joke and kid with my coaches. … But they know when I am serious and that's what counts. … They all had one thing in common. They were good teachers and hard workers. … No one man or two men can do it all. It's a team effort, really an organization effort. A total system. And I think it works.[18]

Alston's and the Dodgers organization's hiring of coaches, and how they were assigned duties, were among the many operational elements that emanated from a very clear sense of how all parts of the organization functioned. There was nothing Orwellian here. Neither was there any superficial "rah-rah" corporate rhetoric on hand. As the organization evolved, leaders like Rickey and then O'Malley developed their many functions carefully and with minute attention to detail. Each component played a role, and each player and employee needed to understand both the content of his job and its place in the broader scheme. The coaches, and Alston's view of them, illustrated this.

In Alston's long tenure, the Dodgers never saw a need for plans in case the manager needed to be removed. Considering the array of Alston's coaches in the late 1950s and early 1960s—Charlie Dressen, Pee Wee Reese, Bobby Bragan, Greg Mulleavy, Pete Reiser—some had been all-star players; some had previously been managers; some would be managers, but while they coached for the Dodgers, there was never much of a notion of anyone "waiting in the wings" to take over should there be a change at the top.

There were occasional rumors. In June 1963, for example, Chicago newspapers reported that several players had raised complaints about Alston, prompting Bavasi to fly to Chicago to speak with them. It was merely rumor, but one coach on the Cubs, Bob Kennedy, perhaps trying to stir up trouble for the Dodgers while they were playing Chicago, mouthed off with supposed authority: "If the Dodgers lose today, Durocher will be manager tomorrow."[19] The Dodgers won the next day, and they went on to win the pennant and the World Series. What actual sources a Chicago coach like Kennedy could have had for such a certain prediction was never clear. Such is often the confident, opinionated nature of many in baseball, and the circulation of such rumors is part of the politics of the game, or any game. (They remain in the never-ending debates of seasons past among baseball history fanatics.) Indeed, if rumormongering serves to disrupt an opposing team's cohesion and quality of play, it is a useful tactic. Alston never paid much attention to such talk, and with his coaches, he readily delegated authority beneath him but felt himself to be fully in command of all on-field matters and decisions. Meanwhile, he fully and happily left all trade, corporate, and business matters to O'Malley, Bavasi, and their assistants. Where on- and off-field areas of purview overlapped, there would always be conge-nial consulting. Meanwhile, all arrangements regarding such things as stadium logistics, travel, and spring training Alston happily left to those above him (and he would never for a moment object to the use of the word "above" here).

Leo Durocher's criticisms about 1962 stand as a glaring excep-tion to the general tone of the operations of the LA organization. Some may have sided with Durocher's assessment of what could and should have been done that season. Of course, Alston did not agree. More importantly, neither did O'Malley or Bavasi. In some of his instincts, O'Malley may have liked the more argumentative, hard-drinking, John McGraw-type skipper he had earlier seen in Dressen, Shotton, and Durocher. But over the years he had certainly come to rely on Bavasi, and with Bavasi's influence, Alston was not to be summarily cast aside. At this juncture, the loss to the Giants in 1962 notwithstanding, nei-ther Bavasi nor O'Malley was pleased with Durocher, especially Bavasi. Bavasi actually wanted to fire Durocher, but Alston advised him not to.

Alston was once a guest at a Jewish War Veterans gathering in Pitts-burgh, and when asked about Durocher, he cast it thus: "We're differ-ent kind of people, Leo and I. He likes the bright lights and all that goes with them. ... I'm still a country boy from Darrtown, Ohio. I'll take the open spaces, a good shotgun, a fine saddle horse, and a good pool table for off-season recreation. Off the field, Leo goes his way, I go mine. He wants to win, so do I. During working hours, we get along fine." Bavasi recalled that he wanted to fire Durocher after he appeared to try to upstage Alston in the media, but he did not fire him because Alston said he deserved another chance. Bavasi had also confided in some reporters that he would quit if Durocher ever replaced Alston. Facing Durocher directly, "When I told Durocher that Alston wanted to keep him," Bavasi remembered with a chuckle, "he wouldn't believe it."[20]

With Alston's blessing, Durocher stayed with the team from 1961 to 1964, later managing the Chicago Cubs from 1966 to 1972 and the Houston Astros in 1972 and 1973. Durocher never won a pennant with either team. Indeed, with the Cubs in 1969 he presided over a 1962

Dodgers-like melt-down on one of his own teams. That season, Chicago appeared to be the likely winner of the NL East division, 1969 being the first season in which the leagues were divided into separate divisions. Durocher's Cubs were in first place all season until September 10. On August 16, they held a lead of nine games. Matters looked secure, but the New York Mets passed them, took the division, and then won the pennant and the World Series.[21] As the Cubs fell before the oncoming Mets, it is not known whether anyone playfully reminded Durocher of his 1962 criticisms of Alston amidst LA's loss to San Francisco. It certainly would have been most unkind. Puckishly, indeed, one could assert that only a reporter who possessed the nature of a Leo Durocher would ever raise such a point. "Nice guys [may] finish last," but they also do not bring up such jabbing questions, even at the very man who first said, "nice guys finish last." Alston's teams responded to the disappointments of 1954, 1958, and 1962 with championships in each of the following seasons, but the 1970 Cubs did not bounce back. Indeed, to some Cubs fanatics, it would not be until 2016 that the team would fully recover from 1969.

The wider point here about baseball management is that, despite any claims about one style being superior, the varying styles of managers can yield varying results. If any one way, between the aggressive, the relatively quiet, or some other manner, could be proven clearly to be better, team owners (and business owners in general) would adopt that one best approach. But no one way works best, as thousands of management manuals and business school texts attest. It is simply too complex a topic for any one formula to apply.

A trivial, but nonetheless revealing aside in the outlook as to the place of coaches in Alston's (and O'Malley's and Bavasi's) organizational scheme came forth in another feature in the years that Leo Durocher coached with the Dodgers. On Alston's staff from 1961 to 1964 and having previously managed both the Dodgers and the Giants, Durocher's contribution to the bumptious layer of the Dodgers' collective personality had been very much part of Brooklyn's charm, but in the environs of Southern California, this "Brooklynism" was a characteristic that appeared more culturally incongruous, and it faded in significance. With Los Angeles, and not just in regard to the loss in 1962, Durocher would be as outspoken as he always had been both as a player and a manager (as well as later when he managed the Chicago Cubs and Houston Astros). Nevertheless, neither he nor anyone could possibly challenge the position Alston held.

At times, Durocher's visibility during his seasons as a Dodger' coach may have appeared to eclipse Alston's in various parts of the media, but this never posed a problem to O'Malley, Bavasi, or Alston. It was never an issue in the actual workings of the team on the field or in any important decisions the team's management made off the field. The issue of Durocher's visibility would actually manifest itself in popular culture but not intrude much into actual baseball matters.

In view of the Los Angeles Dodgers' location in the center of the burgeoning entertainment industry, the producers of several LA-based network television comedy programs came up with scenarios for episodes which intersected with baseball and with the Dodgers specifically. Sometimes individual players would be involved. Pitcher Don Drysdale, for example, appeared on *Leave It to Beaver*, *The Brady Bunch*, and *The Donna Reed Show*. On *Beaver*, the Beav and his friends were able to telephone Dodger Stadium and have a conversation with Drysdale, with the subsequently huge phone bill getting them all in trouble with Beaver's father. On *The Brady Bunch*, the character Greg wanted to be a big league ballplayer, but he got advice from Drysdale to focus on his education so he would have more options as to what he could do in life.[22] Neither O'Malley, Bavasi, nor Alston had the slightest problem with such public appearances by a player like Drysdale. Indeed, they liked the good publicity and public relations such work fostered.

Repeatedly in other 60s TV comedies, various scenarios left the impression that the head figure on the Dodgers was Leo Durocher. In one episode of the popular comedy, *The Beverly Hillbillies*, for example, the character Jethro was discovered to have a great talent for pitching. The man who noticed Jethro and his talent was not Alston but Durocher. (As the story turned out, Jethro needed to use possum fat to grease his fingers to throw well, so he couldn't play.) On *The Munsters*, the behemoth character of Herman gained a tryout with the Dodgers. He was going to be the next Mickey Mantle. At bat, he rocketed one pitch into space, knocked down part of the scoreboard with a line drive, burned a hole in the third baseman's glove with another liner, and bowled over an infielder with his base running. Leo Durocher watched in mild disbelief and shrugged to an associate: "I don't know whether to sign him for the Dodgers or send him to Vietnam." (The latter point was intended as a patriotic comment rather than implying anything punitive.) In yet another comedy of the day, *Mr. Ed*, a show about a man who owned a horse that could speak, the horse was listening to a Dodgers game on the radio and phoned in some advice as to what the Dodgers should do in a particularly tight situation. The advice was addressed not to Alston but again to Durocher. Alston's name never came forth in any of these shows. On *Mr. Ed*, as the advice proved good, Mr. Ed was invited to a Dodgers practice. Mr. Ed's owner, Wilbur Post, having to pretend he'd given the advice, came to Dodger Stadium with his horse. He explained the horse as "a good luck charm." "Wouldn't a rabbit's foot be easier?" queried a bewildered Durocher. On the sly from Mr. Ed, Wilbur then relayed useful advice to the likes of Willie Davis. Mr. Ed also took a bat in his mouth and smacked a delivery from Sandy Koufax off the left field wall for an inside-the-park home run, with catcher John Roseboro leaping out of the way in stark fear as the huge galloping steed slid into home. In all cases it was Durocher, not Alston, who was the frontman here. On TV comedies at least, Durocher could serve as a symbol of Dodgers leadership. As with the sports press, Durocher possessed more thespian talents than Alston.[23]

In a completely different area of the team's relations to the public, the division between the visible work of one of the Dodgers' employees and the actual work of manager Alston came across with utter clarity as well. The Dodgers' radio/TV announcer, Vin Scully, had an excellent relationship with Los Angeles fans. In the early 1960s, many fans would come to home games with transistor radios so they could still listen to Scully while attending the game. Transistor radios were as ubiquitous in the early 1960s as cell phones would become in the early 21st century. Scully was actually able to induce the fans to engage in special cheers and chants as a result of so many fans tuning into his broadcasts while attending the game. Once, Joey Jay of the Cincinnati Reds was called for a balk. Speedster Maury Wills was on base, and Jay wanted to do everything to keep him from stealing. The umpire called a balk because Jay, when coming to his "set" position before delivering to home, was, by rule, supposed to remain set for a full second. The umpire ruled that Jay did not wait the full second. While Cincinnati manager Fred Hutchinson was kicking up a whale of an argument, Scully spoke to the radio audience about the "full second" rule. Then he called upon the fans to help out: "When I say 'A,'" he instructed, "You answer 'B.'" Suddenly, as Hutchinson and Jay were yelling at the umpire, shouts of "B" were coming from all over the stadium. Scully suddenly received a phone call from, of all people, Walter Alston: "Why in the hell is the crowd yelling 'B' in the middle of this argument?" Scully explained it all. The point here was that such links between the club and the fans were utterly extraneous to anything Alston was minding. Here, once Scully explained it to Alston, the intrusion was of no more significance than the question of who appeared on *Mr. Ed*.[24]

Vin Scully had an impact on fans in Dodger Stadium like few other announcers, but there, as in any 1960s TV comedies, there was no hidden message to the effect that Durocher or anyone else but Alston was really in charge of the team. For the forum of entertainment television,

Durocher was simply a better personality. Alston always maintained a quiet dignity that would not mesh with such Hollywood-based TV comedy. Alston had no interest in TV theatrics. (Possibly, his poor acting in high school plays back in Darrtown all those years ago had been more than enough for him.) As he had been before in Brooklyn and with the Giants, Durocher was good copy. His gravelly voice resonated well over TV and radio. He would always interview well with either media, and he proved later to be a good TV baseball broadcaster and analyst. He knew his stuff, and he sounded good over the airwaves. Alston knew all such things were not his métier. He, O'Malley, and Bavasi were each quite content with Durocher taking such peripheral limelight and extra money while he coached for them. It was good for Durocher. It was good public relations, and it did no harm to anyone else. The key was that such matters were completely separate from the actual matters of baseball. There the question of who was in charge was fully established. The Dodgers organization felt no need to maintain any sort of posture of respectability, which, in another organization, could have led some to feel uncomfortable with a coach like Durocher appearing as he did on TV. To the Dodgers' management, respectability was inherent in what they did, how they performed in games, and how logistics behind the scenes of the games were handled. A bit of positive public relations with the general population via the TV entertainment industry, especially in such a media mecca as Los Angeles, was simply a nice little additive. Durocher gaining a little more visibility and extra cash from the TV networks did not bother anyone in the Dodgers' hierarchy either, least of all Alston. He was secure in his relationship and friendship with Bavasi and O'Malley, and if that had ever failed, he would be quite content going home to Darrtown.

10

Winning Is Always
the Best Response

The painful loss to San Francisco in the 1962 National League play-off was certainly not an easy thing to endure, either for Alston or for the Dodgers. At the time and since, some have raised the simple point of just how good a team San Francisco had that year, with such stars as Willie Mays, Orlando Cepeda, Willie McCovey, Felipe Alou, Matty Alou, Harvey Kuenn, Juan Marichal, Gaylord Perry, Billy Pierce, and Jack Sanford. Losing to such a team was hardly a disgrace, but for the Dodgers, the embarrassment and the anguish could not be so easily shrugged off. In previous seasons, Alston had felt the sting of criticisms, especially when it appeared that his lack of outward aggressiveness did not serve the interests of the team. In 1962 he endured many such opinions again.

Back in 1954, Alston's first season in Brooklyn, the Dodgers and Giants fought for the pennant, and after a loss to Chicago, Jackie Robinson snarled to a reporter about Duke Snider being awarded a double on a fly ball which, to Robinson, should have been ruled a home run. Robinson especially complained here that Alston did not contest the call: "The team might be moving somewhere if Alston had not been standing at third base like a wooden Indian." Other players like pitcher Billy Loes voiced some similar comments that season. Alston's alleged lack of aggressiveness did receive some press attention in 1954. In response, Alston remained his usual calm self, something which the New York media was experiencing for the first time. Alston would allude to the fact that the entire history of baseball reveals that arguing with umpires is virtually 100 percent futile, and that a manager can risk more bad calls in future games should he gain a reputation for being too argumentative. Here was a view that, of course, flew directly in the face of the tendencies of such managerial legends as McGraw, Dressen, or Durocher, who believed in contesting every minute detail, or of such players as Ty Cobb and Jackie Robinson, who approached the game the same way. Alston's view did, and does, imply that a certain lack of integrity may exist among some umpires, who should be making calls no matter the past history of any manager or player. As in other sports, some umpires accept the idea of "makeup" calls. Debates, then, over which managerial style yields the best outcomes will never end—on the field, in the press, or in bars. Alston preferred not to argue too much with umpires, although he certainly did so from time to time. He also avoided any direct public answering of critics, be they players or reporters. He answered to Bavasi and to O'Malley, and what occurred between them, after the 1954 season or at any other time, were matters shared with no one else. (Researchers have found no archive and no cache of letters of memoirs that reveal some hidden truths.)

Once O'Malley had come to respect and rely on Bavasi, the three-way relationship remained solid. O'Malley and Bavasi were not going to fire Alston because of pressures from "experts" in the media or from fans through the media. Alston appreciated the loyalty. "You can't work for better people," he wrote. He actually received an offer to manage the Cleveland Indians. Back when he managed in St. Paul and Montreal, such an offer may have been enticing, and, indeed, if any such offer had then come from Cincinnati, he may have taken it and managed in his home-town neighborhood. But once he was firmly in place within the Dodgers' system, he felt, "I've got the best job in the world." Cleveland's offer involved a five-year term. With LA the contracts would continue to be one year at a time, but Alston felt no need to change. "In all my years, I've only asked for a raise once and I got it, but I can't remember when that was." Money was never a major matter for Alston. In 1954, his first salary was $24,000. By the 1970s, he was making a little over $100,000. He was content, and no grumblings in the press would undermine the solidity he felt within the Dodgers' organization.[1]

One response Alston was very happy to present to his critics of 1954 was the Dodgers' season of 1955, as the team ran away with the pennant and won their first World Series. After that victory over the Yankees, critics had little choice but to be mum. Similarly, the 1958 season had been abysmal. A few critics grumbled, but Bavasi and O'Malley remained loyal, and Alston responded by guiding the team to another title in 1959. Winning is always the best response to criticisms. Between the 1962 and 1963 seasons, Alston had another response open to him, as he did receive a tentative offer to manage Cleveland, but he politely refused and did not attempt to leverage anything out of Bavasi and O'Malley via the offer.[2]

After the debacle of 1962, the Dodgers came back for the 1963 season with something to prove. Sandy Koufax's Raynaud's Condition appeared to have been successfully treated. As he now had full feeling in all his fingers, there was nothing holding back his strength and skill. He proceeded to mow down the league. That season, Koufax won the rare "pitcher's Triple Crown," leading the league in wins (25), ERA (1.88), and strikeouts (302), the first pitcher in the history of the National League to break the 300-strikeout mark. Meanwhile, he walked only 58. He threw 11 shutouts, which also led the league, and on May 11, he threw a no-hitter against the Giants. He was voted the league's Most Valuable Player. Koufax had shown signs of such greatness in 1961. He looked like he would achieve much in the first half of 1962, but then came the Raynaud's. In 1963, nothing impeded him or the Dodgers.

Beyond Koufax's remarkable achievements, Tommy Davis hit .324. Maury Wills, slowed a bit with foot trouble, only stole 40 bases but still hit .302. Frank Howard hit 28 home runs. The general team hitting was a trifle light. No one else hit .300, and the team's average was only .251, but the defense was tight and the pitching superb. In addition to Koufax, Drysdale went 19–16, with several of the losses coming by the closest of margins. Johnny Podres, now 30 years old, won 14 games, and Ron Perranoski won 16 as he became the best relief pitcher in the league. Pitching, speed, defense, and hitting when needed proved a good formula. The line-up was stable; the platooning Alston previously felt compelled to employ was gone. Among all non-pitchers on the roster, only 10 Dodgers would play in more than 80 games.[3]

For the critics who had emphasized the idea that Alston was too mild-mannered a manager, an incident on May 6, 1963, did reveal that, when necessary, he could be aggressive and even menacing. The Dodgers lost a game in Pittsburgh. From the game they were to proceed to the airport and fly off to St. Louis. It was a hot day in Pittsburgh. The Pirates were leaving town at the same time, and some Dodgers noted that the Pirates left in a comfortable modern bus, while the one they boarded was old, cramped, and had no air conditioning. Amidst the sweaty ride to the airport, the players' grumbling increased. Some was directed at the bus driver, who had been hired by the team's travelling secretary, who handled all the arrangements concerning transportation. The driver snapped back at some of the players' complaints. In the Pirates' victory that afternoon, the Dodgers committed several key errors, and the driver had the temerity to refer to those errors, saying "If you guys would win some games, instead of kicking 'em away, you might deserve an air-conditioned bus." Alston took control. He ordered the driver to pull over, and with the bus stopped, Alston stood up and addressed the team. His message: if anyone wished to raise any more complaints about the bus or anything else, they could meet him outside the bus right then.

(He would handle the driver as well, but he did that in private, and he did not fire him.) Among the players on the bus was Frank Howard, who stood over 6'7" and weighed about 270 lbs. Alston would later concede that he did wonder what may have happened had a man like Howard taken him up on his offer, but at that moment on route from Forbes Field to the airport, Alston was very much in earnest and too angry to give any rational second thoughts to such a hulking presence as Frank Howard.

His rare show of temper won the day. Not only was the rest of the ride to the airport non-eventful, but the Dodgers proceeded to win 13 of their next 15 games. (Of course, before the first of these wins, after they had flown to St. Louis, the Dodgers drove from their hotel to Busch Stadium in a new, fully air-conditioned bus.) There had been an earlier spring training incident when Alston noticed Koufax and pitcher Larry Sherry coming back to their room after hours. He beat on their door, and, when he got no reply, he kept beating until it opened, breaking his 1959 championship ring in the process. From that moment on, Sherry and Koufax kept proper hours.[4]

The philosopher Arthur Schopenhauer famously mused that there can be no democracy before the age of 18. His point speaks to the psychological dynamics at play in such rare incidents where Alston displayed temper. Granted, all the players were over 18, but the culture of adolescent boys remains very much alive amidst young men engaged in a sport they had each been playing, in most cases continuously, since they were small children. Among such people, an authority figure needs to command acceptance within a masculine mentality where physical prowess is very much a standard. Alston's assertiveness thus worked, not because the players came to feel any sort of overt physical fear of him. Former boxer Billy Martin would do this in several managerial jobs he held, even seriously injuring one of his players on the Minnesota Twins, when, likely in a state of inebriation, he actually assaulted a player.[5] That sort of action was counter-productive, as was Martin's alcoholism more generally.

At a saner level, Alston succeeded in conveying to his players that he could still think and operate within a fully masculine culture. The realization that their manager, though now a grandfather in his 50s, still maintained such sensibilities made players that much more accepting of his leadership. Several writers, including Frank Finch of the *Los Angeles Times*, Bob Hunter of the *Los Angeles Herald Examiner*, and George Lederer of the *Long Beach Independent, Press-Telegram,* claimed the Pittsburgh bus incident helped bring the team together. Whether the incident had that much importance is debatable. Winning 13 of their next 15 games certainly helped here, actual cause and effect never fully proven, of course. Still, such incidents did underscore the point that "the quiet man" had a rage within him when he wanted to utilize it. It was important that the players know this.[6]

Members of the press encountered this rage that occasionally came forth from Alston. Alston made a point of his not caring much, one way or the other, what reporters wrote about him. He emphatically told several writers that he never read sports columns. His concerns focused strictly within the club, and structurally within the management of the organization with O'Malley and Bavasi. Even here, Alston would on occasion lash out verbally at a reporter about some drivel he had clacked.[7] For Alston this willingness to "put on the gloves" was an element that made him effective as a manager within the Rickey/O'Malley organization. As the front office's field manager, Alston was altogether content to support and do the bidding of directives from O'Malley or Bavasi. Were he just a front man for the Dodgers' system, he would have commanded less respect from players or the press. His occasional flarings of temper gave him a presence and an individuality that gave his leadership a character and identity that came solely from him and not just from the context of merely being O'Malley and Bavasi's man on the playing field. Thus, he could stand up to challenges from a star like Jackie Robinson. When the team was winning with apparent ease, as they did in 1955, Alston did not need to take up any of the limelight, and critics who picked away at Alston being a mere figurehead for a club that simply needed to be taken to the park and allowed to play. But in 1956, when winning did not come so easily, Alston could call a team meeting and rage at his players, and they would respond because his words were more than mere vapor. His quiet ways were what fit the organizational scheme that Rickey, O'Malley, and Bavasi had constructed. His edges gave a dynamism that was a necessary ingredient for his part of the team's organization to be effective in the game and with the personnel who played it.[8]

The 1963 Dodgers posted 99 wins. They finished six games ahead of St. Louis. Even though the team was now well-ensconced in Los Angeles, a Dodgers pennant still prompted feelings of NY nostalgia, especially as, once again, the Dodgers were to face the Yankees in the World Series. Aside from the 1959 victory over Chicago, one had to go back to 1920 to find a World Series in which the Dodgers had faced any team in the World Series but the Yanks. This new LA/NYC contest was, of course, anything but a "subway series," but the memories from the seven Yankees/Dodgers World Series from 1941 to 1956 remained very much alive among hundreds of thousands of baseball fans. Among the memories was the fact that the Dodgers had only beaten the Yanks in one of those seven Series. In 1963, the Yankees had won their fourth straight pennant. They completely dominated the American League, winning by 10½ games over second-place Chicago. Mickey Mantle had been hurt some of the season, but in October he was well and still, at age 31, a very powerful hitter. Whitey Ford remained one of the game's best pitchers. Yogi Berra was still with the team, as were Elston Howard, Roger Maris, Tony Kubek, and Bobby Richardson. Some reporters snickered about the Yankees being a little long in the tooth, but, healthy at the season's end, they certainly appeared formidable.

To no one's surprise, Alston picked Koufax to start Game One in New York. Koufax had not lost a game since August 11; he had only lost five games all season. Alston had given Koufax a full week's rest, and no starts after September 25. The Yankees sent out their ace, Whitey Ford, so it appeared the opening game would be a real pitchers' duel. While the decision to start Koufax in Game One of the World Series was unremarkable, Alston made another line-up decision that would prove quite clever. Bill "Moose" Skowron had been the Yankees' first baseman from 1954 to 1962. He had several seasons batting over .300, and in one three-season span from 1960 to 1962, he hit 77 home runs. But after the 1962 season, the Yankees chose to release Skowron. Alston and Bavasi were happy to pick him up as a backup first baseman and for pinch-hitting chores. New York's management appeared wise in letting Skowron go, for under Alston in 1963, Skowron hit a mere .203 and homered only four times. Despite this mediocre performance, Alston believed that Skowron would be up for a duel with his old team. Alston demonstrated managerial wisdom here, as Skowron did indeed hit well. In Game One, he went 2-for-3, his two hits yielding two RBI. In the Series, Skowron hit .385.[9]

In game one, Whitey Ford pitched well for New York, but, in addition to Skowron's surprising play, catcher John Roseboro hit a home run with two runners on base. That would prove more than enough offense. As for the Yankees, meanwhile, Koufax completely throttled them. In the bottom of the 1st inning Koufax struck out the side, doing the same in the 4th. The Yanks' first 14 batters not only went down in succession, only one, Clete Boyer, managed to hit a ball in fair territory, and that was an anemic infield grounder. Otherwise, there were three little foul territory pop-outs and 10 strikeouts. Koufax would strike out 15 that day, setting a new World Series record. Koufax's fearsome speed and breaking ball proved just too much for the Yankees, as well as for their fans. Heads were shaking all over Yankee Stadium. After he struck out the first two Yankee batters in the bottom of the 1st, Koufax appeared to sneer into the New York dugout, as if to proclaim to them: *Not only do*

I know you can't hit me; I also know that you know you can't hit me. The Yankees were not just beaten, they were completely dominated. Yogi Berra did not play that day against Koufax, but he watched carefully and later commented to reporters: "I can see how he won 25 games. What I don't understand is how he lost five."[10]

After winning Game One soundly, 5–2, Alston was anxious to keep the momentum going. In Game Two, he started Johnny Podres, who had masterfully pitched Game Seven for Brooklyn in 1955. It was impossible to determine how many people in the New York area still held sentiments about the Dodgers, but in starting Podres in New York, Alston appeared to be catering to them. (There was, as well, the well-ensconced wisdom in the game that lefties tended to do better in Yankee Stadium.) Now that the Mets were playing in New York, the appearance of former Brooklyn Dodgers like Koufax, Drysdale, Podres, and Alston did appear to arouse fans whenever the Mets hosted them. Much the same happened when Willie Mays and the Giants came to town. Later, the appointment of Gil Hodges as the Mets' manager would prove immensely popular, even before he led them to a championship in 1969. Hodges had indeed been the one Brooklyn Dodgers player who maintained a home in Brooklyn after the move to LA.[11] In Game Two of the 1963 Series, Podres shut out the Yankees for eight innings. LA put up four runs, but New York rallied in the ninth inning. They scored one run and had runners on base. Alston brought in Ron Perranoski, who stopped the Yankees from there.

Up two games to none, the Dodgers returned to Los Angeles. Alston sent out Don Drysdale to start game three. Drysdale had indeed won 19 games that season, but in the minds of some Dodger fans he seemed to be a trifle jinxed; the hitting of the Dodgers supposedly weakened on some of the days he started. Drysdale did lose some close ones, but it was one particular loss that season, on June 28, which gave credence to the scuttlebutt about Drysdale getting little offensive support. The game, against Milwaukee, was a 1–0 thriller, pitting Drysdale against the Braves' legendary Warren Spahn. Milwaukee's one run had come at the very top of the first, thus isolating the score and further magnifying the pure pitchers-duel character of the game. The rest of the way, indeed, neither side could score or even mount a threat. It was a terrific game, and its significance in the collective memory of LA fans remained distinct. In the World Series game against the Yankees (in Dodger Stadium, just like the late June duel with Spahn) it was the Dodgers who scored a run in the first. This perfectly reversed imagery and dispelled yet more the supposed jinx set up by the June loss to Spahn and Milwaukee. From there indeed Drysdale took total command. It was as though he knew that, with the one run, he would likely get no more offensive support (indeed he did not). To LA fans, the big right hander made up his mind to show everyone that one run was all he needed. He took the entire matter onto his shoulders, giving up but three meaningless hits and throttling New York 1–0. Alston was effusive:

> Koufax and Podres were great, but I think Drysdale was their equal at that point in time. He hardly made a bad pitch. His best ones were all at the right time. For instance, in the sixth inning with the tying run at third, he struck out Mantle. I don't think he missed on a pitch all day. You can't do better than that.[12]

With Drysdale's win, the Dodgers appeared not only to be easily sweeping the Yanks but to be squaring all outstanding matters from the season with any such rivals as Warren Spahn and the Braves.

Now up three games to zero, for Game Four, Alston again turned to Sandy Koufax, and the Yankees turned back to Whitey Ford. Each gave up a home run, but the Dodgers pushed across another run in the seventh inning. Koufax had totally dominated the Yankees in Game One. Whitey Ford was actually more dominant this day, as the Dodgers garnered but two hits off him. Alston found Koufax less effective, and in the ninth inning, trailing 2–1, the Yankees threatened to tie the game. Alston made the decision not to relieve Koufax, however. He saw how well Koufax was pacing himself and believed he would come through. With runners in scoring position, Koufax struck out Tom Tresh and Mickey Mantle with curveballs that baffled both hitters. Alston remembered with a smile: "Those were terrific pitches." Mantle remembered too, only he wasn't smiling. After Koufax struck him out, Mantle turned to catcher John Roseboro and yelled in frustration: "How the ____ do you hit this ____?" Roseboro smiled.[13]

The Dodgers swept New York. No team had ever done that to the Yankees in a World Series. Alston's pitchers held New York to an anemic team batting average of .171. New York's pitchers held the Dodgers almost as well; LA hit but .214. Tommy Davis and Bill Skowron were the only ones who hit well. But while New York's pitching was strong; LA's was phenomenal. Having been criticized in the preceding seasons for excessively platooning his players, Alston showed his tactical versatility, as in the Series with New York he used but 13 players, including his four pitchers. Sports commentators and journalists had been taking Alston a trifle lightly. His earlier habit of platooning had served as an allegedly substantive basis for criticisms when he failed to win in 1960, 1961, and 1962. Somehow it seemed he was just not the equal of more traditional, fire-breathing managers like Leo Durocher and Charlie Dressen.

The Dodgers' World Series win in 1963 marked Alston's third title in eight years. In the history of the National League, the only other manager who won three World Series was the legendary McGraw.[14] Thus the press was right—Alston was not the equal of Durocher, Dressen, or others; by at least one key statistical measure, he was their superior. Alston may have been less demonstrative, he may have argued less with umpires, and he may not have been good journalistic copy. Indeed, he behaved differently from most other heralded managers, but this "quiet man's" record was now speaking for itself, not so loudly but quite clearly.

For the 1964 season, the Dodgers were again the favorites to take the pennant. After winning their opener against St. Louis, with Koufax pitching, the Dodgers lost seven games in a row, nine of their next ten. Their hitting was weak and never really recovered. No one hit .300; no

Along with Sandy Koufax, Don Drysdale gave Walter Alston and the Dodgers one of the best starting pitching duos in baseball history. In the early and mid–1960s, the two mowed down virtually every lineup the National League could put forth (and any hitters who were not in awe, especially if they batted right-handed, would snap-to when they saw one of Drysdale's famous brushbacks hurtling their way). In 1965, Drysdale and Koufax combined for 49 wins. When the Dodgers left Brooklyn in 1957, the East Coast press gave much sympathetic coverage to Brooklyn's grievous loss. While no one doubts the authenticity of those sentiments, the LA area would develop their own strong cultural ties to the Dodgers. Photograph 1962 (National Baseball Hall of Fame and Museum, Cooperstown, NY).

one hit 25 home runs. The team's season home run total was a mere 79. As before, the health of Sandy Koufax would be critical. He won 19 games, and he would have likely won more. But in April, he tore a muscle in his left arm while diving into second base against the Cardinals. He missed several starts and was a little less aggressive in his pitching throughout the summer. Then, after a start on August 16, on advice from the club's physician, Alston rested Koufax for the remainder of the season. While Koufax won 19 games and Drysdale won 18, no other pitcher even won eight. With the early April losing streak, LA had fallen to last place. They rose a bit from there. On July 11, they made it to fifth but could do no better. They ended up tied with Pittsburgh for sixth place.[15]

The NL pennant race was exciting that year, with Philadelphia, Cincinnati, and St. Louis battling one another for the lead. St. Louis came out one game ahead of the Phillies and the Reds. San Francisco was in the race most of the year too (finishing three games back), but Alston and the Dodgers never got out of the second division. The critics and fans may have once again been guffawing at Alston and his apparently passive approach to the game. Here Bavasi and O'Malley gave no hints of dissatisfaction, however. Indeed, they not only kept Alston, they let Durocher go.

The undisputed star of Alston's Dodgers, who dominated the National League in the early and mid–1960s, was pitcher Sandy Koufax. Alston called Koufax the greatest pitcher (as well as the worst-hitting pitcher) he ever saw. In October of 1965, the Dodgers won the pennant and were set to face the Minnesota Twins in the World Series. Alston planned to start Koufax in Game One, but the game fell on *Yom Kippur*—Koufax would not play, demonstrating a devotion to his faith that Alston applauded. The Dodgers would lose that game, but came back to win the Series, with Koufax shutting out the Twins in the seventh game (National Baseball Hall of Fame and Museum, Cooperstown, NY).

As he had after the previously disappointing seasons of 1954, '58, and '62, in 1965 Alston led a team on an apparent mission. In 1965, the Dodgers' hitting was again a trifle weak. The team batting average that season was only .245. (It had been .250 even in '64.) A crucial problem here came on May 1, just 17 games into the season; Tommy Davis broke his ankle sliding into second base. He was gone for the season. Davis had led the National League in batting in both 1962 and 1963. In the entire decade of the 1960s, Davis was the one truly outstanding hitter Alston had, and after the 1965 ankle fracture, Davis's speed, and career, were never the same. His 1965 season-ending injury appeared to destroy the Dodgers' pennant hopes. Bavasi picked up a thirty-year-old journeyman named Lou Johnson, who had last played major league ball with the Braves in 1962. He had been in the minor leagues ever since. Johnson would prove a capable player and a good personality and spirit for the team. Maury Wills came back with his old speed and stole 94 bases, and one of Alston's favorites since Montreal, Jim Gilliam, now 36, was the regular at third base and hit .280.

Alston had a team with a maturity and collective spirit that mirrored the devotion to organization that his management style had always embodied. As in 1963, the hitting was good when it had to be. The defense was consistently tight. The starting infield were all switch-hitters, so Alston again needed little platooning. The kind of self-discipline that it usually takes to play well hitting from both sides underscored the kind of maturity that fit well in the system that Alston and the Dodgers' organization always wanted. The team speed was the best in the league, and, once again, the pitching was superb. Koufax's arm was again sound, as was Drysdale's. They combined for 49 wins. (Drysdale also hit .300.) In addition to winning 26 games, Koufax set a record with 382 strikeouts, and he threw a perfect game against Chicago. Bavasi had also acquired a third strong starting pitcher, Claude Osteen, from Washington. He would win 15 games; Podres and Perranoski were still effective. So, with the speed, defense, and impossibly strong pitching, Alston came back from a mediocre season, again answering his detractors with another pennant, edging the Giants by two games.[16]

The New York Yankees' dynasty had finally crumbled in 1965. They finished in sixth place, 25 games out of first. This season the Minnesota Twins won the pennant and were the Dodgers' opponent in the World Series. Like the Dodgers, the Twins had had a losing season the previous year. But in 1965 they produced a potent team. Their offensive power was outstanding with such hitters as Tony Oliva, Harmon Killebrew, Bob Allison, Don Mincher, and Jimmie Hall. Their starting rotation featured Jim "Mudcat" Grant, Jim Perry, Camilo Pascual, and Jim Kaat. One of their scouts, Benny Borgmann, had been Alston's manager in Portsmouth, Ohio, way back in 1938. That little tidbit, and the positive memories of Alston from his 1948–1949 seasons in St. Paul notwithstanding, the Twin Cities were certainly excited to have a winning team playing in their first World Series. (As the former Washington Senators, their last pennant had been in 1933.)

Minnesota hosted Game One on October 6. As became a famous story, Alston had his ace, Sandy Koufax, and the fans fully expected Koufax to start. The trouble was that October 6, 1965, marked *Yom Kippur*, the Day of Atonement, the holiest day in the Jewish calendar, a day of prayer and fasting. Koufax made it clear that he would act in good religious faith. On *Yom Kippur*, he would never pitch nor do anything but pray and fast. This matter had arisen with regard to Koufax in prior seasons. "We always arranged the rotation so he would miss it," recalled Alston. "Several times in other games, he had pitched with only two days' rest so that he would not have to be in the ballpark working on the Day of Atonement. For this," Alston affirmed, "I give him credit. In an age when youth is so often derelict in its duty, Koufax is not ashamed to stand up and be counted." Alston further praised O'Malley for his support here: "You have to give Mr. O'Malley credit, too," he wrote. "The big boss asserted himself promptly when the question was put to him: 'I wouldn't let Sandy pitch on his Day of Atonement if he wanted to,' Mr. O'Malley said, and that ended that."[17]

Many fans around the nation were flummoxed by the whole *Yom Kippur* matter. The levels of appreciation for religious diversity were not yet strong in many parts of the country. Old Dodgers fans throughout Brooklyn certainly knew the score here. But people in many other parts of the nation did not. A few recalled 1934, when the Detroit Tigers were contending for the pennant. Detroit's star was Hank Greenberg, and he had grown up in New York City as an Orthodox Jew. Amidst Detroit's pennant fight with the Yankees that September, Greenberg faced the decision of whether to play on *Rosh Hashanah*. That week a prominent rabbi in Detroit looked through his Torah and Talmud and raised the point that *Rosh Hashanah* was actually a day of joy; hence it was certainly valid to play ball that afternoon. The good rabbi was also a keen Tigers fan! With his rabbi's blessing, Greenberg went out and hit two home runs, and the *Detroit Free Press* printed, in Yiddish, "Happy New Year, Hank!" (א גוט געבענטשט יאר [*a gut gebentsht yar*, Hank!])

Unlike *Rosh Hashanah*, however, *Yom Kippur* could never be described as a day involving any sort of New Year's joy. Permitting anything like the playing of baseball would be unconscionable. On *Yom Kippur*, 1934, indeed, Greenberg did not play, and Detroit lost—the game but not the pennant. Greenberg had been hit by all sorts of anti–Semitic slurs wherever he went. Moreover, he was playing in a city that boasted such notable anti–Semites as Father Coughlin and Henry Ford. Back in 1934, many immigrant Jewish families in America did not know a thing about baseball, but they wept with pride over Greenberg's actions. Koufax always praised Greenberg for the stand he took here. In 1965, no one in the Dodgers' organization was about to do anything but support Koufax in his devotion to his religion. The general public did not capitulate to anti–Semitic extremism as it had back in the 1930s, but more than a little head-scratching was palpable nonetheless. Even more, however, the pride among America's Jews grew immensely with Koufax's decision.

While the story of Koufax not starting Game One of the 1965 Series occupied much space in the media, Alston never said anything more about it to reporters. Besides, he had Don Drysdale for Game One anyway. Here another famous story emerged which has been told in many forms. Drysdale did start the game for Los Angeles against the Twins' Mudcat Grant. Each team scored a run in the second inning. In the Twins' half of the third, their potent lineup got to Drysdale. They rallied for six runs, and during the onslaught, Alston chose to pull Drysdale for a reliever. Two former Yankees greats, Tommy Henrich and Lefty Gomez, were in Minneapolis for the game, and as Alston trudged out to the mound to relieve Drysdale, Gomez turned to Henrich and declared: "I know what Alston is thinking." "No you don't," replied Henrich. After Gomez playfully insisted that he knew, Henrich smirked and relented: "OK, what is Alston thinking?" Gomez nodded: "Alston's thinking 'I sure wish Drysdale was Jewish.'" Some have cast the story that Drysdale himself actually said to Alston "I bet you wish I was Jewish." Given the intensity with which Drysdale always pitched, and given the anger and frustration he was doubtlessly feeling at this point, it is impossible to imagine Drysdale saying anything remotely witty. Whatever he may have said, it would be unprintable. Other sources claim that after the game, which the Twins won, a reporter asked Alston whether he wished Drysdale was Jewish. Then or later, Alston corroborated no other story other than the line being Lefty Gomez's. Such a story certainly fit the extroverted nature of Lefty ("El Goofy") Gomez. Whatever the source, the story was an indication of the depths to which Koufax's not pitching on *Yom Kippur* had penetrated the consciousness of baseball fans.[18]

After their big third-inning rally against Drysdale and the Twins' win in Game One, 8–2, Koufax started Game Two after a day of fasting. Again, the Twins' lineup showed its potency, as they hit Koufax and won easily, 5–1. The Series shifted to Los Angeles, and the prospects looked a little grim for the Dodgers. Alston turned to his third-best starter, Claude Osteen, and he came through with a shutout. That 4–0 victory was critical, lest the Dodgers be down three games to none. In the next two games, Alston went back to Drysdale and Koufax. Drysdale evened the Series with a 7–2 win. Then Koufax crushed the Twins, scattering four hits and throwing a 7–0 shutout. The teams flew back to Minneapolis for Game Six. This time Osteen lost, 5–1, setting matters up for a deciding seventh game.

For Game Seven, Alston faced what he later termed "my toughest decision." In the normal rotation, it was Drysdale's turn to start. Of course, as this was game seven, all matters of what constitutes "normal" were discarded. Alston thought about the situation from several angles. One obvious point was that when Koufax was on his game, there was no touching him. Drysdale was almost as good—almost. Whoever started, Alston would have the other in the bullpen. In this context, Alston knew that Koufax usually needed more time to warm up than most pitchers, so if he had to be brought into the game with runners in scoring position, he could be less effective. The opposite was the case with Drysdale in relief. He could be ready in an instant. Further, if he had to bring in Koufax as a reliever, Alston knew the team could be trailing. He would likely need to pinch-hit for Koufax when his turn to bat came. As Alston had once conceded: "Koufax was … one of the worst hitters I ever saw."[19] Drysdale, on the other hand, was one of the best-hitting pitchers ever. For Alston, there was also a level of pressure he could potentially place on Twins manager Sam Mele. If he started Koufax, turned to Drysdale, and *then* turned to Perranoski if needed, that succession of pitchers would involve a left-hander, a righty, and another lefty. This would make Mele drain his reserves as he would likely switch batters, right/left/right. That all went into Alston's thinking as he considered who would start Game Seven. "I made up my mind that Sandy was preferable when it became fairly obvious late in the sixth game that we weren't going to get to [Mudcat] Grant."[20]

In the actual game, Koufax's performance rendered all of Alston's cogitations moot. He scattered three hits, gave up three walks, struck out ten, and went the full nine innings, shutting out the Twins, 2–0. It was anything but a breeze, however. Koufax was pitching on just two days' rest. He later conceded that he was quite tired and, indeed, did not have much of a breaking ball that day. In consultation with his catcher, John Roseboro, he made the decision to rely on his fastball.[21] It sure worked. Alston and the Dodgers had their fourth World Series in 11 years. No manager in the history of the National League had done that.

With the victory in 1965, Alston was secure in his position with the Dodgers' organization. The one-year contracts would continue, but it was clear that the job was Alston's as long as he wanted it. Alston's status was never in doubt, nor was his salary ever a point of contention. In 1954, O'Malley paid him all of $24,000; by 1966 he was making $65,000.

Before the 1966 season, however, the Dodgers went through a huge salary dispute. Koufax and Drysdale, who had together won 49 games and struck out 602 batters in 1965, decided to hold out. They wanted salary increases, but with baseball's infamous "reserve clause" still in force, players could exercise little leverage against management when it came to salaries or much else. Holding out was the only effective means of applying pressure. Koufax and Drysdale held out through spring training and into April. They hoped that their obvious value to the team would make LA's many fans erupt and put pressure on the team's management to force a favorable agreement. They made noise about pursuing alternative careers in show business and maintained their stand until the regular season was just about to commence. Finally, everyone came to terms. While earning much less than they originally wanted, Drysdale signed for $110,000 and Koufax for $125,000. Alston played no direct role in salary disputes ever, and he said nothing to the press throughout the ordeal, but he was certainly glad to have his two stars back. "It was a joyful reunion for all of us," he recalled with his usual modesty. He was actually worried about whether they had worked out much during the holdout—"their contracts were no concern of mine but their arms were."[22] They were both ready to play.

The 1966 season would prove very similar to the previous one. The Dodgers relied on defense, speed, and pitching. Koufax proved again to be the best in the game. Some were already deeming him the best ever. His pitching elbow was constantly inflamed, however. It proved to be, from all the stress he had put on it over the years of throwing, post-traumatic arthritis. Koufax would demonstrate his strength of character as he persevered through the pain, winning 27 games and posting an ERA of 1.73, each stat led the league, and they were the best season marks he ever achieved. It was Koufax who pitched on the final day of the season to defeat Philadelphia and take the pennant by a game from the Giants.

In the 1966 World Series, Alston faced another first-time AL pennant winner, the Baltimore Orioles. (The now fallen Yankees finished dead last.) In their previous incarnation as the St. Louis Browns, the Orioles had won one pennant in 1944, during baseball's spartan days of World War II (and way back in the 1890s, "The Old Baltimore Orioles," as they were dubbed, had also won three straight NL pennants). Like Minnesota in 1965, Baltimore paid no heed to 19th century or World War II events. Baltimorians were in a state of total excitement over *their* first pennant. They had a potent line-up with three players posting over 100 RBI. Baltimore had John "Boog" Powell and Brooks Robinson. Most importantly, they had the Dodgers' old nemesis from Cincinnati, Frank

Robinson. After the 1965 season, Cincinnati had traded Robinson to Baltimore, claiming he was old at 30. Robinson was incensed over this, and with the Orioles he responded with a vengeance, hitting for a Triple Crown and earning MVP honors. In addition to a powerful offense, Baltimore had a defense that was the equal of the Dodgers.' Luis Aparicio, whom Alston had faced in 1959, was a great shortstop. Brooks Robinson was arguably the best defensive third baseman in the history of the game. Alston would himself describe Robinson's defensive skills as "brilliant." Additionally, Dave Johnson and a young Paul Blair became multiple Gold Glove Award winners at second base and center field.

The question for Baltimore was pitching. They had some young pitchers who had shown signs of greatness, but they were inconsistent during the season. What proved critical for the Orioles during the Series was that their pitching came through, with strong outings from each starter. In the first game, with Koufax having pitched the pennant-clinching last game of the regular season, Alston started Drysdale. Frank and Brooks Robinson touched him for home runs in the first inning. Orioles starter Dave McNally proved weak that day, as the Dodgers came back and scored two runs. But Baltimore reliever Moe Drabowsky came in and pitched brilliantly for 6⅔ innings, striking out 11. The Dodgers could score no more (for the entire Series as it turned out), and the Orioles took the first game, 5–2.

For Game Two, Alston turned to Koufax. The Orioles countered with a 20-year-old rookie named Jim Palmer. Koufax saw his usually splendid defense falter, especially with two fly balls being lost in the sun, resulting in the Orioles scoring three unearned runs. Alston relieved Koufax after six innings, and the Orioles scored twice more to win, 6–0. Jim Palmer would go on to a Hall of Fame career, but in 1966 he was very much an unknown quantity. In this, his rookie season, Palmer had shown flashes of greatness, but not with any consistency. On this day, he came through, however, and Koufax and the Dodgers were shut out. In Game Three, the Orioles started another young pitcher, Wally Bunker. The Dodgers countered with Osteen. Osteen gave up but three hits, and the Orioles scored but one run. Meanwhile, off Bunker, LA scattered six hits and, once again, were shut out. In Game Four, Alston came back with Drysdale. The Orioles again sent out Dave McNally. Each pitcher gave up but four hits, but one hit off Drysdale was a solo home run by Frank Robinson. It would be the only run of the game.

The Dodgers' pitching had once again been quite effective. In the Series, the Orioles hit but .200. Meanwhile, the Dodgers hit an anemic .141. Some noted grimly that even the infamous 1919 Chicago "Black Sox" had hit for a higher average. It was like the 1963 World Series in reverse. The Orioles' pitching held LA cold. LA's pitching was solid, but their offense was absent, and their usually excellent defense had slipped in Game Two. In that game, Willie Davis lost two fly balls in the sun, but he made a fantastic catch in Game Four, saving a home run. It may have saved the day, but the Dodgers simply could not score. It was a terrible letdown for Alston and the club, not just to lose, as they had in 1956, but to be swept. To put a sense of finality on the severity of it all, soon after the Series was over, Sandy Koufax, at the mere age of 30, announced his retirement. The arthritis in his left elbow was just too much to endure any longer.

11

Midst the Days
of Hope and Rage

With the retirement of Sandy Koufax, the fortunes of Alston and the Dodgers would undergo a complete reversal. One had to go back to dark times of the 1930s to find a Dodgers team that had strung together a disheartening succession of second-division finishes. Ever since Brooklyn's pennant way back in 1941, the sad old patterns of the team as a perennial tail-ender appeared to have been reversed. (The World War II years were not important in the evolution of the Dodgers here. These extraordinary times completely disrupted the team's development, but they did the same to everyone else.) After the war, the Dodgers reestablished and kept up their newly found standards of success. They went forth, tying for the pennant in 1946 and winning it in 1947 and 1949. They lost the pennant only on the last day of the season in 1950, tied in 1951, won in 1952, 1953, 1955, 1956, and 1959, tied in 1962, and again won in 1963, 1965 and 1966. It was a full 20+ years of steady top-level baseball, always winning or at least in full contention. Aside from the Yankees, no baseball team had ever shown such consistent excellence for so long. But after 1966, the long line of successful pennant contending appeared to be over. The Dodgers' farm system could not summon up another Koufax or noticeable talent. Obviously, such qualities as Sandy Koufax possessed could not be summarily rolled forth like a new automobile on an assembly line, and no one understood that better than Alston.

When the team gathered for spring training in 1967, reporters incessantly asked Alston and others what the Dodgers would do now that Koufax had retired. Repeatedly, Alston could only speak in generalized points about letting the organization work and produce the best talent it could. Many reporters and fans were not satisfied with such vague answers, of course, but it was not as though Alston was hiding something from the eagerly probing reporters. He knew that he had to do the best he could with what talent remained from the prior pennant-winning years, with any new talent his minor league teams could give him, and with anyone Bavasi could procure in the trade market. Bavasi conceded that with Koufax's retirement, his effectiveness in the trading area was all the more daunting. He admitted: "Now they know I'm desperate."

The 1967 Dodgers would fall far. The hitting was even weaker than it had been in previous seasons where Koufax and Drysdale carried them. The team batting average that year was .236. No one hit .300 (or even .280). Among the pitchers, Drysdale fell to 13 wins. Osteen led the team with 17 wins, but he also had 17 losses. The previously remarkable team speed was no longer imposing. In 1963, Maury Wills had stolen 104 bases; in 1967 the entire team stole a mere 57. In the National League race that year, the Dodgers finished eighth, with only the still-hapless Astros and Mets faring worse. The 1958 season had been that bad; 1954 and 1962 had each been disappointing as well, but following each of those poor seasons, Alston and the Dodgers had come back to win both the pennant and the World Series. In 1968, however, there would be no such rebound. In 1968, the team again finished eighth. Two seasons in a row in the second division—this had not occurred since 1938. In those pre–Branch Rickey, pre–Larry MacPhail days, the Dodgers were indeed the hapless "Bums" from Brooklyn. Thoughts of such a bleak future did not rest well with the trendy fans in Los Angeles.

For Alston, his tasks as a manager appeared to turn toward patient teaching and away from focus on individual game tactics to get a desired edge in critical games which may decide that often thin difference between first and second place. The situations which produced these more exciting priorities now seemed long gone. Alston's image as "the quiet man" continued, and now, amidst some impatience among fans, it was an image that did not resonate as it once had. It now appeared to possess no elusive inner qualities that were special, and which somehow lay beyond journalistic grasp. The resulting impatience of reporters (or fans) were matters with which Alston would continue to show his usual outward calm. The key here, as always, was that Bavasi and O'Malley believed in him, as well as in the system they had all helped construct. Alston had always been good at nurturing and developing talent. He showed that again and again in Nashua, Pueblo, St. Paul, and Montreal. If he had to become more of a teacher/instructor than a pennant-drive tactician, he would readily make the adjustment.

Back in 1965, Alston had a 23-year-old second baseman, Jim Lefebvre, who hit poorly in much of the spring and summer. Alston's description of how he handled Lefebvre illustrated the kind of touch he employed with so many of his players, one that showed as much a grasp of psychology as of the finer points of baseball. Alston recalled:

> Jim came back to the bench with his head down .... He was obviously discouraged. I called him to my side and asked if he'd like to have me tell him what was wrong. ... He said, "Please tell me." I said: "It's no mystery, Jim. It's the same as I've told you all along. ... You're still upper-cutting the ball, only now it's worse than ever and you're striding too soon. You've developed the habit of dropping your back shoulder because you're not waiting for the ball, and you're swinging too hard. ... If you'll keep your shoulders level—and I know you can—and try to take a level cut, you'll start hitting the ball again."[1]

In the next inning, Lefebvre stroked a single to left field. Two innings later, as Lefebvre was stepping out of the dugout to his next at-bat, Alston made a point of hollering to him: "Just stay level." Lefebvre homered to left field and went three-for-four that night. After the game, Alston stopped by Lefebvre's locker. "I had," Alston recalled, "a big grin on my face which hardly matched the one on his. I said 'Dammit, Jim, if you'll just listen to the old man now and then, I'll make a .300 hitter out of you yet.'"

Alston's point here was not to brag about possessing any particularly keen insight into batting. Rather it was to emphasize "that being a con man is part of a manager's job, especially with kids. ... Maybe" he conceded, "Lefebvre wasn't swinging quite as badly as I described it, and maybe he didn't swing much more levelly after our talk, but it did get him to thinking. ... So he stepped up the next time with more confidence than before, and you've won half the battle when you make a young player think he can do it." That season, Lefebvre hit only .250, but in September, after the little chat with Alston, during the team's pennant drive, he hit .321 with 20 RBI.[2]

Alston would continue to show this sort of patience and self-effacement. The team's losing records of the late 1960s were certainly discouraging, but Alston never aggravated matters with outbursts of temper. The press would be of no help here, of course. Displays of temper would have made for good stories, but Alston did not worry about the press very much; he never did. Alston, Bavasi, and O'Malley continued to have faith in their organization and made sure everyone did their jobs to the utmost. The needs of reporters, no matter the noise, continued to sit on the periphery as far as the organization was concerned.

Bad news continued to come to LA nonetheless. Beyond the general disappointments in the seasons of 1967 and 1968, even when any hint of good news for the Dodgers arose it would be subverted by wider issues. In the spring of 1968, for example, one particularly remarkable pitching record was set in Los Angeles, but it came amidst terrible news that overshadowed everything. The wider political context of the events here deeply affected all the Dodgers and their standing, not just in baseball but in the nation's more general culture. In 1968, although Koufax was gone, Don Drysdale had continued to pitch well for the Dodgers, and he was especially effective that spring. The old jinx that seemed to follow Drysdale continued very much as before—the team never appeared able to score runs for him. The only difference now was that this now appeared to be a curse which befell all the other Dodgers pitchers too. In 1968, Drysdale appeared to take matters into his own hands. He simply refused to give up any runs. In May and early June, he went on a remarkable pitching streak. From May 14 to June 8, Drysdale did not allow a run in 58 consecutive innings. This set a record for consecutive scoreless innings, a mark that has since been topped only once (in 1988, by another Dodger, Orel Hershiser). The previous record of 55⅔ innings had been set way back in 1913 by Hall of Famer Walter Johnson (who also had little supporting offense from his usually hapless Washington Senators). It was a great record for Drysdale, but, sadly, the setting of the mark came amidst tragedy.

On June 5, approaching the record, Drysdale's hurled his sixth consecutive shutout. That set a National League record for scoreless innings, previously held by the Giants' old ace, Carl Hubbell. Drysdale threw his sixth shutout in Los Angeles on a Tuesday evening. That same night, Senator Robert Kennedy won the California Democratic Presidential primary election. In his victory celebration speech at the Ambassador Hotel in Los Angeles, Senator Kennedy, although not much of a baseball fan himself, went out of his way to mention, to the delight of the crowd: "I'd like to express my high regard for Don Drysdale" and his new pitching record. Everyone cheered loudly, and Kennedy added that he hoped he would have Drysdale's support in the rest of the Presidential campaign. The crowd cheered even louder. Kennedy thanked everyone: "Now it's on to Chicago [for the Democratic Party Convention]," he proclaimed, "and let's win there." Then he flashed the "Peace" sign to the crowd and left the stage. Just a few minutes later he was assassinated.[3] As the tragic news rapidly spread about Los Angeles and the rest of the world, the significance of Drysdale's achievement obviously paled, and any impetus to celebrate the record felt utterly inappropriate. For Alston it may have aroused a few of his memories from April 1945, when he was doing so well and enjoyed much local praise for his managing of the Dodgers' farm team in Trenton, New Jersey, but the string of early-season victories came at the time of the death of President Franklin Roosevelt. The nation's wider events in the spring and summer of 1968 certainly diminished the sense of achievement in the work of Don

Drysdale. The team would again finish in eighth place, ahead of only the still seemingly hapless Houston Astros and New York Mets. Adding to it all, on August 15 that summer, Alston's mother passed away.[4]

The wider social history of the late 1960s eclipsed most of the Dodgers' successes and failures in the same time period. Back in Brooklyn, the Dodgers had been very much part of the working-class culture that stood with a happy, poke-your-tongue-out defiance at Gotham's elites, represented in sports by the Yankees and the Giants. For many immigrant groups, notably the East-European Jews, growing attachments to the Dodgers had also proven to be a major component of their broader assimilation into American culture. The fact that such sets of social dynamics among Brooklyn's immigrant and working-class populations also came to be part of the causes that the Dodgers and Jackie Robinson led in regard to racial justice and integration, rendered the popular culture legacy of Brooklyn's organization and community spirit ever more ennobled. Such proud Brooklyn legacies would devolve toward ones of decidedly different tones as the team reestablished itself in Los Angeles.

The Dodgers' triumphs in 1965 and 1966 took place amidst some horrible urban tumult in the economically poor sections of Watts in downtown Los Angeles. Amidst these vicious riots, some hoped that the Dodgers' success could stand as a symbol of something contrastingly positive—how black and white players, coaches, and managers could do wonders when they worked together. But the wealthy and poor communities in the LA area apparently existed in complete disregard, ignorance, and even contempt of one another. How well the Dodgers' success in 1965 helped bring together the otherwise torn community was a matter for speculation. The 1965 Watts riots were the first of the major inner-city African American insurrections. (Detroit's and Newark's eruptions came later, as of course did the great number of riots that exploded after the death of Dr. Martin Luther King Jr. in 1968.) It was in LA that the first LBJ-era urban riots occurred, and there no journalist noted a figure from any sports team in the region successfully building bridges between various peoples and neighborhoods to promote forms of peace and understanding amidst the city's ugly troubles. Over the next years, few sports figures in other cities would fare much better, but the contrast between the wealthy and impoverished regions of a city, with the local sports franchise appearing to rest on the comfortable side of the divide, was an image that in 1965 first tinged LA, the Dodgers, and Alston.

Alston himself never spoke out in regard to social/economic issues that gripped Los Angeles in the mid–1960s. Despite managing there for almost 20 years, his actual roots in the LA area never grew terribly deep. During the baseball season, he always rented a house near Dodger Stadium and lived quietly. In the off-season, he always went home to Ohio. (In many seasons, Lela Alston stayed home in Ohio.) In regard to racial issues, the Dodgers' record had certainly been a proud one with Branch Rickey, Jackie Robinson, and all they did as the first team to break baseball's racial barrier. Some of Alston's contributions here—most notably, as the manager of the nation's first racially integrated professional baseball team of the 20th century in Nashua, New Hampshire—was certainly part of this proud legacy. But now the issues and the geography had shifted dramatically. In Los Angeles, the Dodgers no longer appeared to sit on the historical cutting edge in regard to baseball's issues, let alone to wider matters facing the nation.

Events surrounding the construction of the Dodgers' new stadium revealed a different set of images that the team presented to segments of the local population as they implanted themselves in their new locale. Dodger Stadium was built in a section of Los Angeles known as Chavez Ravine. Prior to the stadium's construction, that little valley had been home to thousands of people, many of whom were rather poor Mexican Americans. These people, including a retired U. S. Marine, Cruz Cabral, who had served with honor and won several medals during World War II, were given but superficial regard by city planners with respect to their property rights. This arose in regard both to the needs to construct Dodger Stadium as well as to more general "Great Society" efforts to construct federally funded public housing in this and other parts of the city. This paradox in regard to the LBJ-era efforts for better public housing, imposed with no apparent regard to on-site cultures and sensibilities, would emerge in many cities. In LA, this sad paradox also came to ensnare the Dodgers. Local Mexican Americans in Chavez Ravine found themselves summarily evicted from their homes and with notably little compensation. One woman in the community, Aurora Vargas, tried to stand her ground in her home and was seen kicking and screaming as four city deputies forcibly carried her out of her house on Malvina Avenue. Minutes later, the bulldozers rumbled forth and flattened her home, as well as those of Cruz Cabral and many others.[5] It was a bit of urban renewal that would have delighted such a New York figure as Robert Moses ("If the ends don't justify the means, what does?"). The irony here was that, just a few years before, Walter O'Malley had cast himself as someone who left Brooklyn, in part, because he did not care for the hard-boiled, socially callous ways of such ruthless New York City planners as Moses, especially as Moses was anything but helpful with respect to O'Malley's desire to build a new stadium.

Once settled in LA, however, O'Malley now appeared to preside over some of the very same sorts of high-handed self-delusions and tyrannical actions associated with the likes of Moses. The on-field success of the Dodgers from 1959 to 1966 enabled many fans and reporters to overlook matters that had, sometimes literally, been pushed aside in the name of progress. A new stadium, the Dodgers' success, and all the wealth and fame they brought to the region—these were the primary concerns. Victories would supposedly wash over all other uncomfortable points. An old adage here, "a rising tide lifts all boats," may have resonated among some of the wealthy, but among the poor there were neither affecting tides nor pleasure craft to be lifted. The well-heeled fans in the LA area did indeed come to love their Dodgers, but the region's devotion seemed largely an animation of the middle-class and wealthy sections of the region far more than the poorer ones, much as, even more than, the Yankees and Giants had prompted back in New York City. This certainly marked a very different set of social dynamics than those beloved "Bums" had aroused back in Brooklyn.

The era of the Watts riots was one of the first signals to wealthier people, in LA and elsewhere, that the forgotten poor of the nation were not going to remain silent, let alone feel or express gratitude for what any Great Society was purportedly doing for (to) them. Instead many grew ever more intent upon showing that a nation ostensibly devoted to "liberty and justice for all" would be compelled to take note of them, one way or another. The Watts riots were an early sign of a commitment by poor people to call attention to their forgotten selves, and to do so, as Malcolm X had put it, "by any means necessary."

On top of such bitter developments that continued to evolve through the middle of the decade, the year 1968, so divisive as it was with tragedies like the deaths of Martin Luther King and Robert Kennedy, underscored the point that any sense of optimism about the future was at least naïve and likely futile. Many areas of the sports world reflected this new outlook, one that was more radical than liberal, more divisive than inclusive, and more rageful than hopeful. The idea that in this era a successful sports team could somehow ameliorate so much inter- and intra-community pain appeared rather far-fetched. The Dodgers' mediocre play at the time merely highlighted how out of touch were those who had made the case that the planting of such enterprises in the LA area as professional sports teams would be good for the lives and the prosperity of all Angelenos. The proverbial "circus without bread" would hardly suffice in ancient Rome; in America in the late 1960s, *panem et circenses* seemed all the more absurd.

The world of sports both mirrored and in some ways actually

helped shape the emergence of more divisive radical impulses that were emerging in American society and politics in the late 1960s. New sports heroes came forth who displayed decidedly different attitudes in regard to key questions of race and identity, and to propriety in the behavior of athletes. As this counterculture was developing in sports, the place of the Dodgers, and of baseball in general, which had once been squarely in the avant-garde amidst strivings for racial justice, would go through a dramatic shift.

A classically liberal concept idealized a world in which color of skin should have no meaning in anyone's life, as Dr. Martin Luther King had famously dreamed: what should matter is not the color of skin but the content of character. This ideal was fading before new political and social outlooks which emphasized the role of race in one's political identity. Debates raged widely in sports, in politics, and in the general hubbub of American life. Well into the 21st century, these debates have never ended. They have merely taken on different forms. The mid– and late–1960s marked a time when the assertions of racial consciousness and pride came forth with the utmost of verve and enthusiasm, or, as some critics may prefer, with a strong, smug, adolescent certainty. In various sports, major figures embraced views and fired imaginations especially among many young, urban, African American men.

A prominent young sociologist of the era, Harry Edwards, developed theories amidst the new racial assertiveness, holding that a great measure of the quality and the tonality of the athletic expressions of many young African American men was coming forth, not in spite of the political anger and assertiveness they were feeling, not even regardless of it, but decidedly because of it. The key was that certain athletes took rage and channeled it into their athleticism to make them excel even further. As had been already evinced in the music of Miles Davis and Charlie Parker (in contrast to the outwardly happy, seemingly non-threatening imagery presented by such an older figure as Louis Armstrong), a coolly focused rage was now ever more in evidence in many sports, and it proved inspiring, as a most compelling point here was that the pure quality of the resulting athletic performances was undeniably great. Professional football had produced its greatest running back, Jim Brown. Basketball presented such dominant stars as Bill Russell and later Kareem Abdul Jabbar. In track and field came Olympic medalists Tommy Smith and John Carlos. Even in the traditionally staid sport of tennis, there was the compelling figure of Arthur Ashe. Most famousin this context, of course, was the heavyweight boxing champion, Muhammad Ali. Each was the very best at what they did in their respective sports, and in each lay the conviction that the content and character of their athletic excellence was not coincident to but bound up in both their politics and their racial identities.

It appeared less and less tenable to hold onto a classically liberal position—that your politics are, in effect, your own business, while your work, be it in sports, music, or anything else, is to be understood and appreciated as an entirely separate matter. Most important here was the fact that it was not just the African American athletes who were forging this new confrontational ground. Quite the contrary, theirs was a view that grew as these athletes felt themselves imposed upon and often in most blunt and harsh manners. If the Federal government had taken a liberal, noblesse oblige position about politics' coincidental relationship to sports, the whole shift in more radical directions in so many genres of American popular culture and sports may have evolved in markedly different and less visible and aggressive manners. But, undeniably, it was the Federal government in 1967 which had, with the utmost sniggering conspicuousness, singled out Muhammad Ali and told him that he was not entitled to his own politics and religion. (The Supreme Court would later slap the government down for this, but that took over three years.) It was the Federal government that stated that Ali would not be allowed to fight professionally if he followed his religion and his conscience and refused military conscription to serve in the War in Vietnam. The government arrogantly and consciously crossed a line here, and when they did so, such sensibilities and outlooks crystallized as they did among so many other athletes, who came forth in support of Ali, with many then defiantly merging their political/religious consciousness with their athleticism.

Sentiments of defiance among racially and politically conscious athletes were certainly present before April 1967, when the Federal government stripped Ali of his heavyweight title. The government's actions served greatly to increase the sense that all who displayed such convictions were doing so in direct defiance of authorities who were aware, wary, and apparently more than a bit fearful of what young African American athletes were doing. The government's actions could certainly be intimidating. In their smug arrogance, some government figures as Lyndon Johnson, J. Edgar Hoover, and Richard Nixon may not have been able to conceive their impact yielding anything but intimidation. Their actions, however, could also, and certainly did, ennoble many who now summoned their courage and chose paths of confrontation and resistance ever more defiantly. Any notion of Johnson, Hoover, or Nixon, that the emerging radicalism from the nation's African American community could be blunted by the intimidation of star athletes proved utterly wrong.

Amidst the political polarization occurring here, where the world of sports was affected, noteworthy was the fact that baseball appeared to lag noticeably behind the principal forces of action and change. Some of this may have been mere image, but it appeared to have substance as well. Immediately after Muhammad Ali was stripped of his title in the spring of 1967, Jim Brown, through his Negro Industrial and Economic Union, called for a meeting of support for Ali. The meeting took place on June 4, 1967. To be sure, this meeting occurred during the major league baseball season, and not during the seasons of professional football and basketball. So simple matters of availability and schedules may have been at work here. Still, the meeting conspicuously drew many NFL stars, along with basketball's Bill Russell and Lew Alcindor.

Conspicuously absent at the gathering were major league baseball players. In contrast, indeed, that same year, several baseball players made a special good will tour of Vietnam, including Pete Rose, Ernie Banks, Tony Conigliaro, Jerry Coleman, Lefty Gomez, and Joe DiMaggio. Coleman, Gomez, and DiMaggio were of an older generation, and the mixture of old and current players was part of the positive message organizers hoped to impart to the troops, as well as to the nation—that generations past and present appreciated the service and sacrifices of the men in Vietnam. Amidst the politics of the age that saw, and often celebrated, a gap between older and younger generations, the baseball players' tour of Vietnam also conveyed a sense that the national pastime was somehow not up to date with the latest trends. Instead, it appeared in harmony with their elders, and in apparent accord with President Lyndon Johnson, whose administration had just then taken away Muhammad Ali's title.

In the late 1960s, aside perhaps from golf, no major sport in the nation cast a more conservative aura than did major league baseball. Internally, the collapse of both the Yankees and the Dodgers jumbled the traditional order of leadership within the game. Meanwhile, the kind of heroes that baseball put forth appeared, in some cases, to have roots in slightly older times. Outwardly at least, Willie Mays, Henry Aaron, and Ernie Banks all presented joyous, quiet, peaceful, non-threatening imagery. Some African American players, like pitcher Jim "Mudcat" Grant and Curt Flood, would show sympathies with new confrontational styles of political action and discourse, but they were conspicuous exceptions (and Flood would pay a steep price for his defiance). Some like Roberto Clemente certainly embodied the ideals of a fierce pride in identity driving him into extraordinary levels of achievement. But because the identity Clemente asserted here, as a black Puerto Rican, lay on the periphery of the political foci which occupied the sports and general news headlines of the day, his impact was minimal, a marginality further underscored by his playing in Pittsburgh, far from the nation's primary media centers.

In the context of his views on African American identity and on the War in Vietnam, one idea that Muhammad Ali conspicuously advocated was that Black men and women in America needed to raise themselves up and direct themselves away decidedly from the harmful habits that were plaguing many poor urban communities. Drugs, crime, and other forms of self-destructive indulgence were all on the rise in many inner-city communities. Here, in response, Ali openly advocated that people strive "to live a clean life." Other outstanding stars like Jim Brown and Bill Russell represented similar sentiments both in their expressed thoughts as well as in their deeds—against drugs, against gangs, against crime, and against thoughtless violence.

Some baseball players, on the other hand, openly flaunted their enjoyment of recreational drugs and of general non-conformity. Mark Fidrych, Bill Lee, and Phillip "Dock" Ellis were notorious in this regard. On June 12, 1970, Dock Ellis pitched a no-hitter for Pittsburgh against San Diego and later claimed to have done it while tripping on LSD. Ellis regularly displayed much of the clenched-fist outlooks of the African American radicalism of the day. His mention of taking acid on the field had many on the drug-crazed side of late–60s American politics chuckling heartily. Fidrych and Lee were not at all hidden in their enjoyment of marijuana, and they clearly came forth as parts of the so-called "counter-culture" that flourished among the nation's middle-class white youth. In the context of what Muhammad Ali and others were advocating and representing about a righteous life, such baseball players as Ellis, Fidrych, and Lee were then decidedly "cool" but not the least bit "clean." Other slightly older, but athletically better baseball players of the era like Al Kaline, Brooks Robinson, and Carl Yastrzemski certainly lived in clean exemplary manners, but they did not embody any of the "cool" aura that was part of the appeal of a Muhammad Ali, a Jim Brown, or a Bill Russell. (As a compulsive gambler and an open politically conservative/straight-arrow, Cincinnati star Pete Rose thus symbolized someone who was then neither "cool" nor "clean.")

Amidst all these dynamics in sports and popular culture, Alston and the Dodgers clearly fit into the mode of a Brooks Robinson or a Carl Yastrzemski—clean but hardly cool. While Alston and the Dodgers had once led the cause of integration, those events now appeared in the distant past in the eyes of the nation's youth. Teenagers of that time, born after 1950, had few if any direct memories of the early days of baseball's desegregation. To that generation, a desegregated athletic team was completely unremarkable. Even the hero of baseball's historic breakthroughs in racial integration, Jackie Robinson, was someone few young people of the late 1960s had actually seen as a player. By the late 1960s, Jackie Robinson had also fallen away in his appeal as a leader and spokesperson for justice among African Americans, both young and old. Robinson, indeed, spoke out directly against some of the positions taken by radical groups of the late 1960s like the Black Panthers, and he befriended several Republican leaders, including Richard Nixon, whom he had supported against Kennedy in 1960.

The evolution of Jackie Robinson's fate in the causes of African Americans paralleled a contemporaneous transformation in boxing. Floyd Patterson had once been the heavyweight champion. While champion he had stood as a symbol of pride for many white and African Americans, and he (more specifically his manager) intentionally avoided bouts with several fighters who had mob connections. But Patterson eventually lost his title to a clear representative of "mean streets" African America—Charles "Sonny" Liston. Patterson's two losses to Liston, both in the first round no less, appeared to underscore the naiveté that some sensed in the simple notion of racially blind integration magically eclipsing all of the nation's racial sins. Walter Alston's attitudes toward race appeared to fall into that very sort of unsophisticated, naïve category. Liston, of course, subsequently lost the title to Cassius Clay. Then, when Patterson later tried to win the title back against Muhammad Ali (to whom he still referred as "Clay"), declaring, in conscious disdain for Ali and his politics, that he was going to win the title back for America, he not only failed, he failed in a most humiliating way. In the bout, Ali toyed with Patterson and defeated him easily. Very much because of Ali's verbal taunts and superior skills in the ring, Patterson came to be regarded as weak and even as a bit of an Uncle Tom. Beneath the radar and the senses of the sports press, Ali actually held Patterson in high esteem. Patterson would indeed later be the only man Ali allowed to refer to him as "Cassius Clay," Ali simply declaring, "He earned it." Patterson did, but outwardly, like Jackie Robinson, he appeared a relic from a bygone era. Like Robinson, Patterson would also befriend Richard Nixon.[6] Jackie Robinson and Floyd Patterson (like Louis Armstrong) had done much outside their immediate areas of sports and entertainment to try to address wrongs the nation had committed against African Americans. Now the new ways in which racial views were being articulated and addressed left many such older figures appearing to stand far outside the mainstream of the avant-garde. Posterity may reveal that each had done a great deal of service to so many, of all races, and still had something politically pertinent to say, but in their immediate times, each appeared decidedly passé and socially irrelevant.

Walter Alston was similarly firm in his belief that he and the Dodgers organization were free of racial prejudice, and he was quite proud of that. He went out of his way to note that he always felt "lucky to have come in contact with men like Campanella, Robinson, Jim Gilliam, Maury Wills, and Johnny Roseboro."[7] These were players who appeared to represent older times. Any mention of such former stars had little impact on young people who were looking upon the likes of Bill Russell, Jim Brown, and Muhammad Ali as role models and guides. When a younger Walter Alston had managed the Nashua Dodgers back in 1946, he encountered and fought vehemently against racial taunts hurled at Roy Campanella and Don Newcombe. He detested the racism of the fans he heard spewing words like "n_____" at his players. He was openly willing to fight folks in towns like Lynn, Massachusetts, who used such language. Those experiences now appeared to be of a distant past.

Moreover, Alston was now witnessing radicals, entertainers, and musicians who shrugged at such early acts of opposition to segregation. (As Miles Davis had poignantly titled one of his famous pieces: "So What?") Some "hep" African American entertainers, comedians, and commentators were also employing such racial language and vocabulary that Alston had genuinely despised as part of their means of expression of identity. It was a different world, one which Alston did not really understand. In past years, his stamps of strength that came in his defense of racial integration in baseball, as well as in his considerable abilities with a rifle, with a pool cue, or (if need be) with his fists, had all been part of how his leadership in the game of baseball could resonate as legitimate among players, white or black.

In the context of the politicization of sports and popular culture in the late 1960s, an older man like Alston, especially as he now led what appeared to be a floundering team that had long ago seen its better days, came across as elderly, out of touch, and completely un-hep. Given the images associated with anything socially trendy in the late 1960s, the outward imagery Alston cast could certainly strike casual observers in a starkly contrasting manner. He had married his high school sweetheart, presumably having never dated another. He was not divorced. He was a grandfather. He never drank during the season. He never played poker. He had given up smoking cigarettes, and certainly never smoked anything else. Metaphorically and literally, while some of the New Age's culturally *à la page* were considering the appeal of the music of the Four Tops vs. the Temptations or of Miles Davis vs. Ornette Coleman, here was a rural Ohioan who knew no Motown groups and whose own musical tastes straddled the likes of Lawrence Welk and Whoopie John.

Once when sitting with two of his players early in the afternoon before a game, Alston was listening to them discussing their previous night out at a club in Manhattan. With complete honesty and naivete, Alston asked them: "What is it you do exactly in a night club?" Learning that all one did was sit and drink, Alston simply could not understand. Playing cards or pool over a glass of milk made sense to him. Sitting and doing nothing seemed ridiculous.[8] Among the "with it" youths of America of the late 1960s and early 70s, a smug, often false, sense of projection could be at work in regard to any judging of their elders. If someone then appeared so utterly out of touch in such matters as popular music and entertainment, how good could such a person be at something else that was important? How could such an out-of-touch old person be able to lead young men playing professional baseball? The logic here may have made as much sense as judging how well a surgeon of the day could perform a procedure on the basis of how much he or she knew about Bob Dylan, but the implied sense of someone being out of touch was always present, an all-too-easy catch-all notion of pseudo-awareness into which many could lapse.

As Alston was now approaching sixty, his previously intimidating physical prowess had faded. He could still shoot better than 'most anyone, be it with a gun or with a pool cue. In the off-season between 1969 and 1970, he broke 90 several times in single turns at straight pool, and his prowess in skeet shooting remained top-notch. Knowing how out of touch his skeet shooting friends were in comparison to the youth culture of the day, Alston chuckled about his affinity for skeet shooting with the tongue-in-cheek point that "Outside of baseball people, I know of no other group that likes to agitate as much as skeet shooters."[9] Such a statement hardly placed Alston in line with some genuine political agitators of the day, and Alston knew this as well as anyone. If he had actually thought rural Ohio skeet shooters to be agitators, he would have obviously had no clue as to what was occurring in Harlem or Oakland.

With a shotgun, Alston's only targets were clay birds. With the likes of Kennedy and King being victims of shootings, many young African Americans wondered about being able to shoot back at a real target. Amidst such political and personal contemplations, proficiency at such a thing as skeet shooting (presuming many urban youths of 1970 ever cared or even knew anything about this) had little-to-no resonation. Much of the world seemed to have passed Alston by, and as he seemed so clearly out of touch with much of the nation's popular music and culture, his unflappable, quiet manner led many less-than-astute baseball fans to leap all too readily to some sort of notion that he was not really in command when running a ball club. He was culturally "square" to the nth degree, but with all things baseball (itself seen as the least hep of all the major sports), he was anything but clueless. Nonetheless, the out-of-touch image would persist among the casual baseball public.

In 1972, President Richard Nixon took it upon himself to make public his selections for a 1945–1970 National League All-Star team. He named Alston as the manager. Upon learning of his selection, Alston demurred: "I'd be the last one in the world to argue with the President of the United States." Then he added with a slight smile: "He hasn't seen us play lately, has he?" Alston had a slick wit when he wanted to use it, but amidst the blindingly bright lights of political controversies in the late 1960s and early 1970s, such little nuances would go largely unnoticed. On another occasion, in January of 1971, sports writers in Chicago voted to award Alston their J. Louis Comiskey Memorial Award for his "long and meritorious service to baseball." Receiving the award, Alston quipped: "I must rate pretty good here. Joe Pepitone's chauffeur even met me at the airport." Joe Pepitone had been a solid but not great player with the Yankees from 1962 through 1969. One problem in New York was that he enjoyed the city's night-life a bit too much. He was traded to the Cubs, where he played from 1970 into 1973. There his night-life habits continued to compromise his potential, especially so in Chicago, for the Cubs, still without lights in Wrigley Field, played all their home games in the early afternoon, leaving Pepitone with less recovery time from his nightly activities. Alston's little barb indicated how well aware he was of such matters among players in the National League. His voicing such a point certainly spoke contrarily to those who preferred to see him, in his famous quietude, as out of touch with the modern game.[10]

Commentators, journalists, and historians who have studied America's popular culture in the tumultuous era of the late 1960s/early 1970s have come to no consensus as to whose views marked the true cutting edge. There is no one set of facts that is salient; no one outlook supersedes all others. At the time, though, certain views did appear to gain ascendancy and were popularly regarded to constitute desirable qualities. In the sports world, people like Walter Alston and the Dodgers, their earlier work on behalf of racial justice and integration notwithstanding, appeared about as far away from the world of the cool and the hep of the late 1960s as one could imagine.

In their typically quiet manner, Alston and the Dodgers' organization did, nonetheless, go through a revival, although, amidst this, their level of social outreach to the poorer communities of Southern California was never great. Their focus was on matters inherently baseball in nature. In 1969, as the leagues each split into Eastern and Western divisions, the Dodgers were in the NL West. They finished in lowly fourth place (of six), much the same as their two previous second division finishes in 1967 and 1968, Don Drysdale's pitching heroics that spring notwithstanding. But in 1969, they did play better than .500 ball (85–77) for the first time since Sandy Koufax retired. The following year, they improved slightly to 87–74, good enough to finish second behind the game's emerging powerhouse, the Cincinnati Reds. A few of the Dodgers' old stars from former winning seasons were still with the team, including Willie Davis (age 30), Maury Wills (now 37), and Jim Lefebvre. Meanwhile, Alston and Bavasi were busy making trades as well as developing new talent from within their organization.

Several young prospects were starting to emerge. Bill Russell, Bill Buckner, and Steve Garvey were just 20–21 years old when they began playing with LA in 1969 and 1970. Alston often expressed delight in the idea of homegrown talent. It confirmed his tradition-driven belief in the Dodgers' system. It seemed to link quite nicely in his mind with the faith he always held in the family and small-town Ohio solidity, no matter, indeed especially if, such values appeared antiquated or corny in the late 1960s and early 1970s. With Steve Garvey especially, as his father had earlier driven a bus for the Dodgers when they traveled to spring training games in Florida, Alston felt a further affirmation of some traditional values he felt sadly to be ebbing in the general culture around him. The explicit references Alston cast here underscored a political outlook that now appeared decidedly old-fashioned in politically hep circles. Garvey, Alston happily noted, "used to ride along [with the team] when he was ten or eleven. He used to ride quietly along, as all good little boys should be seen and not heard. ... Steve finally became our bat boy on the road." Such an old-fashioned expression as "seen and not heard" certainly marked a different sort of ideal than the views many African American youth were hailing or that people like Muhammad Ali and Roberto Clemente were asserting. But Alston's small-town Ohio roots remained entrenched, and he was anything but ashamed of them. Indeed, Alston took pride in proclaiming, with some overtones to which many could take umbrage, then or since: "I think there are a lot of complaints [referring to social protests among athletes and about the nation at large], but not too many in our game. Our [LA's] bunch this year [1969] is as good a group as we've ever had. I don't think you get *those kind of people* in baseball very often [emphases added]."

Garvey himself played both football and baseball at Michigan State University. There he was not conspicuous or outspoken about political issues that enveloped so many college and university students in the late 1960s. After finishing at Michigan State, Garvey signed with the Dodgers, where he always exhibited a clean, "all–American boy" image. Jim Lefebvre's behavior and image were similar. Lefebvre had also been a batboy for the Dodgers when he was young. His emergence as a potent hitter in the Dodgers' lineup pleased Alston greatly. In an age of non-conformists, Alston was, in every way, someone who believed in "the [Dodgers'] System." And he built a new and talented squad largely from within its own ranks and sensibilities. Another prominent sports coach in the LA area, Alston's friend, UCLA basketball coach John Wooden, exhibited a similarly strong, unapologetic entrenchment in traditional values. His views were devoid of racial prejudice certainly (in notable contrast to such a reactionary figure of the era as University of Kentucky basketball coach Adolph Rupp), but, like Alston's, Wooden's sensibilities appeared decidedly in contrast to many of the purportedly more "hep" outlooks that dominated the socially trendy circles of the nation's youth culture.[11]

Beyond their successes with home-grown talent, Alston and Bavasi contributed to some of the Dodgers' reemergence via the trade route. Of note here, they acquired Dick Allen in 1971 and Frank Robinson in 1972. Neither stayed with the team long, however. A certain conspicuousness came with these standout players. This conspicuousness derived, not just from the fact that, in the 1960s and early 70s, Allen and Robinson were among the true mega-stars in the game. Both had been saddled with images of aggressiveness that lingered among some in the press and not always in positive ways. This was especially the case with Dick Allen. The negative aura here grew further because of Allen's and Robinson's short stints with LA. This brevity added to issues and questions concerning the Dodgers' (and baseball's) outlooks on racial matters and politics of the time. Alston's interjections and overrulings of judgments made by Maury Wills when he was team captain had prompted similar questions. In 1964, for example, Wills took the liberty to alter some of the team fines for such infractions as missing a sign, failing to bunt, or not hustling. Alston stepped in and reset the levels, asserting that such matters were his purview as manager.[12] Some of the issues that arose amidst such concerns were a trifle edgy, tinged as they were with connections to racial matters. All possible responses were, and remain, subject to interpretation and debate. At the time, their conspicuousness was undeniable, and they contributed to the image of Alston and the Dodgers' (and of baseball's) aura of undue conservatism.

By the time he came to Los Angeles in 1971, Dick Allen had developed a reputation in certain baseball circles as a troublemaker. Without any doubt, Allen had been a victim of several vicious forms of racism.

Allen had been willing to raise protests about his treatment, especially when he played in Philadelphia, where he had first signed in 1960. When he joined the Phillies' organization, Allen was sent to the minors for seasoning and development. The Phillies unfortunately sent him to Little Rock, Arkansas, where he was subject to a volume of racial insults and taunts, including "n____!" On several occasions, his car was vandalized. Once up with the Phillies, there were more incidents. One teammate, Frank Thomas, taunted him defiantly. When Thomas called Allen "boy," a fight ensued. With stories of such incidents flying about the rumor mills among Phillies fans, the city's baseball enthusiasts came to regard Allen as some sort of bad actor and began regularly booing him, hurling more racial insults, and even throwing coins and transistor radio batteries at him. In response, and quite logically, Allen began donning a batting helmet when he took the field at first base and once toed the word "BOO" in the infield dirt while in his position there, conspicuously answering his critics with his own comment.[13]

Amidst all this tumult, Allen's on-field play was tremendous. He made the All-Star team several times. In 1966, he batted .317 and hit 40 home runs with 110 RBI. He did drink beer and smoked tobacco, however, and he liked to play the horses. This lent support to his bad image. In 1969, he went to a racetrack in New Jersey and, after getting caught in traffic, failed to arrive at a home game on time. For this he was fined and suspended. In retaliation, Allen stayed away from the Phillies for nearly a month, only returning upon the team's leaders promising to trade him. "I can play anywhere," he quipped, "first, third, left field, anywhere but Philadelphia." Allen's so-called "strike" of 1969 engendered a great deal of press coverage, and it was virtually all negative. Allen seemed one of the few athletes in baseball whose words and deeds mirrored the defiant African American protests that were so strong in other sports and in the society at large. Baseball's general reaction to Allen, especially in Philadelphia, further underscored the especially conservative aura that surrounded the national pastime in contrast to the other major sports.

Allen's reputation certainly preceded him as the Phillies traded him to St. Louis after the 1969 season. Allen played well for the Cardinals, however, and there were no controversies. St. Louis manager Red Schoendienst, the same man who had played with Alston in Rochester back in 1943, openly praised Allen. Schoendienst declared simply: "Allen did a fine job for us, and we never had any problems with him."[14] In 1971, Allen joined Alston and the Dodgers. Alston felt he needed help at third base. Allen had playing experience there, and he was more than willing (as he had said, he'd play anywhere except Philadelphia). Dodgers publicist Red Patterson was effusive: "That Allen is unbelievable. He reported at his lightest weight since high school. [He] has worked like a rookie and has even been on the field at 7:45 to take extra work."[15]

Allen proved solid at third base. He also did well playing left field and first base. His fearsome power hitting was the main thing Alston wanted, and here Allen proved to be a major contributor to the Dodgers' offense. In 1971, Allen played virtually every game. His power came through, as he led the team in home runs (23) and RBI (90). His batting average of .295 was the second-best mark on the team; only Willie Davis's .309 was higher. As in St. Louis, Allen gave no evidence of troublemaking while with the Dodgers. Some talk did circulate that he would not take part in community outreach efforts that O'Malley's office wanted to develop. Still, coach Danny Ozark declared, "Allen did a great job for us in L.A. He was a great baserunner, the best I ever coached. I'd take the extra base with him, and I don't think he was ever thrown out the entire year."[16]

Even if the claims of non-participation in community outreach efforts were true, at all the on-field levels with which Walter Alston concerned himself, Allen proved an excellent member of the team, and in 1971 the Dodgers fully rebounded into contention. That summer they were in the NL West division race to the final day. Despite Allen's great play, injuries to Bill Singer, Bill Grabarkewitz, and Bill Sudakis proved critical, and Alston's Dodgers fell back in the summer, trailing the leading Giants by as many as 11 games. They started September eight games out. Then they played very well, finishing the season just one game behind San Francisco (the Giants subsequently lost the NLCS to Pittsburgh). With his team overcoming such obstacles and finishing so close to the top, Alston was voted National League Manager of the Year.[17] Having lost so narrowly, and feeling he needed to improve his pitching strength, that December, Alston and Bavasi were able to procure Tommy John from the Chicago White Sox. But they had to trade Dick Allen to get him. Chicago also gave LA a mediocre infielder named Steve Huntz in the deal, supposedly to fill the void Allen's departure left at third base. Huntz never played a game for LA, however. Meanwhile, Tommy John proved an outstanding pitcher for the Dodgers. From 1972–78, missing all of '75 with the famous and now-named "Tommy John" surgery, he would win 87 games in six seasons.

Allen would play very well in his three seasons in Chicago. In 1972 he was voted American League MVP, and he twice led the AL in home runs and once in RBI's. From there he returned to Philadelphia, where the earlier tensions had greatly mellowed, both with the club and with the fans. Eventually, Allen was inducted into the Philadelphia Sports Hall of Fame. The controversies that had dogged the early part of Allen's career had left an aura, and LA's willingness to depart with him after just one season suggested that the team was somehow uncomfortable with him as well. There is no actual evidence of that. In counterpoint, some may have wanted to project elements of racism being apparent in any perceived senses of opposition to someone as allegedly controversial as Dick Allen. For Alston and the Dodgers, Allen's excellent play added to the legacy the organization had built since the time of Jackie Robinson. Yet Allen's short stay in LA, like Jackie Robinson's late-career bristlings of temper when Alston first managed in Brooklyn and reduced Robinson's playing time, yielded notions of racial tensions somehow lurking somewhere just beneath the surface of the club. There was vastly more image than reality involved here. Had LA kept Allen, given especially Allen's subsequent excellent play with the White Sox, some could speculate as to what could have come forth for the Dodgers. Debate and speculation there can never end. Tommy John certainly pitched well for Los Angeles, but Allen played excellent ball with Chicago. Such are the vagaries of trades and "what if's" in baseball or in any sport.

Had Allen played another season in LA, he would have been a teammate of Frank Robinson's. Like Allen, Robinson had gone through controversy earlier in his career, illustrated by an altercation he had with Braves third baseman Eddie Mathews. Mathews took exception to Robinson's especially hard slides. Robinson did this with everybody. It was the kind of hard-nosed, intense style of play he always displayed, but many white players begrudged such displays of intensity coming from an African American. That controversy had largely vanished by 1966, and this contrastingly positive imagery grew by leaps and bounds amidst Robinson's extremely successful seasons in Baltimore, where he led the Orioles to four pennants in six years. When Robinson came to Los Angeles, he was 36 years old. In the 1972 season, he played only 103 games, hit 19 home runs, and batted .251. After the season, Robinson expressed a desire for more playing time. His dissatisfaction again generated some intimations of racially-tinged issues at play in the Dodgers' organization. Again, the varying perspectives here were more impressionistic than substantive.

As in 1971, in the 1972 season, the Dodgers finished second. But while they had nearly edged the Giants for the NL West championship, in 1972 the Dodgers' second-place finish found them 10 games behind the increasingly powerful Cincinnati Reds. Robinson played well for the Dodgers, but he had injured his wrist in a collision with the outfield wall in St. Louis. Another veteran Alston had procured, Manny Mota, was also slowed by pulled leg muscle problems. With Allen gone, the 1972 Dodgers had shown defensive weakness at third base. Alston also wanted more depth in pitching. So the Dodgers dealt Robinson and several others, including infielder Bobby Valentine, to the California Angels and received pitcher Andy Messersmith and third baseman Ken McMullen. Messersmith would pitch well for LA. Meanwhile, the Angels were actually quite eager to get Robinson. Their new General Manager, Harry Dalton, had been GM with the Orioles when Robinson played there, and Dalton was especially keen on getting Robinson back on his team. There was simply no way that Alston and the Dodgers wanted to get rid of either Frank Robinson or Dick Allen, and neither Robinson nor Allen ever spoke negatively of Alston. Alston himself was straightforward: "Allen never caused me any real trouble. We had a little bit in common—we both loved horses—and we talked about them a good bit. ... [Elsewhere] when the game started Richie gave you 100 percent." With Robinson, Alston recognized he was moody, but, he shrugged, "a lot of people are. You learn to live with them. Frank was a sound baseball man. He still swung a good bat though ... he had lost a lot of his speed."[18]

The short tenures of Dick Allen and Frank Robinson with the Dodgers were completely understandable. Wider issues of race could encourage consignments of wider social or political meaning, but neither Robinson nor Allen ever expressed any thoughts along such lines, and neither was ever one to duck away from controversy. Nonetheless, the two each spending but a single in LA lent a vague accentuation to senses that the Dodgers organization, like the leadership of contemporaneous major league baseball in general, had shied away from various sorts of racial controversies, contributing to the casting of a conservative aura over the game, all in marked contrast with many other sports of the day.

In the late 1960s and early 1970s, pro basketball's former Lew Alcindor presented the public with Kareem Abdul Jabbar. The NFL had Ahmad Rashad, born Robert Earl Moore. Of course, Muhammad Ali was the epicenter of all such matters, be they personal, political, or of sports. Meanwhile, among major league baseball players of that era (or since), such name changes and all the political symbolism they carried came forth with—no one. To the historian and commentator, the issue of names cannot be cast as *the* principal litmus test, but the contrast that baseball presented to the sports public of this strident time was striking. For this and many other reasons, baseball appeared to have lost much the absolute centrality it had formerly held as "the national pastime." Major League Baseball's leaders revealed their own awareness of this changing status in 1973 when they attempted to institute the game's major innovation of the modern era—the Designated Hitter Rule. The American League accepted it, while the National League, including Alston and the Dodgers, did not. If Alston (or O'Malley or Bavasi) held any sentiments at odds with their League's stand against the institution of the DH, they never made their views public, nor has any archival source ever since been found which reveals any exception taken privately. The two leagues have never resolved the point that, ever since, they have played different games. At the time the NL, including Alston and the Dodgers looked ever more conservative. In 1947, they were the avant-garde; in 1973 they seemed of the Old Guard.

For the LA Dodgers in the late 1960s and early '70s other such politically-tinged contrasts also sat among the Southern California sports public as they viewed the area's teams. Other LA squads of the era, like the Rams and the Lakers, contrasted with the placid image of Alston's Dodgers. The Lakers had Jimmy McMillan, Elgin Baylor, and, above all, Wilt Chamberlain, who, while admitting to having voted Republican in 1968, still cast a menacing specter of a "bad dude." Similarly, the Rams boasted the "Fearsome Foursome" defensive line, which included such glowering hulks as Deacon Jones and Roosevelt Grier. The "bad ___ed" nature inherent in the appeal of such towering figures as Wilt, the Deacon, and Rosie had no counterpoint in the Dodgers' organization. Alston's Dodgers' appeared comparatively mellow, less glowering, and quite white. Alston's friend, John Wooden, and his UCLA basketball teams maintained a similarly prim and proper image.

One player on the Dodgers in these years, Bobby Valentine, was critical of Alston. Perhaps projecting his own outlook as a young man who came of age in the era of the late 1960s and early 1970s, Valentine described Alston as a man who "tries to avoid confrontations, not because it is a way of smoothing things out, but because he doesn't know what to do in a crisis. He just hopes the crises will go away."[19] Valentine did not cite specific incidents to illustrate his criticism. (Alston's work in 1971 that led to him receiving the Manager of the Year award speaks to anything but the disengaged figure Valentine cast.) Valentine believed Walter Alston did not like him, or care for challenging questions or the general brashness that Valentine put forth. Valentine would be one of the players the Dodgers traded to the Angels with Frank Robinson in order to get pitcher Andy Messersmith.[20] Whether Alston was uncomfortable with Valentine, or whether he more simply wanted Messersmith, who would win 20 games for the Dodgers in 1974, remains a matter of speculation.

Like any good manager, Alston never said anything personal about players who were traded away. When a player is traded, it is always easy (and understandable) for him to believe some personal reasons had to enter into the willingness of the manager to dispense with him. With a person of such unashamed brashness as Valentine, such self-focus and possible egotism may have magnified his preoccupations. When Valentine was with the Angels the following season, he and another former Dodger, Bill Grabarkewitz, directed verbal jibes at Alston; Angels manager Bobby Winkles asked them to cease such gossiping with the members of the press. Reporters were sorry not to receive more good copy from Valentine or Grabarkewitz, but the reporters could dig up no other such stories, and no one else spoke of Alston like that.[21] Whether anything of a personal nature influenced Alston here cannot be determined fully, but little appeared to affect him that way. Further, if Alston was aging and mellowing into some sort of old man who avoided crises and merely hoped they would vanish on their own, it would follow that his game management would have grown increasingly ineffective. But, under Alston, the Dodgers continued to be pennant contenders throughout the 1970s. It would be quite a stretch to assert that the Dodgers' success here came regardless, let alone in spite of Alston.

Such thoughts as Valentine's reinforced the Dodgers' "safe" image that served as a further hint of evidence for critics and fans who wanted to see the national pastime as somehow more conservative and who sought, as well, to account for the Dodgers' failure to get over the hurdle of competition in the early–1970s NL West, especially against the Cincinnati Reds. Baseball's conservative aura in the 1970s was apparent to many observers of the day, but assertions of the Dodgers' significance in that general image involved much oversimplification. Alston and the Dodgers were trying to do all they could to beat Cincinnati. Here the reasons for the failures were not so much anything the Dodgers did or did not do, and they were certainly not due to any forms of racism, nor were they due to any aging or mellowing of Alston. The trouble for LA, and for the rest of the NL West, was simply that, for most of the 1970s, the Cincinnati Reds were simply too strong. Alston conceded the Reds were "a tremendous ball club."[22] And indeed they were always on lists any of the game's experts compile when they name the best teams in the history of baseball. The fact that Alston and the Dodgers consistently challenged Cincinnati in these years is more a point of praise than criticism. What if they had kept Dick Allen and not taken Tommy John; what if they had kept Frank Robinson and not gone for Andy Messersmith? Such speculations were there for debate in the region's many cafés, barbershops, and bars, and they could fuel other speculations about racial issues, but the substantive point remained that Alston and the Dodgers were making choices with an eye on how to gain an edge over, as it happened, one of the truly great clubs in the history of the game. In contrast to such criticisms as those of Valentine, another contemporary, Dave

Bristol of the Cincinnati Reds, reflected about Alston quite differently: "Every time I sit in a dugout opposite that man," Bristol acknowledged, "I learn something."[23] In counterpoint to the specific political meaning some may have wished to cast as a result of the trading of Robinson and Allen, Cincinnati's great second baseman, Joe Morgan, also stated, "I'd like to play for a couple of seasons for Walt Alston. It must be a wonderful experience. I look across from our dugout into theirs and see him sitting there, never screaming, never losing his cool. No matter what the score is, he seems to be always the same, always in charge of things, completely in charge." Alston's archrival manager of the 1970s Reds, Sparky Anderson, could not have put it more frankly: "I could never be as good as him."[24]

From 1971 through 1976, the Dodgers under Alston were a power in the NL West in every

By the 1970s, Alston was completely secure in his position as manager of the Dodgers. Some players and scribes carried forth with mutterings and rumors that he was out of touch with his players as well as with much of the detail in the running of the ball club. Such rumors spun about the press and the baseball public. Alston felt no need to lend them credibility and gave them no notice. He quietly went about his business. In his last six seasons at the helm of the Dodgers, his teams were consistent winners. Indeed, they always gave the powerful Cincinnati Reds (often acknowledged as one of the greatest teams of all time) a stiff fight for the title in the National League West, and in 1974 Alston's Dodgers won the NL West title (and the NL pennant) over the Reds. Photograph 1974 (National Baseball Hall of Fame and Museum, Cooperstown, NY).

season. After 1971, when they were beaten by one game by the Giants, they were the only team to challenge the Cincinnati Reds, finishing second to them in 1972, 1973, 1975, and 1976. In 1973, after trading away such veterans as Allen and Robinson, Alston moved more fully in the direction of youth. Here he began to form what became known as the "Kiddie Infield." Each member of this infield that the team brought up—Steve Garvey, Davey Lopes, Bill Russell, and Ron Cey—would become a standout who played together for a long succession of seasons. In 1973, the Dodgers would rebound. They played well, winning an impressive 95 games. Unfortunately, the deeply talented Cincinnati Reds won 99.

Alston stuck with his youth movement, and before the 1974 season he made a key procurement, obtaining relief pitcher Mike Marshall (in exchange for Willie Davis). That season, Alston and the Dodgers actually beat the hated Reds by four games and went on to defeat Pittsburgh for the NL pennant. Once again, Alston was voted Manager of the Year.[25] Alston had built a remarkable team, with one of the strongest infields in the history of the game. It just happened, however, that through the 1970s, Cincinnati, with such stars as Pete Rose, Johnny Bench, George Foster, Joe Morgan, Tony Perez, and Dave Concepcion, was just a little better. As it was, the 1974 title marked Walter Alston's seventh pennant. (The Oakland A's defeated them in the World Series, that Oakland team, like Cincinnati of those years, also being one of baseball's outstanding teams, one of the few to win three successive World Series.) Alston's seven pennants exceeded every manager in the history of the National League except John McGraw. In the American League, only Casey Stengel, Connie Mack, and Joe McCarthy won more.

In 1976, again finishing second to Cincinnati in the NL West, Alston announced his retirement just before the close of the season. That summer there would be some problems on the Dodgers. Their offense did not produce runs at key times. Friction between players grew. Cincinnati ran off with a big lead, and by August it appeared they were not to be headed. Some reporters, quoting anonymous sources, criticized Alston's leadership, with the implication that the team should have been more aggressive and intimidating. Amidst the frustrations, Alston lost his temper and shouted at a reporter, Allan Malamud of the *Los Angeles Herald Examiner*. Alston called him "an overstuffed pig." Given the language of such managers of the time as New York's Billy Martin, this was hardly strong stuff, but coming from Alston, it was quite surprising. Two days after the incident with Malamud, Alston telephoned him and apologized. He was still a bit peeved, as he commented to other reporters: "The only thing is, he can write his [opinions] in the newspapers and I don't get much chance to make mine heard."

Alston was certainly feeling the pressures of unfulfilled hopes among the fans and local reporters. (In that same month of August, Alston's father passed away.) Talk-radio programs were full of callers asserting that the Dodgers needed to make a switch at the top. In late September,

Alston did announce his retirement with four games left in the season. While only anonymous sources were quoted in criticism of Alston, upon his announcement, Don Sutton, Steve Garvey, and Bill Buckner (as well as Sparky Anderson) spoke in praise of his work. Was there any force-out from management here? Be it O'Malley, Bavasi, or anyone else in the Dodgers' offices, no one has ever gone on record to affirm that.[26]

The Dodgers still won an impressive 92 games in 1976. The trouble was, once again, that Cincinnati won 102 games. No one could stop the 1976 Reds. They won the pennant, swept the Phillies in the NLCS, and swept the Yankees in the World Series. Amidst the heat and the pennant race disappointments, Alston did register his 2,000th win that summer. He was then only the sixth manager to reach that mark. His final total of 2,040 is currently ninth on the game's all-time list.

The Dodgers turned the 1976 team over to Alston's old friend and coach, Tommy Lasorda. Lasorda took the team that Alston had helped form with stars like Steve Garvey, Davey Lopes, Bill Russell, Ron Cey, and Don Sutton, and proceeded to win the next two NL pennants. Alston had thus guided three sets of Dodgers clubs to the top. He inherited the Brooklyn Dodgers that won so steadily in the mid–1950s. Then he built the Koufax/Drysdale teams of the early and mid–1960s. From there, in the early 1970s, he built an entirely new squad that stood with the best teams of the day. He won a pennant with them, pushed and pressured the phenomenal Cincinnati squads in every season, and saw the team continue to win after stepping down. Winning with three distinct generations of teams in 23 years was, by any yardstick, a remarkable feat of organizational and managerial skill.

12

Extra Innings and Post-Game Analysis

Near the end of the famous 1989 baseball movie *Field of Dreams*, the character Terence Mann (played by James Earl Jones) delivers a climactic oration in which he proclaims: "The one constant through all the years ... has been BaseBall [with a decided emphasis, as underlined, on each of the 'Bs']. America has rolled by like an army of steamrollers. It has been erased like a blackboard, rebuilt and erased again. But baseball has marked the time. ... This game is part of our past.... It reminds us of all that once was good, and that could be again." Such convictions about baseball being Americans' true marker of time have often come forth, both before and after the movie and novel.[1] These convictions touch upon what many fans like to sentimentalize about baseball and what appears to differentiate the game from all other sports as to its significance in American culture—that it does more than merely reflect its times, it stands beyond them, imparting meaning in and of itself.

Beyond mere personal preference, one point of evidence as to baseball standing apart from the other major American sports is the simple fact that it is the one major team sport that does not utilize a clock. It thus operates more as a traditional small-town farm than as a modern big-city office or factory. (One of baseball's famous philosophers, Yogi Berra, reflected this idea when someone asked him, while on the ball field, "What time is it?" Yogi's reply: "You mean right now?") Rooted more in past times, beyond many immediate points of familiarity, baseball has come to appear less meaningful to some people, usually urban, suburban, and younger, but the game still arouses great sentimentality among many of its fans. So many of baseball's sentimentalists enjoy conceptions of the game in small-town, rural contexts. The casting of *Field of Dreams'* location in Iowa/"Heaven" and one of its characters, Archibald "Moonlight" Graham, from Chisholm, Minnesota, were chosen out of that very sentiment. These selections certainly made the story resonate better than it would have had the ballfield been set in the Bronx/(Hell) and Moonlight Graham had hailed from Cleveland. (The image, memory, and sensation of an industrial river that catches on fire would have certainly disrupted the lovely pastoral setting that both the novelist and the filmmaker desired.)

Walter Alston's career and much of his work with the Dodgers do present several likenesses with *Field of Dreams*. Especially poignant were Alston's small-town rural Ohio roots. Here several comparisons between Alston and Moonlight Graham are striking. As players, Graham and Alston each got to the majors, but for only the last weeks of a single season—Graham in 1922 with the Giants; Alston in 1936 with the Cardinals. Each played in only one game, and for both it was the last game of the season. Unlike Graham, Alston did get to bat once in the majors (and he struck out on three pitches).

Alston, of course, did stay in the game rather than "hang 'em up," as Doc Graham did after his proverbial cup of coffee in the majors. But while their career paths completely diverted from there, each became a star in his hometown for what he did in life. For each, their relationship to their Midwestern community was central. Graham's Chisholm, Minnesota, and Alston's Darrtown, Ohio, gave both men a profound grounding, revealed in simple, proud affirmations. In the film, Graham declared: "I was born here; I'll live out my days here, and I'll die here—with no regrets." Alston felt the same way.

Alston's roots in Darrtown, Ohio, exemplify what makes baseball appear timeless to so many of the game's devotees. Compared to the clock-driven, team sports of the modern age like football, basketball, and hockey, many purists love to see baseball convey an innocence of spirit. No matter the harsh words critics have tossed at Middle America—provincial, unsophisticated, deplorable—indeed in some ways because of them, the small-town culture of Middle America endures, with many continuing to find it ennobling. Baseball's ongoing attraction is both a cause and an effect here. For many in small-town Middle America, Alston's roots in Darrtown, Ohio, serve as perfect examples of the game's enduring mythos. Among Alston's Ohio townspeople lies a *Gemeinschaftlichkeit* that finds joy in the holding of allegiance to organizations and to institutions whose lifecycles stretch beyond those of the individuals within them, a team concept in the widest sense. To proud small-town Midwesterners, slights from allegedly more sophisticated urbanites merely deepen their local affections.

In small Midwestern communities like Alston's Darrtown, everyone knew one another. There were no secrets; neighbors trusted one another implicitly. A person's word was his bond. Men like Alston's father incurred financial debts and faced them squarely, never skirting them with legalistic trickery. The more modern urban/suburbanite may make use of such maneuvers as declarations of bankruptcy as a means of evading the consequences of debt. Such ways were foreign to such people as the Alstons. Corporate banking and financial tricks were indeed part of the *gesellschaft* that flourished in an industrializing America, a development and a culture that came after the rural "Butternut" society that settled such Southern Ohio communities as Darrtown. The term *gesellschaft*, not coincidentally, was also the word that Germans came to use for the institutional entity that was the limited-liability corporation, as well as for the idea or perspective of a wider society that sits beyond such minutiae-focused entities as small towns, i.e., the *gemeinschaft* which was the heart of Alston's Darrtown. As Alexis de Tocqueville had surmised, in praise of the common people of American he met in the late 1820s in such townships as those in rural Ohio, Alston came from a place where democratic and community ideals were lived and celebrated, all without any need to study the pertinent philosophical and intellectual foundations, or the pathways of subterfuge that may lie in counterpoint to such community strictures. To Tocqueville, these people had become Cartesians without studying the pertinent philosophical texts in formal ways. While certainly not the only means, learning and playing baseball was a kind of replacement curriculum here, perhaps secondary in importance only to the Bible or the Constitution.

Much of the continued resonance of baseball's pastoral imagery in the popular imagination rests on these sorts of points which underscore the pleasing contrasts that lie between baseball and the other, more recently invented major team sports, all clock-driven, more urban, and modern in their foundations. Examples like Walter Alston underscore how baseball represents those elusive Middle American ideals, while other team sports appear more generically modern.* Over much of the 20th century and well into the 21st, this cultural division has appeared in many forms. It has been the basis of both earnest social philosophizing from George Will as well as good comedy from George Carlin. Baseball is rural while football is urban (in a similar vein, amateur golf once presented America with Bobby Jones, while professional golf gave us Walter Hagen). Baseball is Jeffersonian, while football is Hamiltonian; baseball is William Jennings Bryan, while football is

---

*Devout baseball fan, journalist George Will, with his usual dry sarcasm, described professional football as the perfect embodiment of modern life—episodes of extreme violence interrupted by an endless series of committee meetings.

Theodore Roosevelt. The contrasting metaphors, both humorous and serious, are many, and here Walter Alston's roots with the Southern Ohio "Butternuts" do indeed contrast with those of professional football, which are more strongly rooted in Yankee-settled Northern Ohio industrial towns, like Canton.

By no means unscathed, baseball has survived many challenges to its place as America's true marker of time. In the early 20th century, the game lived through the disdain put forth by several smug self-styled "Progressive" outlooks which sought to elevate a modern urban world, symbolized by such sports as football, to a position not merely different than but decidedly above the supposedly simpler mentalities of older times that baseball embodied. President Theodore Roosevelt was especially energetic as he exhorted America's young men to take on all challenges before them like the players on a football squad. While some young Americans may have been influenced here, in the post–Progressive years of the 1920s, baseball did not appear to have yielded much in regard to its status. Baseball's leaders readily grasped, absorbed, and exploited the same marketing and advertising modalities that football and other rising sports had begun to employ.

It was not until the advent of television that professional football challenged baseball as the nation's most popular form of sports entertainment. Television did indeed render the traditional game less appealing, especially as the small, quickly moving ball was harder to follow on the screen than was the larger, more slowly moving football (or basketball). Throughout the competition for media market shares and status, however, the sentimentalities surrounding the pastoral aura of baseball endured, albeit not quite so fully, and there lay the basis of some of Terrance Mann's plea that baseball "has marked the time." Alston's career, his accomplishments, and his serene manner also mark clear illustrations of what endured.

Well beyond the marketing impact of television, another more profound and rather somber challenge that can readily be, and has often been raised in reaction to any tenderness that people may wish to conjure about baseball involves thorny issues of race. Few significant themes in the cultural history of America can escape inspection via this vital lens. In the context of sentimentalities about the baseball of older times, the mention of race certainly does compromise the nobility in any notion of the game purportedly embodying "all that once was good." In *Field of Dreams*, the casting of James Earl Jones, beyond the fact of the dramatic power of his wonderful bass-baritone voice, as the person who delivered the great oration about the game helped diffuse at least a bit of the glare surrounding the exception that racial issues invoke about positive generalizations as to what baseball of older times continues to embody and symbolize for America. (Doubtlessly, this was a matter of which the film's directors and producers had to have been conscious.)

Even if expressed naively, so many notions about what "once was good" in America do indeed refer to baseball when it was played in times of extensive Jim Crow hegemony. It is by no means far-fetched to consider whether Ted Williams or Joe DiMaggio would have set quite as many marks as they did if they had to face Satchel Paige once or twice a month. Would such catchers as Bill Dickey or Mickey Cochrane have held quite as dominating reputations as they held against base stealers if they had had to try gunning down the likes of James Thomas "Cool Papa" Bell? How would Lefty Grove or Carl Hubbell have fared pitching to Martin Dihigo or Josh Gibson? (In any meaningful reverse form, each of those questions prompts intriguing thoughts as well.) The issue of race marks an exception to any notions of the essential goodness of baseball of earlier times, and it is a point of exception that can never be summarily disregarded. The French-born American, later Professor and Provost at Columbia University, Jacques Barzun may have once famously pronounced: "Whoever wants to know the heart and mind of America had better learn baseball."[2] Barzun's "study guide" for "the heart and mind of America" would appear to need a little revision and require some learning about race as well. At the intersection of these two themes of undeniable importance to the nation's collective cultural meaning, while there is much bitter conflict, the legacy of Walter Alston and the Dodgers provides ground for some happier points of communion and harmony. In the grasping of America's history and its culture, whether by immigrants, school children, documentary producers, or anyone else, the question of whether the processes should hold an overall positive or negative tone is a central element in the debates about what is essential in the nation's history, debates that will never end. Whatever tonality one may ultimately prefer, a look at the various mixings of baseball and race is certainly a way of going to the heart of the issue.

In the decades from the end of World War II through the 1950s, 1960s and 1970s, much of America's legacy of Jim Crow did unravel. During these years, the collective leadership of the Dodgers, with Branch Rickey, Walter O'Malley, Buzzie Bavasi, Walter Alston, and Vin Scully, did embody a *Field of Dreams* notion of an institution that "marked the time." Here it was not just a matter of baseball standing alone, like a small Midwestern farm, with a newer America of urban factories and offices rolling by. In the days of Alston and the Dodgers, the team rolled with the times. This involved being a truly central part of the great changes in the America that was dismantling so many of the entrenched customs and laws of segregation. At the same time, the nation's population was also growing and expanding to numerous locales that previously lay outside the nation's mainstream. Alston and the Dodgers played major roles in all of this too.

In the post–1945 years, unlike earlier decades, as various parts of America rolled by with one identity and political impulse following another, the glaring exception of race does not undercut or dilute sentimentalities that may arise about Alston and his Dodgers. Their work involved activities that meant a great deal to the game, as well as to the entire nation in its evolution and maturation beyond the sensibilities of Jim Crow. That cannot be denied, but by the mid–1960s, many of the fundamental features of racially-focused politics in America departed from the older, relatively straightforward liberal ideals of equality regardless of race and turned more towards varied concepts of identity based on race. Within this, Alston and the Dodgers, as well as baseball in general, appeared to fall away from the cutting edge, in sports or in wider areas of political discourse. In addition to the impact of television rendering other sports more watchable, stars in other sports emerged as the ones who much more visibly "marked the time." Some of the contemporaneous views of Walter Alston then cast him as being out of touch, or even hostile. There were inaccuracies in these characterizations; he never showed or expressed anything hostile to such sports figures as Muhammad Ali, Jim Brown, or Kareem Abdul-Jabbar. Still, common perceptions clearly cast the sports world's "cutting edges" of political change as emerging elsewhere.

It was not just Alston and the Dodgers who fell away and appeared relatively antiquated in public perceptions as to where any social "cutting edge" may lie. In the 1960s and 1970s, for example, major league baseball never presented even one player who changed his name, and by implication, at least some of his identity, as, so visibly and influentially, did such people as Kareem Abdul-Jabbar or Muhammad Ali. (No African American player in major league baseball ever recorded such a name change.) Not just here, but in many other ways baseball seemed to recede into the political backdrop of the sports world. Forms of new identity politics and the personal assertiveness among leading sports figures came forth far more in boxing, basketball, football, track and field, and even tennis. At the time, perhaps only professional golf cast a more conservative aura than did the old national pastime of baseball. Whether baseball was genuinely out of touch with newer trends in American and African American culture and politics was, and still is, ultimately a matter of personal judgment. Some certainly saw it so; others still do. Some can point to a few ball players who exhibited some of the "hep" political and personal styles of the age. Well into the 21st century, still others continued to see too many aspects of identity politics to involve *cul de sacs* which, despite their many points of outer attractiveness, may suffuse more than elevate, and ultimately divert impressionable young people onto more narcissistic pathways which prove injurious to their individual progress, as well as to the wider progress of various sectors in the nation's economy and culture, especially the impoverished ones.[3] Here again, the issues are matters both of judgment and often of heated debate. It has been so since the first divisions of such philosophies and tactics were fervently argued among leaders like Dr. King and Malcolm X.

Walter Alston stood affirmatively with Dr. King, rendering judgment solely on the content of the character of a player's ability without regard to race, religion, or ethnicity. Certain public and media images notwithstanding, there were then no problems, much as some wanted to believe there were, between Alston's Dodgers and the forceful, previously controversial personalities of Dick Allen or Frank Robinson. Similarly, had Alston managed the Dodgers during Jackie Robinson's heyday, he would not have reduced Robinson's playing time, a matter which did cause friction. Alston understood and respected Robinson's hostile reactions to the age-induced diminutions of his playing time. Any athlete of Robinson's caliber will not go gently. His resistance to the inevitable coming of twilight was part of what made him great in the first place, and Alston knew this as well as anyone. Even though Robinson was subsequently willing to raise criticisms of such groups as the Black Panthers, in his final public appearances, he would be among the noteworthy voices calling for African Americans to be named major league baseball managers. When Frank Robinson was appointed manager of the Cleveland Indians in 1975, Walter Alston was as delighted as anyone.

The vagaries in the validity of the *Field of Dreams*–inspired notions of baseball being for America the ultimate marker of time, reminding us of what was good and can be good again, are certainly complicated by the issues of race. Even accepting the glaring points that racial issues expose, Walter Alston and the Dodgers of the post–1945 decades did provide important road markers of classical liberalism. From there, as succeeding generations rolled by, some turned to alternative views. Others held firmly to classic egalitarian values which the Dodgers were instrumental in raising and bringing to the center of the nation's conscience amidst "Baseball's Great Experiment."

In addition to being in the avant-garde in the nation's first post–1945 steps to end Jim Crow laws and customs, in the ending of other legacies of prejudice in modern America, Alston's Dodgers were also at the forefront. Anti-Semitism in the nation had been severe for many generations. Writers on the subject point to the obvious time of World War II, with the fight against the glaring terrors of Nazism, being critical in the ending of many older, blatant forms of prejudice against Jewish Americans. The notable writer and literary critic, Irving Howe, emphasized that many Americans had formerly been openly anti–Semitic in their outlooks and policies, with many more choosing to enable such prejudices by indulgently capitulating to the more blatant anti–Semites among them. With the War, Howe said, many Americans came to feel levels of guilt as they tacitly recognized both the past actions they had indulged and the idea that they too would have probably "looked the other way," just like the majority of Germans in the Nazi era. The guilt, quipped Howe, was so pronounced that even Henny Youngman became popular. (Not a bad literary turn: Making a point about Jewish assimilation through the use of a Henny-Youngman style joke about Henny Youngman!)

In succeeding generations, many more subtle forms of antisemitism lingered. Having been a focal point in the Americanization of so many generations of Jewish immigrants in Brooklyn, the Dodgers continued to be a point of cultural identity for many Jewish Americans even after the team moved to Los Angeles. Regarding the markedly lesser but still considerable barriers that Jewish Americans faced, Arn Tellem, a noted sports agent in baseball and basketball, and later an executive with the Detroit Pistons, cast matters quite nimbly, and with some of same the bitterness-tinged humor of Irving Howe: Up to the time of his generation (Tellem, born in 1954), the significance of a Bar Mitzvah, he noted, had always involved its marking of the point when an American Jewish boy came fully to the realization that he had a greater chance of owning a major league baseball team than he would ever have of playing for one.[4] Within the humor of this casting lay a remaining, and still somewhat uncomfortable social gap which somehow continued to hold matters of professional athletics out of the realm of the possible for young Jewish Americans. The earlier legacies of such athletic stars as Hank Greenberg or Sid Luckman notwithstanding, in the mid–1960s, the world of sports continued to represent to many Jews that exclusive club, that school, that neighborhood, that profession, that line that could still not be crossed. Without question, the role of the Dodgers' Sandy Koufax in this transformation was monumental. For young Jewish boys, and perhaps for girls as well, the extraordinarily self-disciplined Koufax completely and utterly obliterated that line as he blew away the likes of Mickey Mantle and the New York Yankees and Harmon Killebrew and the Minnesota Twins. (As Mickey Mantle snarled in frustration to a chuckling John Roseboro after striking out against Koufax at a critical moment in Game Four of the 1963 World Series: "How the ____ do you hit that ____?") Mantle couldn't, nor could anyone.

Making Koufax's triumph completely exhilarating was the fact that he so visibly, and without a hint of posturing, combined his pitching dominance with an even more utterly unambiguous commitment to his Judaism on the day of *Yom Kippur* in 1965, when he quietly refused to pitch the first game of the World Series. No Jewish American of that generation, especially those living in environments where anti–Semitic outlooks and verbal (as well as the occasional physical) assaults remained both pronounced and unashamed, can ever forget that October day. Significant here is the point that the Dodgers' Walter Alston and owner Walter O'Malley both expressed complete support of Koufax, with statements involving not merely an absence of ambivalence, but complete respect and admiration. Their imprimatur was that much more heartening. Koufax was acknowledged to be the very best and, unlike such situations that a Joe Louis or a Hank Greenberg had faced, there was no such added verbiage as "although colored..." or "despite his religion...." It was now and forever simple. Koufax was the best, period, and much of whatever was left of the old walls came a tumblin' down.

Irving Howe, Arn Tellem, and so many others may have used humor as effective means in their responding to Judaism's sufferings and survival even against Nazism. With neither humor nor with any explicit commentary, what Koufax communicated was a response strictly through his deeds on the pitching mound, as well as at an Orthodox Synagogue in 1965. And, as his pitching was the very best, the message stood utterly alone with nothing else needed to accompany it. In American culture, expressions via baseball could, and can, thus be versions of Immanuel Kant's "categorical imperative" or Arthur Schopenhauer's "thing in itself." Just as Tocqueville's democratic Americans did not need to read Descartes, the children and grandchildren of Jewish immigrants did not need to read Kant (and they certainly did not need to read Schopenhauer). They simply watched Koufax. Here Alston and the Dodgers helped assemble the syllabus.

Branch Rickey had earlier wanted Jack Robinson to help defeat Jim Crow *not* by fighting back against it but by eclipsing it via the professional message of undeniably great ball playing. Alston echoed these sentiments and tactics for Rickey with the African American players he first managed, Don Newcombe and Roy Campanella, in New

Hampshire. Rickey's chosen tactics proved quite effective, though they certainly took a personal toll on both Robinson and Newcombe. Rickey grasped the idea that pure excellence in the field of play was the best way for elite athletes to demonstrate in favor of desired political changes, for here all good baseball fans could only perceive the content of the character of the player Rickey placed before them. (Later generations wanted to do more than present any mere demonstrations of excellence in their professions. They sought, as well, to fight back both within and beyond the spheres of their professions. Each of these approaches, philosophies, and attitudes had its own often-conflicting justifications. Debates as to the efficacy of the different outlooks will never end.) One of the points revealing the wisdom in Rickey's vision came forth in a little incident many years later. The matter concerned the Georgia-born Frederick "Dixie" Walker. Walker was one of the Dodgers, indeed the best and most famous of them, who had asked Rickey to trade him rather than play with Jackie Robinson. (They were teammates for one season.) Before he died in 1982, Walker was asked if, after the passage of so many years, he now had anything to say about Jackie Robinson and the whole integration issue. Walker's response underscored the point of baseball being, for him too, "the categorical imperative" (and, yet again, in perfect Tocqueville fashion, completely innocent as Walker was of any formal philosophical grounding): Dixie Walker simply acknowledged that Jackie Robinson was a great ballplayer, "as outstanding an athlete as I ever saw." (Walker would further note: "A person learns, and you begin to change with the times.") By the direct means of being "outstanding" at what he did, Sandy Koufax helped beat down vestiges of antisemitism in the same profoundly simple way. Throughout this sort of progress, a constant enabler, themselves also utilizing Tocqueville's Cartesianism-without-Descartes preparation and methodology, was Walter Alston and the Dodgers.[5]

Yet another example of the social change that the Dodgers represented came just after Alston retired and left matters in the hands of his protégé, Tommy Lasorda. This also involved a pitcher and his impact on another still-to-be-assimilated American minority: Mexican Americans. The pitcher was Fernando Valenzuela. In the Dodgers' move to Los Angeles, Alston and the team lost much of the previous position they held in Brooklyn, where they had played an important role in the acculturation and integration of so many residents of that diverse, working-class borough. The Dodgers served as a kind of icon, an image and a basis for a fondness and an idealization of the nation's culture, all to facilitate the gaining of a greater sense of national belonging for everyone. In the 1960s and 1970s, throughout the LA area, the team appeared to hold its greatest thrall of the region's toney, wealthier classes. This made them rich, but it also made them appear more socially staid and less vital.

Fernando Valenzuela's arrival on the Dodgers in 1980, under the wing of Tommy Lasorda, changed so much in regard to the team's links to the poorer Mexican population of Southern California, that region's counterpart of the East European immigrants and African American migrants of earlier times in Brooklyn. With a different tenor and vocabulary, of course, the legacy of what Robinson, Campanella, Newcombe, Gilliam, Wills, and Koufax had meant to earlier generations of minority fans in Brooklyn rolled forth again. The Dodgers' long-time broadcaster for Spanish-language television and radio, Jaime Jarrin, was quite explicit:

> I maintain that there is no franchise ever or anywhere that has had the impact on popular culture—or on culture at large—than the Dodgers have. Starting with Jackie Robinson..., [onto] Sandy Koufax [who] became an icon for a whole generation of assimilated Eastern Europeans, and on to Fernando Valenzuela, [Hideo] Nomo [of Japan], and right through Hyun-jin Ryu [from South Korea] and Yasiel Puig [from Castro-era Cuba]. What franchise has affected that many people in such an important way? Not to mention what the Dodgers meant to the business of sports with westward expansion.[6]

With regard to the significance of the Dodgers and Mexican Americans, baseball had certainly presented noteworthy Hispanic players in seasons prior to Fernando Valenzuela. Some, most notably Roberto Clemente, presented overt challenges to the fact that Hispanics had not been integrated into the many dimensions of baseball's institutions and, more importantly, of America's social mainstream. In one major respect, the exposed gap actually involved so much more than an overlooked population that needed to be integrated into America's game. Most American Hispanics, including Clemente, came from regions of Latin America whose players and fans could (and did) legitimately claim their own styles of ball playing to be worthy of respect and as much part of their own culture as were the styles of fans and players in the United States and Canada. Further underscoring the challenge that Roberto Clemente and Latin ball brought to the game lay the fact that generally Clemente did not speak English terribly well. This is why, although the matter arose inadvertently, it was altogether fitting that, when the Pirates defeated the Orioles in the seventh game of the 1971 World Series and Clemente, named the Series MVP, spoke to a national audience, he did so in Spanish *and* with no translation provided. The NBC TV network may have felt embarrassed not to be ready with a translator, but it was quite appropriate that the matter was left standing quite proudly on its own as it came forth. As with Sandy Koufax, where his pitching brilliantly spoke for itself, Clemente's play was, alone, more than enough, and any verbal expressions of pride which then came forth from him had no need for (and may have been better without) any wider communicability; they were poignant as they were.

This same issue of language was a challenge that faced the Dodgers when they played Fernando Valenzuela. Like Roberto Clemente, Valenzuela had little to no adequacy with the English language when he first came up. The key was that the Tommy Lasorda did speak Spanish. With the Dodgers thus providing the needed accommodativeness, it would be Valenzuela who ignited a spark among Mexicans in Southern California. Previously ambivalent about baseball in America, now by the tens of thousands, Mexican-Americans all over Southern California, as well as in parts of Nevada and Arizona, became rabid Dodgers fans. "Fernando-mania," as it was called, marked a new level of cultural assimilation that was part of baseball's, and the Dodgers', long-standing contributions to the sport and to the nation.

The inclusion of Valenzuela and his impact on California's Mexican American community, as well as subsequent appearances by Asian-born ballplayers, is appropriate here, because Walter Alston was not and never saw himself as a singular force in the political change and cultural assimilation efforts of the post–1945 Dodgers. He was, and always felt proud to be, a part of collective legacies which "marked the times" in all these turbulent years. In Darrtown he was part of a wider *Gemeinschaftlichkeit*. With the Dodgers, he was part of the leadership that started with Rickey and continued with O'Malley, Bavasi, Lasorda, Scully, Jarrin, as well as himself, one that lasted so long, contributed so much, and won so consistently.

Beyond being a major part of this collective effort, a feature that Alston uniquely contributed came from his straightforward persona that was rooted in his small-town Midwestern origins. With people like Alston, the solidity of small-town Middle America endured in the nation's culture, no matter derision from more trendy locales. The pings and dents that may have come with name-calling like "corny," "provincial," and "deplorable" may have had some impact, but they have never come close to being annihilating. As Indiana's famous poet. James Whitcomb Riley, nodded with a smile long ago: "Out here 'corny' is good." Walter Alston embodied that world, and so much that was good about it, and he did this as well or better than any figure of his day in sports. While Alston's leadership style had some detractors (whose criticisms usually involved their own projections), he won like few others ever did.

It was pleasing for some critics to project their impatience with the calm of the smoothly operating Dodgers management system by raising claims of Alston being out of touch. He was out of touch with many areas of American popular culture in the late 1960s and 1970s. That may have signaled the casual observer and reporter to project senses of diminished competence whenever the Dodgers did not win. To this same end, some fans and scribes often muttered to the effect that Bavasi and the O'Malley family protected Alston. The obvious rejoinder here would ask: if Bavasi and Walter O'Malley were so utterly competent in their work, why would they burden themselves with someone of any lesser quality as their field manager? So many successful managers have been targets of such projection. Stengel, Weaver, McCarthy—each put up with scribe and fan projections to the effect of "push-button manager" and "with that talent, I could manage the team too; anyone could." The fact was that Alston was always in touch with every aspect of the game before him, as all his opposing managers knew quite well. His outward style did not have the bombast and crowd-pleasing/arousing ways of such contemporaries as Earl Weaver or Billy Martin. Additionally, into his final season, Alston's teams would win 90 games per season. What stopped them was not any lack of fire or excess of calm. What stopped them was simple: Cincinnati, with Johnny Bench, George Foster, Joe Morgan, Pete Rose, et al. From 1970–1976, Alston's teams kept pace with and put pressure on the Big Red Machine, a team that was certainly one of the best of all time, something that can also be said of the 1972–1974 Oakland A's, who beat Alston's Dodgers in the 1974 World Series, the one year LA actually beat the powerful Reds. The combination of being un-hep with respect to the popular culture of the 1970s, be it leisure suits, disco, drugs, or divorce (Alston's life touched none of this) and coming close but not quite winning it all gave entitlement to fans who, amidst their fashions, their music, their divorces, and cocaine, criticized those who failed where they felt narcissistically entitled.

So much of the cultural context of LA in the 1970s has long vanished, and what remains may not be terribly healthy. Alston and the Dodgers exhibited a steady constancy that marked the time through so many of the years since 1945. Even as the great Yankees dynasty fell, the Dodgers remained standing. They rolled forth first with a dynasty from 1946 to 1956. Then they saw it erased. In the late 1950s into the mid–1960s, Alston helped build it back up. It was erased again, and he helped build yet another. In these same years, so many movements in America indeed rolled by like armies. Wars, desegregation, protests, riots, and so many other events appeared to be tearing the nation apart. Various movements rose. Each was noisily erased or superseded by another.

In their own ways, Alston, along with Bavasi, O'Malley, Lasorda, and Scully, each helped construct an entity (like baseball in the wider sweep of the nation's history) which, amidst all such frenzied movements, marked the time for generations of fans and became a link into the broader movements of time.

The Dodgers organization rolled on and on, calmly producing star players and maintaining a tradition of winning. Other teams came forth with star players too. When the infamous baseball reserve clause finally ended in 1975, several teams, notably the rebuilding New York Yankees, simply purchased the talent they wanted. Alston's Dodgers bought few such stars. They brought forth their finest talent in the traditional way—through their own system. Alston himself rose this way, becoming a minor league manager within Branch Rickey's vast organization. He learned his trade as he handled the chores of so many components within the team's organization. Thus he knew, intimately, how the many components operated and contributed to the general functions of the team. He could readily see any little problem well before it could fester and grow into something significant. He seldom showed frustrations, in large measure because he was always so prepared. Others, less schooled in such minutiae as Alston had learned, incurred and often grew accustomed to more chaotic modes of functioning and dysfunctioning. They could not duplicate and may not have even grasped the exceptional managerial processes at work for so long with Alston and the Dodgers. It all looked so simple and easy, but such deceptive images are so often at hand with regard to true greatness in any athletic endeavor.

When Alston retired from managing the Dodgers, the acclaim came forth from the team, from the LA community, and from all of baseball. Alston accepted the praise with his usual calm grace. Then he and Mrs. Alston quietly packed up their belongings in Los Angeles and went back to their old home in Darrtown. He provided consultation work for the Dodgers and came to some spring trainings. Generally, he stayed home, enjoying himself at his expert woodworking, shooting, and pool. To the people of Darrtown, he was the same "Smokey" they had known for decades, and life went on happily as always.

In early 1983, Alston suffered a major heart attack. He had shown heart problems as far back as 1968. Back then, a Los Angeles physiologist, Richard Hill, monitored Alston's heart during several games, using tiny hidden electrodes (the same kind NASA had developed for astronauts). Despite Alston's placid exterior, during games his heart rate would rise as much as 30 percent. Switching pitchers late in a game gave him the greatest stress (as would an occasional wild throw that found its way into the dugout).[7] At that point, on advice from Dr. Hill and others,

Alston did give up cigarettes and drinking. He would drink lightly in the off-season. From there, Alston's cardiac health appeared to steady. With the heart attack of 1983, Alston survived, but he would never fully recover. Gall bladder difficulties also arose. He was weaker, and his prior capacities at such passions as guns and pool all faded. This too he quietly accepted. Still in a weakened state from his heart attack, Alston could not go to Cooperstown that August, when he was inducted into the Baseball Hall of Fame. He certainly wanted to go, but he was more than happy to have his grandson go in his place. (The youngster was a fair ballplayer in his own right.) The poor health from the heart attack did not abate, and on October 1 of the following year, Walter Alston passed away. His final resting place, of course, was in Darrtown.

Reflecting on Alston soon after he had passed away, two people who knew him well, Dodgers broadcaster Vin Scully and *LA Times* sportswriter Jim Murray,reflected on his character. Their statements were noteworthy, ever more so because of their similarity. Scully spoke of how he always imagined Alston being the type of man "who could ride 'shotgun' on a stage[coach] through Indian territory" in the old days of the American West. Murray wrote that Alston "was a man you'd most like to be next to you in a lifeboat or a foxhole." Murray embellished: he was "one of the most unafraid men I have ever known. Almost everyone has the smell of fear, the hint of panic, the look of swallowed hysteria at one time or another. Alston's throat was always flat." As a manager, Alston's nature was such that he could never be motivated by fear of failure.

Way back in 1938, Benny Borgmann, Alston's manager on the pennant-winning club in Portsmouth, Ohio, touched on the same idea when he noted that one never heard an alibi from the young man.[8] (Aren't all alibis motivated by some sort of fear? Perhaps that is a principal aspect of alibis that makes them especially irritating for coaches and managers to endure; they denote both fear as well as a deeply ego-ingrained denial of that fear which renders improvement much more unlikely. Alibiers are always seeking reassurance for themselves; they think about themselves, not about the team, and they are usually the last to see it.) Alston never injected ego into his managerial decisions. He never needed to second-guess himself and never cared to. Alston was a man genuinely devoid of inner turmoils. He encountered none in his upbringing; problems, yes, including real economic poverty, but no genuine turmoils, much less the images that cynics ever since Sinclair Lewis have attempted to raise about small-town America. Alston was a frank man, a friendly man, one who could occasionally get angry, always with reason, but he didn't let such feelings linger, and if others could not see that, it was their shortcoming and not his. Inter-personal dramas were never part of Alston's life. Whatever the tasks to which he devoted himself, be it teaching, carpentry, hunting, skeet shooting, or pool, his focus would be singularly on the task at hand. Alston had read no such writings as those of Immanuel Kant, but to him each task in which he was engaged was its own categorical imper-ative. Naturally grasping everything thus, he would always achieve the very highest levels to which his abilities could take him—not quite to the major leagues as a player but to the very top as a manager.

When it came to his chief profession of managing a baseball team, Alston's keen ability led him to achieve like few others. He knew every aspect of the business as well as anyone who ever turned in a line-up card to an umpire. He won often and with a consistency matched by very few. He rarely spoke about anything outside the realm of baseball. Reporters noted that one did not talk with Alston about popular or clas-sic books or music or about anything philosophical. There were only dis-cussions of hit-and-run choices, the balk rule, the infield-fly rule, and the wisdom of the designated hitter. Baseball was his business, and where he practiced it, that was all he did. That was what Branch Rickey saw in Alston: a manager who had the ability to achieve the best things on a ball field, and who could provide Rickey with the necessary assistance in his wider political efforts, all without irritating, personality-based diver-sions. Mr. Rickey chose well.

Alston's 2,040 victories rank him with only nine other major league managers who won more than 2,000 games. Such a mark signifies a manager in whom players, general managers, and owners had to have felt a great level of confidence and comfort. As both Tommy Lasorda and Don Drysdale mentioned, independently of one another: "If you couldn't play for Alston, you couldn't play for anybody." Alston was able to command such confidence because of the quiet assuredness with which he went about his business. Unlike so many other coaches and managers, there was never a hidden meaning with Alston in whatever he did. He was friendly and neighborly, yet quite private, and his pri-vacy was such that no one sensed anything hidden beneath the surface. Therein lay a basis for which a few found fault with him—no perceived sense of any of proverbial "fire in the belly."

When asked to criticize Alston, a few umpires did chuckle a bit about the fact that he was never effective at arguing a call. In that regard, one could easily counter with a simple question: how many times did any argument, even if it was louder, longer, or more detailed, lead to a reversal? (With little doubt and with very few exceptions, most hon-est answers would be: "Never.") Other criticisms of Alston also focused on his quiet nature. When Alston passed in 1984, even the *New York Times* saw fit to include a bit of this criticism in their obituary. But such criticisms tended to involve projections of the personalities of the critics more than revealing anything about Alston himself.[9] He was actually as passionate about winning as anyone, and as devoted as any to the honing of all the managerial, strategic, and tactical details necessary for consistent winning. He was the same at skeet shooting, at pool, carpentry, the teaching of science and industrial arts, and with anything else he did.

Along with Alston's 2,040 victories that ranks him high (#9) on the list of winningest managers, his won/loss percentage of .558 ranks third (behind only Joe McCarthy and John McGraw) among those with 2,000 victories. Alston was a winner virtually every year he managed. Alston, McCarthy, and McGraw achieved greatness with some common traits—keen eyes for talent, coolness under the heat of fierce competition, effective employment of game tactics, handling and motivating players and coaches. Otherwise, as with great managers in any field, each worked with a tonality that was a natural extension of his personality. Good managers always have to be truly who they are; anything else is an artifice whose presence invariably causes discomfort and muddies the clarity of what is to be executed in the tasks at hand. McGraw was always pugnacious and fiery. McCarthy was outwardly phlegmatic and unobtrusive, but, beneath such an exterior, he was always completely in charge. Alston displayed a similar outward calm, one which did not quite fit some people's senses of what was appropriate for the tenor of his time. But as with McCarthy, Alston's calm also belied an intensity and desire for steady winning and excellence. Alston excelled specially at working within a leadership team, first with Branch Rickey, and from there with Buzzie Bavasi and both Walter and Peter O'Malley, the elder and younger. The smoothness of operation that came forth brought a consistency of quality seldom matched.

As in every sport, the difference between winning and second place can often be quite slim. Consistently losing by wide margins readily promotes an examining of ways one could improve. Winning often, and coming close just as often, can reveal not so much what needs to be improved, but rather how a few matters of simple luck going one way or the other can mark the difference. In golf, for example, any student of the game's history is in awe of Jack Nicklaus's mark of 18 major tournament victories. Perhaps even more awesome is that Nicklaus finished second in major championships 19 other times, with the margin of difference often being but a stroke or two (and on several occasions that one stroke being a clear matter of pure luck going the way of the winner). Not just winning so often, but being in full contention that many other times is a striking mark of the man's greatness. Alston's Dodgers teams finished first eight times, and they came in second eight times, including several seasons where they fell just shy of the marks set by the great Cincinnati Reds teams of the 1970s; no disgrace there certainly. (Joe McCarthy similarly won nine pennants and seven times came in a close second.) With the margin between winning and second place often so close, anyone, from Alston to McCarthy to Nicklaus, who wins so often and comes close just as often, sets quite a standard for his life's work. In his own life, Alston always enjoyed good company. For his work in baseball, he earned such a place for himself in posterity.

Chapter Notes

Introduction

1. Fred Hutchinson, quoted in *The Sporting* News, July 16, 1966, 6; September 14, 1963, 6, Clippings File, National Baseball Hall of Fame and Museum, Cooperstown, NY.

2. Walter Alston, with Jack Tobin, *A Year at a Time* (New York: Word Books, 1976), *passim.*

3. *New York Times*, October 2, 1984, 29.

4. *The Sporting News*, July 27, 1983; *USA Today*, October 2, 1984, section C, 1–2, Clippings File, National Baseball Hall of Fame and Museum, Cooperstown, NY.

5. Alexis de Tocqueville, *Democracy in America*, Book Two, Chapter One, 1; https://www.marxists.org/reference/archive/de-tocqueville/democracy-america/ch20.htm.

Chapter 1

1. Alexis de Tocqueville, *Democracy in America*, Volume II, Henry Reeve, trans. (Auckland, NZ: The Floating Press, 2009), *passim;* David McCullough, *The Pioneers: The Heroic Story of the Settlers Who Brought the American Ideal West* (New York: Simon and Schuster, 2019), *passim.*

2. *Hamilton Evening Journal*, August 7, 1925, 14; August 14, 1925, 11; September 2, 1930, 13; April 3, 1931, 12; October 7, 1931, 13; *Hamilton Daily News*, October 9, 1930, 7; October 14, 1931, 10; May 11, 1933, 16.

3. Walter Alston, with Jack Tobin, *A Year at a Time* (New York: Word Books, 1976), 7.

4. The literature on the relevant social history backdrop to pre–Civil War reforms in such states as Ohio is vast; for purposes of discussing its significance in regard to the background of Walter Alston, a good summary of the patterns of pre–Civil War political divisions between conservatives and reformers in Midwestern states can be found in: James M. McPherson and James K. Hogue, *Ordeal By Fire: The Civil War and Reconstruction*, Fourth Edition. (New York: McGraw Hill, 2009), 23–24, 101; On the 1860 election's voting statistics in Ohio: http://78ohio.org/1860-presidential-election/.

5. The resistance in the North to many aspects of Republican reform efforts in the Civil War and Reconstruction era is also an area in which there has been much scholarship. For purposes regarding the pertinent background of Walter Alston, the distinguished scholar David Herbert Donald outlined succinctly, for general audiences and for students, the theme of what he termed "Racism as a Limit to Change." While explaining Southern resistance to changes in the status of the former slaves after the Civil War, and the reestablishment of the power of the White Southern ruling classes, the acquiescence of most of the Northern states to the South's construction of Jim Crow was highly significant. Illustrating this, Professor Donald pointed to Northern states, like Ohio, themselves voting down resolutions to give African Americans equal rights in suffrage; Donald further quoted newspapers specifically in Cleveland, fervently applauding President Andrew Johnson's vetoes of Civil Rights and Freedmen's Bureau Bills soon after

the Civil War. See Bernard Bailyn. Dallek, Davis, Donald, Thomas, and Wood, *The Great Republic: A History of the American People*, 4th ed. (Lexington, MA: D.C. Heath, 1992), Part 4, Chapter 20, 27–36.

6. Regarding this phenomenon of "capitulation," see C. Vann Woodward, *The Strange Career of Jim Crow* (New York: Oxford University Press, [1955] 2002, 67.

7. Fred Hutchinson, quoted in *The Sporting News*, July 16, 1966, 6, Clippings File, National Baseball Hall of Fame and Museum, Cooperstown, NY.

8. *Hamilton Evening Journal*, August 24, 1925, 12; August 9, 1928, 16; August 28, 1928, 16; *Hamilton Daily News*, August 13, 1928, 2.

9. Alston, *A Year at a Time*, 16, 26; Walter Alston and Sy Burick, *Alston and the Dodgers* (Garden City, NY: Doubleday, 1966), 3.

10. Alston, *A Year at a Time*, 14–15; Alston and Burick, *Alston and the Dodgers*, 22–23; *Los Angeles Herald-Examiner*, October 1, 1964; Bill Gleason column, October 8, 1966, Clippings File, Cooperstown.

11. *Hamilton Evening Journal*, April 20, 1929, 23.

12. *Hamilton Evening Journal*, October 22, 1926, 17; January 16, 1928, 13; *Hamilton Daily News*, March 4, 1927, 2; March 12, 1927, 24; November 14, 1927, 11; May 8, 1929, 11.

13. *Hamilton Evening Journal*, February 12, 1929, 7; February 25, 1929, 8.

14. *Hamilton Evening Journal*, March 17, 1938, 12; Alston and Burick, *Alston and the Dodgers*, 21.

15. *Hamilton Daily News*, September 27, 1929, 21.

16. Alston, *A Year at a Time*, 8–9; Alston and Burick, *Alston and the Dodgers*, 25–27.

17. *Hamilton Evening Journal*, January 6, 1933, 10; *Hamilton Daily News*, December 8, 1933, 15; April 13, 1934, 14; December 11, 1934, 2; January 11 1935, 14; *Sandusky Star Journal*, March 14, 1933, 7; January 4, 1935, 16; *Coshocton Tribune*, January 4, 1935, 8; *Piqua Daily Call*, January 8, 1934, 6; *The Sporting News*, September 14, 1963, 6.

18. Alston, *A Year at a Time*, 28–30.

19. *Ibid.*; *Cincinnati Enquirer*, April 28, 1960, 17.

20. *Hamilton Daily News*, December 31, 1930, 7.

21. *Hamilton Daily News*, June 12, 1934, 8; June 19, 1934, 8; August 24, 1934, 14; September 4, 1934, 8; Walter Alston and Sy Burick, *Alston and the Dodgers* (Garden City, NY: Doubleday, 1966), 16.

Chapter 2

1. Alston, *A Year at a Time*, 36–38; Alston and Burick, *Alston and the Dodgers*, 27.

2. Alston, *A Year at a Time*, 38; Alston and Burick, *Alston and the Dodgers*, 33.

3. *Greenwood* [Mississippi] *Daily Democrat-Times*, June 18, 1935, 3; July 4, 1; July 8, 3; July 9, 3; July 30, 3; July 31, 3; August 1; https://www.baseball-reference.com/register/team.cgi?id=be0f739e.

4. *Zanesville Times Recorder*, September 2, 1936, 10.

5. *Charleston Daily Mail*, May 28, 1936, 69; *Charleston Gazette*, May 28, 1936, 5, 17; *Beckley Post Herald*, June 5, 1936, 8; July 24, 8; July 26, 8; Alston and Burick, *Alston and the Dodgers*, 31, 34.

6. *Charleston Gazette*, June 1, 1936, 10; June 3, 13; July 1, 10; July 30, 14; August 1, 6; August 2, 14; *Beckley Post Herald*, May 28, 1936, 8; *Charleston Daily Mail*, November 29, 1936, 13.

7. *Bluefield Daily Telegraph*, September 2, 1936, 8; *Monitor Index and Democrat* (Moberly, MO), September 19, 1936, 5; *Hamilton Daily News*, September 11, 1936, 15.

8. Alston, *A Year at a Time*, 49–50; Alston and Burick, *Alston and the Dodgers*, 27–30; https://www.baseball-reference.com/players/g/guttedo01.shtml.

9. Alston, *A Year at a Time*, 49–51; Alston and Burick, *Alston and the Dodgers*, 29.

10. Cubs–Cardinals Game., September 27, 1936; http://www.baseball-almanac.com/box-scores/boxscore.php?boxid=193609270SLN; Alston and Burick, *Alston and the Dodgers*, 30.

11. *Hamilton Daily News*, March 4, 1937, 16.

12. Alston and Burick, *Alston and the Dodgers*, 31.

13. *Syracuse Herald*, April 27, 1937,

16; April 9, 29; https://www.baseball-reference.com/register/team.cgi?id=5daf512d.

14. *Corpus Christi Times*, July 7, 1937, 9; *Abilene Reporter News*, July 7, 1937, 6; *Galveston Daily News*, July 13, 1937, 6; https://www.baseball-reference.com/register/team.cgi?id=25193e3b.

15. *Galveston Daily News*, October 3, 1937, 16; *Abilene Reporter News*, July 9, 1937, 2.

16. *Portsmouth Times*, March 16, 1938, 8; April 19, 1938, 8.

17. *Coshocton Tribune*, September 21, 1938, 7; September 19, 2; *Massillon Evening Independent*, September 21, 1938, 9; *Portsmouth Times*, September 27, 1938, 2; December 7, 10.

18. *Portsmouth Times*, May 13, 1938, 20; May 25, 12; May 26, 16; August 13, 5; August 23, 9; September 25, 20; October 9, 16; *The Sporting News*, October 25, 1965; Clippings File, Cooperstown.

19. *Portsmouth Times*, May 3, 1948, 14.

20. *Portsmouth Times*, September 25, 1938, 21; April 11, 1939, 8, July 11, 8.

21. *Thomasville (GA) Times Enterprise*, July 21, 1939, 6; *Portsmouth Times*, May 23, 1939, 8; June 16, 19; July 11, 8, December 10, 10.

22. *Porstmouth Times* May 26, 1940, 22; June 12, 11; June 24, 1; June 25, 16; June 29, 7, June 30, 7, 19; July 12, 9; *Dayton Daily News*, June 30, 1940, 19; *Zanesville Times Signal*, July 13, 1940, 5; August 10, 7; *Massillon Evening Independent*, August 10, 1940, 5; *Lima News*, June 26, 1940, 13; *Mansfield News Journal*, June 26, 3.

23. *Portsmouth Times*, June 16, 1940, 19; *Massillon Evening Independent*, July 19, 1940, 17; Clippings File, Cooperstown.

24. *Portsmouth Times*, July 13, 1940, 9; July 28, 20; August 9, 12; August 21, 10; September 5, 16; *Lima News*, June 26, 1940, 13; *Mansfield News Journal*, June 26, 1940, 3; *Massillon Evening Independent*, April 2, 1941, 11; July 24, 16; *Zanesville Times Signal*, July 13, 1940, 7; April 2, 1941, 9; Alston, *A Year at a Time*, 23.

25. *Portsmouth Times*, August 17, 1940, 5; September 7, 7; September 8, 21.

26. Letters from Robert Ireland to Elmer Daily and from Daily to Ireland, March 30, 1941, and April 10, 1941, Clippings File, Cooperstown.

27. *The Sporting News*, February 14, 1970, 32.

28. *Zanesville Times Signal*, May 20, 1941, 10; June 15, 9; *Portsmouth Times*, April 2, 1941, 10; June 20, 17; July 12, 7; August 29, 17; September 4, 17; Alston, *A Year at a Time*, 58.

29. *Zanesville Times Recorder*, February 28, 1942, 8; May 2, 8; May 25, 6; June 7, 7; August 14, 12; August 15, 8; *Zanesville Signal*, March 27, 1942, 1; April 21, 7; May 14, 14; July 8, 5; *Massillon Evening Independent*, May 1, 1942, 16; *Hamilton Daily News Journal*, May 4, 1942, 11; *Newark Advocate*, May 1, 1942, 11; *Portsmouth Times*, September 2, 1942, 8; *Rochester Democrat and Chronicle*, April 18, 1943, 1C; https://www.baseball-reference.com/register/league.cgi?id=bb78f699; https://www.baseball-reference.com/register/team.cgi?id=1fe3a636.

30. Alston, *A Year at a Time*, 58.

31. *Buffalo Evening News*, February 4, 1944, 28.

32. *Hamilton Daily News Journal*, March 16, 1943, 6; April 20, 11; *Rochester Democrat and Chronicle*, March 25, 1943, 22; March 27, 14; March 29, 20; April 1, 24; April 13, 21; April 18, 1C; Richard Goldstein, *Spartan Seasons: How Baseball Survived the Second World War* (New York: MacMillan, 1980), passim.

33. *Syracuse Herald Journal*, May 23, 1943, 36; May 30, 26; June 6, 43; June 20, 34; June 23, 17; June 27, 30; June 29, 30; *Rochester Democrat and Chronicle*, May 6, 1943, 22; May 24, 18; June 6, 1C; July 27, 16; https://www.baseball-reference.com/register/team.cgi?id=577cc23c.

34. https://www.baseball-reference.com/register/league.cgi?id=3e5b2fa5.

35. *Rochester Democrat and Chronicle*, April 2, 1944, 1C; May 18, 24; May 20, 20; May 23, 18; *Syracuse Herald Journal*, September 16, 1944, 9; https://www.baseball-reference.com/register/team.cgi?id=577cc23c; https://www.baseball-reference.com/register/league.cgi?id=e2e5d15f.

36. *Trenton Evening Times*, July 27, 1944, 20; *Lebanon [PA] Daily News*, July 29, 1944, 2; *Frederick [MD] News Post*, August 4, 1944, 9; Alston, *A Year at a Time*, 59–60; Alston and Burick, *Alston and the Dodgers*, 33–5.

37. *Trenton Evening Times*, July 26, 1944, 10; July 28, 16.

38. *Trenton Evening Times*, June 19, 1944, 12; July 27, 20; August 1, 1944, 10; August 2, 10; August 4, 18.

39. *Trenton Evening Times*, August 2, 1944, 10; August 17, 18; August 24, 21; August 28, 12; August 30, 11; August 31, 20; September 13, 12; Alston and Burick, *Alston and the Dodgers*, 36.

40. *Trenton Evening Times*, April 3, 1945, 12; April 5, 20; April 9, 12; April 6, 20; April 10, 12; April 11, 16.

41. *Trenton Evening Times*, April 13, 1945, 20; April 16, 1.

42. *Trenton Evening Times*, August 1, 1945, 14; September 13, 20; September 14, 19; *Lebanon Daily News*, June 14, 1945, 6; September 7, 19; *Gettysburg Times*, August 4, 1945, 3; *Hagerstown* (MD) *Morning Herald*, December 22, 1945, 10; https://www.baseball-reference.com/register/team.cgi?id=0151bbe0; https://www.baseball-reference.com/register/team.cgi?id=814aee9c.

43. *Hopewell* (NJ) *Herald*, June 28, 1944, 3.

44. Alston, *A Year at a Time*, 60–61.

45. *Trenton Evening Times*, August 17, 1945, 24.

46. Alston, Walter, with Si Burick, *Alston and the Dodgers* (Garden City, NY: Doubleday, 1966), 16.

Chapter 3

1. *Nashua Telegraph*, April 9, 1946, 12; *Zanesville* [OH] *Signal*, April 12, 1946, 9.

2. *Providence Journal*, April 5, 1946, 13.

3. *Manchester Union-Leader*, April 12, 1946, 18.

4. *Portland Press-Herald*, April 19, 1946, 26; April 27, 11.

5. Roy Campanella, *It's Good to Be Alive* (Boston: Little, Brown, 1959), 118–119.

6. Harold Rosenthal, "He Made a Difference for the Dodgers," *Saturday Evening Post*, April 8, 1950; Michael Madden, "Nashua, N.H., Was Safe Haven," *Boston Globe*, March 28, 1997; Jules Tygiel, *Baseball's Great Experiment: Jackie Robinson and His Legacy* (New York: Oxford University Press, 1983), 146; Charlie Bevis,

The New England League: A Baseball History, 1885–1949 (Jefferson, NC: McFarland, 2008), 256–261.

7. Bevis, *The New England League*, 259–63.

8. Alston, *A Year at a Time*, 62; Alston and Burick, *Alston and the Dodgers*, 45–49.

9. Kenneth T. Jackson, *The Ku Klux Klan in the City, 1915–1930* (Chicago: Ivan R. Dee, 1992); Robert Alan Goldberg, *Hooded Empire: The Ku Klux Klan in Colorado* (Champaign: University of Illinois Press, 1982); William Rawlings, *The Second Coming of the Invisible Empire: The Ku Klux Klan of the 1920s* (Macon, GA: Mercer University Press, 2016) John Craig, *The Ku Klux Klan in Western Pennsylvania, 1921–1928* (Bethlehem, PA: Lehigh University Press, 2016), *passim*.

10. Alston and Burick, *Alston and the Dodgers*, 47–8.

11. *St. Louis Post-Dispatch*, March 11, 1983, Clippings File, Cooperstown.

12. Frank Graham, *New York Journal-American*, quoted in *Montreal Gazette*, March 29, 1950, 18; Alston, *A Year at a Time*, 62.

13. *The Sporting News*, February 14, 1970, 32.

14. *Nashua Telegraph*, November 13, 1946, 10; Alston, *A Year at a Time*, 63.

15. *Nashua Telegraph*, September 3, 1946, 11; September 4, 9; February 3, 1947, 9; November 6, 1950, 10.

16. *Nashua Telegraph*, September 4, 1946, 9; September 9, 9; October 3, 18; December 30, 11; September 5, 1947, 12; December 27, 1947, 7; April 9, 1947, 12; *Daily Kennebec Journal* (Augusta, ME), July 13, 1946, 3; *Syracuse Herald Journal*, August 8, 1950, 21; Alston, *A Year at a Time*, 64.

17. Alston, *A Year at a Time*, 79–80.

18. *Nashua Telegraph*, January 31, 1947, 12.

19. *Nashua Telegraph*, September 4, 1946, 9; December 30, 11; February 8, 1950, 10.

Chapter 4

1. https://www.baseball-reference.com/register/team.cgi?id=db3e78bb.

2. "The Legacy of Al Campanis," http://

www.espn.com/espn/otl/story/_/id/7751398/how-al-campanis-controversial-racial-remarks-cost-career-highlighted-mlb-hiring-practices.

3. *Pueblo Chieftan*, April 9, 1947, 15.

4. *Pueblo Chieftan and Saturday Star-Journal*, September 23, 1978, 5.

5. *Pueblo Chieftan*, February 23, 1947, 10; March 2, 13; March 21, 13; March 30, 13; April 9, 15; *Hamilton* [OH] *Daily News Journal*, April 29, 1947, 10; *Nashua Telegraph*, February 20, 1947, 15; April 7, 8; *Council Bluffs* [IA] *Nonpareil*, September 22, 1947, 7; *Atlantic* [IA] *News Telegraph*, September 22, 1947, 6; *Waterloo* [IA] *Daily Courier*, September 22, 1947, 13; *Beatrice* [NE] *Daily Sun*, September 22, 1947, 6; https://www.baseball-reference.com/register/team.cgi?id=adde2b1f.

6. *Nashua Telegraph*, December 27, 1947, 7.

7. Alston, *A Year at a Time*, 7, 64.

8. *St. Paul Dispatch*, March 20, 1948, 8; April 15, 29.

9. *St. Paul Dispatch* April 21, 1948, 35; April 26, 13; April 27, 22.

10. *St. Paul Dispatch*, May 18, 1948, 23; June 2, 28; June 10, 35; https://www.baseball-reference.com/register/player.fcgi?id=bankhe001dan.

11. *St. Paul Dispatch*, May 6, 1948, 36.

12. *St. Paul Dispatch*, May 5, 1948, 31; *Wisconsin State Journal*, May 6, 1948, 26.

13. *St. Paul Dispatch*, June 5, 1948, 6, June 21, 14; July 7, 25; August 5, 30; August 14, 7.

14. *Kokomo* [IN] *Tribune* July 2, 1948, 8; *Brainerd* [MN] *Daily Dispatch*, October 7, 1948, 16; *Atchison* [KS] *Daily Globe*, October 7, 1948, 8; *Hamilton* [OH] *Daily News Journal*, October 9, 1948, 10; *St. Paul Dispatch*, August 16, 1948, 13.

15. *St. Paul Dispatch*, August 19, 1948, 34.

16. *St. Paul Dispatch*, September 9, 1948, 35; September 20, 16; September 21, 20; October 5, 25; October 7, 35.

17. *St. Paul Dispatch*, October 5, 1948, 24.

18. *Hamilton* [OH] *Daily News Journal*, January 27, 1949, 16; September 23, 15.

19. Alston, *A Year at a Time*, 41, 52, 56.

20. *St. Paul Dispatch*, July 28, 1949, 29; September 12, 19; *Terre Haute Star*, September 13, 1949, 10; *La Crosse Tribune*, September 13, 1949, 14; *Wisconsin Rapids Daily Tribune*, September 13, 1949, 7; *Sheboygan Press*, September 13, 1949, 18; *Rhinelander Daily News*, September 13, 1949, 6.

21. *Terre Haute Star*, April 15, 1949, 29; *Sheboygan Press*, April 15, 1949, 14; *Waukesha Daily Freeman*, April 15, 1949, 11.

22. Alston, *A Year at a Time*, 82.

23. *St. Paul Dispatch*, March 28, 1949, 16; March 29, 20; March 31, 36; April 6, 36; April 18, 15; April 20, 39; May 9, 16; May 10, 26; May 11, 35; June 8, 29; August 18, 28; https://www.baseball-reference.com/register/team.cgi?id=29b8bafa.

24. *St. Paul Dispatch*, June 10, 1949, 23; July 6, 28; July 18, 14.

25. See Rex Hamann, *The Millers and the Saints: Baseball Championships of the Twin Cities Rivals, 1903–1955* (Jefferson, NC: McFarland, 2014), *passim*.

26. *Hamilton Daily News Journal*, September 9, 1949, 20.

27. *Syracuse Herald Journal*, March 10, 1950, 42.

28. *Montreal Gazette*, March 8, 1950, 16.

29. *New York Daily News*, March 24, 1950, quoted in advance in the *Montreal Gazette*, March 22, 1950, 8.

30. Quoted in *Syracuse Herald Journal*, March 10, 1950, 42; *Montreal Gazette*, March 10, 1950, 18.

31. *Montreal Gazette*, March 8, 1950, 16.

32. *La Presse* [Montreal], March 7, 1950, 33.

33. *Montreal Gazette*, March 24, 1950, 18; March 25, 8.

34. *La Presse* [Montreal], April 24, 1950, 35; May 2, 39; *Montreal Gazette*, April 21, 1950, 18.

35. *La Presse*, May 5, 1950, 38; *Montreal Gazette*, April 29, 1950, 10.

36. *Montreal Gazette*, March 29, 1950, 18; March 31, 30; April 17, 18; May 8, 20–21; September 20, 17; Arthur Mann, *Saturday Evening Post*, May 1, 1950.

37. *Montreal Gazette*, August 21, 1950, 16.

38. *Montreal Gazette*, May 20, 1950, 13; June 26, 18.

39. *Montreal Gazette*, June 12, 1950, 18; June 17, 8; August 8, 14.

40. *Montreal Gazette*, June 23, 1950, 16.

41. *La Presse*, September 12, 1950, 38; *Montreal Gazette*, September 15, 1950, 18; September 16, 9; Sepember. 18, 18; September 19, 17; September 20, 17.

42. *Montreal Gazette*, September 2, 1950, 18.

43. *Syracuse Post Standard*, May 4, 1950, 47; *Norwich* [CT] *Sun*, May 4, 1950, 6.

44. *Montreal Gazette*, July 7, 1951, 16; *Hamilton Daily News Journal*, September 5, 1951, 12; *Syracuse Post-Standard*, September 30, 1952, 24.

45. *New York Times*, April 10, 1947, 1, 31–32; Stanley Coben, *Dodgers! The First 100 Years* (New York: Birch Lane Press, 1990), 83; Alan H. Levy, *Joe McCarthy: Architect of the Yankee Dynasty* (Jefferson, NC: McFarland), 321–322.

46. *Syracuse Post-Standard*, August 13, 1951, 19; August 28, 12.

47. *Hamilton Daily News Journal*, September 15, 1951, 3; September 20, 28; September 22, 6.

48. *New York Times*, July 14, 1955, Clippings File, Cooperstown.

49. *Syracuse Post-Standard*, July 5, 1951, 47; July 10, 20; May 13, 1953, 14; https://www.baseball-reference.com/register/team.cgi?id=2bd95206.

50. Alston, *Alston and the Dodgers*, 159; https://www.baseball-reference.com/players/r/roepr01.shtml.

Chapter 5

1. Alston, *A Year at a Time*, 52.

2. *Ibid.*, 52–53.

3. *The Sporting News*, February 14, 1970, 32.

4. *Ibid.*, July 1, 1972, 40.

5. See, for example, Sam Hays, *Response to Industrialism, 1885–1914* (Chicago: University of Chicago Press, 1957), 109.

6. Alston and Burick, *Alston and the Dodgers*, 13.

7. Wells Twombly, "Forever Alston," *San Francisco Examiner*, November 5, 1971, Clippings File, Cooperstown.

8. *New York Times*, undated article from 1953, Clippings File, Cooperstown.

9. Alston and Burick, *Alston and the Dodgers*, 14.

10. *Ibid.*, 13–15; *New York Times*,

November 24, 1953, Clippings File, Cooperstown.

11. Alston and Burick, *Alston and the Dodgers*, 15–16.

12. *Ibid.*, 19; *New York Times*, Alston obituary, October 2, 1984; *New York Times*, November 24, 1953, Clippings File, Cooperstown.

13. O'Malley's words made it into the papers, major and minor, at the end of 1953: *Oneonta* [NY] *Star*, December 30, 1953, 12.

Chapter 6

1. Alston and Burick, *Alston and the Dodgers*, 60–61; Alston, *A Year at a Time*, 106–7.

2. *New York Times*, undated article from 1953, Clippings File, Cooperstown.

3. *The Sporting News*, November 2, 1963, 8.

4. *New York Times*, undated article from 1953, Clippings File, Cooperstown.

5. Alston and Burick, *Alston and the Dodgers*, 41; Mal Mallete, "Boss Man of the Bums," 1957, Clippings File, Cooperstown.

6. *Ibid.*, 42–43.

7. *Ibid.*, 43; Alston, *A Year at a Time*, 105–6; Bill James, *The Bill James Guide to Baseball Managers from 1870 to Today* (New York: Scribner, 1997), 225; Jane Leavy, *Sandy Koufax: A Lefty's Legacy* (New York: Harper Collins Publishers, 2002), 82–87; David Falkner, *Great Time Coming: The Life of Jackie Robinson from Baseball to Birmingham.* (New York: Simon and Schuster), 216–228; Rudy Marzano, *The Last Years of the Brooklyn Dodgers: A History, 1950–1957* (Jefferson, NC: McFarland, 2008); *San Francisco Examiner*, August 26, 1964, 56; Clippings File, Cooperstown.

8. Alston and Burick, *Alston and the Dodgers*, 62; https://www.baseball-reference.com/teams/BRO/1954.shtml.

9. Alston, *A Year at a Time*, 108–9; https://www.baseball-reference.com/leagues/NL/1954.shtml; https://www.baseball-reference.com/teams/BRO/1954.shtml.

10. Quoted in Gene Schoor, *The Leo Durocher Story* (New York: Julian Messner, 1955), 174.

11. Alston and Burick, *Alston and the Dodgers*, 63.
12. Alston, *A Year at a Time*, 109–10; https://www.baseball-reference.com/leagues/NL/1955.shtml; https://www.baseball-reference.com/teams/BRO/1955.shtml.
13. Alston, *A Year at a Time*, 111; "Jackie Robinson Steals Home," Youtube video: https://www.youtube.com/watch?v=6XY-XshGhMU; https://www2.bing.com/videos/search?q=1955+world+series+&&view=detail&mid=7D728A3D96E8710FA78B7D728A3D96E8710FA78B&&FORM=VRDGAR; https://www2.bing.com/videos/search?q=1955+world+series+game+7+entire+game+on+video&&view=detail&mid=E3FB6C99EA91049933DEE3FB6C99EA91049933DE&&FORM=VRDGAR.
14. Alston, *A Year at a Time*, 112–13; "1955 Brooklyn Dodgers Talk about World Series against Yankees," Youtube video: https://www.youtube.com/watch?v=KdR1kcMOBSs.
15. *Ibid.*, 113–115; https://www2.bing.com/videos/search?q=1955+world+series+game+7+entire+game+on+video&&view=detail&mid=E3FB6C99EA91049933DEE3FB6C99EA91049933DE&&FORM=VRDGAR.
16. Alston, *A Year at a Time*, 115; "1955 Brooklyn Dodgers manager Walter Alston comments on team's baseball season," Youtube video: https://www.youtube.com/watch?v=HTxE7KTS5S0.
17. Alston, *A Year at a Time*, 115.
18. Alston, *A Year at a Time*, 115–16; "Walter Alston wins Winchester Outdoorsman of the Year," Youtube video, February 1, 1956: https://www.youtube.com/watch?v=DIPjqmjc4d0.

Chapter 7

1. Alston and Burick, *Alston and the Dodgers*, 89.
2. Alston, *A Year at a Time*, 118–20.
3. https://www.baseball-reference.com/teams/BRO/1956.shtml.
4. *New York Times*, October 11, 1956, 67.
5. Murray Kempton, "Sal Maglie ... A Gracious Man," *New York Post*, October 9, 1956; see also David Halberstam, ed., *The Best American Sports Writing of the Century* (Boston: Houghton Mifflin, 1999), 170–73; https://www.baseball-reference.com/boxes/NYA/NYA195610080.shtml; https://www.baseball-reference.com/boxes/BRO/BRO195610090.shtml; https://www.baseball-reference.com/boxes/BRO/BRO195610100.shtml.
6. Alston, *A Year at a Time*, 123; https://www.baseball-reference.com/boxes/BRO/BRO195610100.shtml.
7. *Washington Post*, February 27, 1977; *New York Times*, November 6, 1975; *Los Angeles Times*, February 6, 1994.
8. Alston, *A Year at a Time*, 124.
9. Alston and Burick, *Alston and the Dodgers*, 100; Alston, *A Year at a Time*, 127; Dick Young, "Obit on the Dodgers," *New York Daily News*, October 2, 1957; see also David Halberstam, ed., *The Best American Sports Writing of the Century* (Boston: Houghton Mifflin, 1999), 174–77.
10. Alston and Burick, *Alston and the Dodgers*, 44.
11. Alston, *A Year at a Time*, 125–126.
12. Alston and Burick, *Alston and the Dodgers*, 96–97; Alston, *A Year at a Time*, 126–127; https://www.baseball-reference.com/leagues/NL/1957.shtml.

Chapter 8

1. Alston, *A Year at a Time*, 124, 126, 142.
2. Alston and Burick, *Alston and the Dodgers*, 49, 99; Alston, *A Year at a Time*, 127–128, 132–133.
3. Alston, *A Year at a Time*, 127.
4. https://www2.bing.com/images/search?view=detailV2&ccid=CmdcBY0A&id=F652B0DBA04E969D84E42880660D1B7B74F7D40A&thid=OIP.CmdcBY0AIPfdaS0TzhUIawHaFp&mediaurl=http%3A%2F%2Fwww.andrewclem.com%2FBaseball%2FDiag%2FMemorialColiseum1958.gif&exph=480&expw=630&q=LA+Coliseum+Baseball+Dimensions+Field&simid=608002655217650732&ajaxhist=0.
5. Alston, *A Year at a Time*, 129.
6. *Ibid.*
7. Philip J. Lowry, "Ballparks," chapter 5; John Thorn and Pete Palmer, eds., *Total Baseball*, 2d ed. (New York: Warner Books), 290.

8. Alston, *A Year at a Time*, 96.

9. Alston and Burick, *Alston and the Dodgers*, 96, 100–101; Alston, *A Year at a Time*, 129.

10. Alston, *A Year at a Time*, 128.

11. https://www.baseball-reference.com/players/m/moonwa01.shtml.

12. Alston, *A Year at a Time*, 141.

13. Alston and Burick, *Alston and the Dodgers*, 102–105; Alston, *A Year at a Time*, 131–133, 135–136; https://www.baseball-reference.com/teams/LAD/1959.shtml.

14. Alston, *A Year at a Time*, 137–38; http://www.baseball-almanac.com/ws/yr1959ws.shtml.

15. Alston, *A Year at a Time*, 141.

16. *Ibid.*, 141; https://www.baseball-reference.com/postseason/1959_WS.shtml.

17. Quoted in *The Sporting News*, September 14, 1963, 6.

Chapter 9

1. http://www.baseball-almanac.com/asgmenu.shtml.

2. https://www.azquotes.com/author/23490-Walter_Alston; http://www.baseball reference.com/awards/hof.shtml.

3. https://www.baseball-reference.com/teams/LAD/1960-schedule-scores.shtml.

4. https://www.baseball-reference.com/teams/LAD/1961-schedule-scores.shtml.

5. Alston and Burick, *Alston and the Dodgers*, 117.

6. Walter Bingham, "No Pennant for Platoons of Dodgers: A Season of Struggling to Win with Percentage Baseball is Doomed When the Best Plans of Walter Alston Go Awry," *Sports Illustrated*, September 18, 1961; https://www.si.com/vault/1961/09/18/617165/no-pennant-for-platoons-of-dodgers.; *Alston and the Dodgers*, 117–118, 122.

7. *Alston and the Dodgers*, 152, 156–157.

8. https://www.mayoclinic.org/diseases-conditions/raynauds-disease/symptoms-causes/syc-20363571.

9. http://www.baseball-almanac.com/teamstats/schedule.php?y=1962&t=LAN.

10. Alston, *A Year at a Time*, 166–167; *Alston and the Dodgers*, 116.

11. *Ibid.*

12. http://baseballeras.blogspot.com/2015/06/leodurocherandthe1962 Dodgers.html; Gerald Eskenazi, *The Lip: A Biography of Leo Duroche*, (New York: William Morrow, 1993, 289–291; Alston, *Alston and the Dodgers*, 57.

13. https://www.baseball-reference.com/boxes/LAN/LAN196210030.shtml.

14. *Alston and the Dodgers*, 117; Alston, *A Year at a Time*, 167.

15. Gerald Eskenazi, *The Lip*, 290–293.

16. This statement by G. B. Shaw gained fame when it was quoted in Ken Burns' famous documentary *Baseball*: "Inning Two: 'Something Like War (1900–1910).'" https://www.youtube.com/watch?v=J3o4EWGVbpY (30:00 mark); the circumstances for Mr. Shaw coming to make such a statement involved the Chicago White Sox and John McGraw's New York Giants steaming across the Atlantic and playing a series of post-season exhibition games in Great Britain in October of 1924. Shaw attended one game, held in London, and he wrote an article about it for the *London Evening Standard*. (It is the same article that yielded Shaw's famous comparison of baseball and cricket: "Baseball has the great advantage over cricket of being sooner ended.") Mr. Shaw's article, "Baseball Is a Mad Game," was later reprinted in *Sports Illustrated*, September 3, 1962, 65.

17. *Ibid.*, 159.

18. Alston, *A Year at a Time*, 164–165; *Alston and the Dodgers*, 116.

19. Quoted in James, *Bill James Guide to Baseball Managers, From 1870 to Today* (New York: Scribner's, 1997), 227.

20. Alston, *Alston and the Dodgers*, 57, 67; *San Francisco Examiner*, August 26, 1966, 56; Clippings File, Cooperstown.

21. https://www.baseball-reference.com/teams/CHC/1969-schedule-scores.shtml.

22. https://www.youtube.com/watch?v=He6PxbLfpBI; https://www.youtube.com/watch?v=eexB8e8VfaY.

23. "The Beverly Hillbillies S01E029 The Clampetts and the Dodgers," Youtube video: https://www.youtube.com/watch?v=n_ZgtiGkR0c; "Herman Munster Tries out for the Dodgers," Youtube video: https://www.youtube.com/watch?v=

OKBpn13P5oQ; "Mr. Ed Plays Baseball," Youtube video: https://www.youtube. com/watch?v=NlVr45CHOuA.

24. Steve Rushin, "There and Back," *Sports Illustrated*, vol. 121, no. 5, August 11, 2014, 33.

Chapter 10

1. Alston, *A Year at a Time*, 167–168.
2. *Ibid.*, 167.
3. Alston, *Alston and the Dodgers*, 121; https://www.baseball-reference.com/ teams/LAD/1963.shtml.
4. Alston, *Alston and the Dodgers*, 118–20; Alston, *A Year at a Time*, 169; *The Sporting News*, October 11, 1963; September 14, 1963, 6; *San Francisco Examiner*, August 26, 1964, 56, August 5, 1971, Clippings File, Cooperstown.
5. Jonathan Mahler, *Ladies and Gentlemen, The Bronx is Burning: 1977, Baseball, Politics, and the Battle for the Soul of a City* (New York: Farrar, Straus and Giroux, 2005), 24.
6. Alston, *Alston and the Dodgers*, 118; Alston, *A Year at a Time*, 163–164; *The Sporting News*, October 11, 1963; September 14, 1963, 6; Clippings File, Cooperstown.
7. Harvey Frommer, *Baseball's Greatest Managers* (New York: Lyons Press, 1985), 10.
8. Leonard Koppett, *The Sporting News*, October 11, 1963, Clippings File, Cooperstown.
9. Alston, *A Year at a Time*, 171–172; Alston, *Alston and the Dodgers*, 124.
10. Hall of Fame website, https://baseballhall.org/discover-more/stories/inside-pitch/koufax-calls-it-quits; Baseball Reference, https://www.baseball-reference.com/boxes/NYA/NYA196310020.shtml.
11. Roger Kahn, *The Boys of Summer* (New York: Harper Perennial Modern Classics, 2006), Chapter 11, "One Stayed in Brooklyn."
12. Alston, *A Year at a Time*, 172; Alston, *Alston and the Dodgers*, 125; https://www.baseball-almanac.com/box-scores/boxscore.php?boxid=196306280LAN.
13. Alston, *A Year at a Time*, pp. 171–73; Alston, *Alston and the Dodgers*, p. 124–26; http://www.thepeskypole.net/2011/10/koufax-vs-mantle-no-

comparison.html ; Jane Leavy, *Sandy Koufax: A Lefty's Legacy*, 137–40.
14. Alston, *A Year at a Time*, 172; Alston, *Alston and the Dodgers*, 123.
15. Alston, *Alston and the Dodgers*, 128–129; https://www.baseball-reference.com/teams/LAD/1964-schedule-scores.shtml.
16. https://www.baseball-reference.com/teams/LAD/1965-schedule-scores.shtml; Alston, *Alston and the Dodgers*, 130–131.
17. Alston, *Alston and the Dodgers*, 166.
18. *Ibid.*, 168; http://www.espn.com/classic/s/merron_on_green.html; http://www.aish.com/j/f/What-Jewish-History-Forgot-Amazing-Events-During-the-High-Holy-Days.html.
19. Alston and Burick, *Alston and the Dodgers*, 117.
20. Alston, *Alston and the Dodgers*, 159, 167–169.
21. "Sandy Koufax's Game 7 in 1965: One for the Ages," Fox Sports website, https://www.foxsports.com/mlb/just-a-bit-outside/story/sandy-koufax-1965-world-series-game7-los-angeles-dodgers-minnesota-twins-102715.
22. Alston, *A Year at a Time*, 189.

Chapter 11

1. Alston and Burick, *Alston and the Dodgers*, 133–134.
2. *Ibid.*
3. "June 5, 1968: The Last Hours of RFK," http://nymag.com/news/politics/47041/index5.html.
4. *The Sporting News*, August 31, 1968; Clippings File, Cooperstown.
5. https://www.scpr.org/news/2017/10/31/77135/remembering-dodger-stadium-when-it-was-chavez-ravi/.
6. See Alan Levy, *Floyd Patterson: A Boxer and a Gentleman* (Jefferson, NC: McFarland, 2008); W. K. Stratton, *Floyd Patterson: The Fighting Life of Boxing's Invisible Champion* (New York: Houghton Mifflin Harcourt, 2012), *passim*.
7. Alston, *Alston and the Dodgers*, 44.
8. Jim Murray, *Los Angeles Times*, October 1, 1984, Clippings File, Cooperstown.
9. *The Sporting News*, February 14, 1970, 32.

10. *Ibid.*, July 22, 1972; January 30, 1971, Clippings File, Cooperstown.

11. Alston, *One Year at a Time*, 134, 179; Clippings File, Cooperstown.

12. *The Sporting News*, August 15, 1964; Clippings File, Cooperstown.

13. Frank Fitzpatrick, "50 Year On, the Dick Allen-Frank Thomas Fight Still Resonates," *Philadelphia Inquirer*, July 2, 2015; https://www.philly.com/philly/sports/phillies/311524701.html.

14. https://sabr.org/bioproj/person/92ed657e "Cardinals Sacrifice Richie Allen's Home Run Power to Shore Up Team's No. 1 Headache in '70-Defense," *Jefferson City* (MO) *Post Tribune*, October 6, 1970, 9.

15. Jim Ogle, "Inside Pitch," unidentified newspaper column, March 26, 1971, Clippings File, Cooperstown.

16. Craig Wright, "Dick Allen: Another View," SABR *Baseball Research Journal* 24 (1995), republished with permission at http://www.whitesoxinteractive.com, 12. https://sabr.org/bioproj/person/92ed657e.

17. *The Sporting News*, October 9, 1971; October 21, 1971; Clippings File, Cooperstown.

18. Alston, *One Year at a Time*, 196.

19. *Sports Illustrated*, March 11, 1974; *New York Times*, October 2, 1984.

20. *New York Times*, October 2, 1984, 29; *New York Times*, June 22, 1992, https://www.nytimes.com/1997/06/22/sports/manager-still-has-detractors-but-not-among-the-mets.html.

21. *The Sporting News*, May 26, 1973; Clippings File, Cooperstown.

22. Alston, *One Year at a Time*, 200.

23. *The Sporting News*, April 25, 1970, 20.

24. *New York Times*, November 29, 1972, 51; *The Sporting News*, October 29, 1971, October 3, 1976, Clippings File, Cooperstown; https://www.nytimes.com/1972/11/29/archives/angels-get-dodgers-frank-robinson-aging-star-key-in-7man-trade.html.

25. *The Sporting News*, October 24, 1974; Clippings File, Cooperstown.

26. *St. Louis Globe-Democrat*, August 26, 1976, section B, 1; *Los Angeles Evening Press*, August 25, 1976, section B, 8; *Los Angeles Herald-Examiner*, April 17, 1976, section D, 2; Clippings File, Cooperstown; Michael Fallon, *Dodgerland: Decadent Los Angeles and the 1977–78 Dodgers* (Lincoln: University of Nebraska Press, 2016), Chapter 2.

Chapter 12

1. W.P. Kinsella, *Shoeless Joe* (New York: Houghton Mifflin, 1982).

2. Jacques Barzun, https://www.brainyquote.com/quotes/jacques_barzun_118702.

3. See Christopher Lasch, *The Culture of Narcissism* (New York: W.W. Norton, 1979), Chapter Five, "The Degradation of Sport," 100–124.

4. Steve Rushin, "There and Back," *Sports Illustrated*, vol. 121, no. 5, August 11, 2014, 60; Leonard Dinnerstein, *Anti-Semitism in America* (New York: Oxford University Press, 1994), *passim.*; Irving Howe, *The World of Our Fathers* (New York: Schocken, 1994), radio interview, done in regard to the newly-published book, Madison (WI) Public Radio, 1977.

5. Dunnell, Milt, "Dixie Lived Down the Racist Image of Robinson Case," *Toronto Star*, May 19, 1982; Berkow, Ira, "Dixie Walker Remembers," *New York Times*, December 10, 1981; *NY Times*, May 18, 1982; Lyle Spatz, "Dixie Walker," Society for American Baseball Research, https://sabr.org/bioproj/person/74909ba3; Harvey Araton, "The Dixie Walker She Knew," *New York Times*, April 1, 2010.

6. *Sports Illustrated*, August 11, 2014, vol. 121, issue 5, 72.

7. *The Sporting News*, August 17, 1968, Clippings File, Cooperstown.

8. *USA Today*, October 2, 1984, section C, 1–2; *Portsmouth Times*, October 9, 16; Clippings File, Cooperstown.

9. *The Sporting News*, July 27, 1983, *USA Today*, October 2, 1984, section C, 1–2; *New York Times*, October 2, 1984, 29, Clippings File, Cooperstown.

Bibliography

Adler, David A. *Campy: The Story of Roy Campanella*. New York: Viking Penguin, 2007.

Allen, Dick, with Tim Whitaker. *Crash: The Life and Times of Dick Allen*. New York: Ticknor & Fields, 1989.

Allen, Maury. *Brooklyn Remembered*. Champaign, IL: Sports Publishing, 2005.

_____. *Jackie Robinson: A Life Remembered*. New York: F. Watts, 1987.

Alston, Walter, with Jack Tobin. *One Year at a Time*. Waco, TX, Word Books, 1976.

Alston, Walter, with Si Burick. *Alston and the Dodgers*. Garden City, NY: Doubleday, 1966.

_____. *Complete Baseball Handbook: Strategies and Techniques for Winning*. New York: Brown and Benchmark, 1984.

Amoruso, Marino. *Gil Hodges: The Quiet Man*. Middlebury, VT: Paul S. Eriksson, 1991.

Bailey, Budd. *Jackie Robinson: Breaking Baseball's Color Barrier*. New York: Cavendish Square, 2016.

Barber, Red. *The Broadcasters*. New York: Dial Press, 1970.

_____. *Rhubarb in the Catbird Seat*. Lincoln: University of Nebraska Press, 1968.

_____. *Walk in the Spirit*. New York: Dial Press, 1969.

Bavasi, Buzzie, with John Strege. *Off the Record*. Chicago: Contemporary Books, 1987.

Bennett, Doraine. *Jackie Robinson*. Fortson, GA: State Standards, 2008.

Berra, Yogi, with Dave Kaplan. *What Time Is It? You Mean Now? Advice for Life from the Zennest Master of Them All*. New York: Simon & Schuster, 2002.

Bjarkman, Peter C. *Duke Snider*. New York: Chelsea House, 1994.

Bragan, Bobby, as told to Jeff Guinn. *You Can't Hit the Ball with the Bat on Your Shoulder: The Baseball Life and Times of Bobby Bragan*. Fort Worth, TX: The Summit Group, 1992.

Brandt, Keith. *Jackie Robinson: A Life of Courage*. Mahwah, NJ: Troll Associates, 1992.

Breslin, Jimmy. *Branch Rickey*. New York: Viking, 2010.

Campanella, Roy. *It's Good to Be Alive*. Boston: Little, Brown, 1959.

Caro, Robert. *The Power Broker*. New York: Alfred A. Knopf, 1974.

Chalberg, John C. *Rickey & Robinson*. Wheeling, IL: Harlan Davidson, 2000.

Clavin, Thomas. *Gil Hodges: The Brooklyn Bums, the Miracle Mets, and the Extraordinary Life of a Baseball Legend*. New York: New American Library, 2012.

Cohen, Stanley. *Dodgers! The First 100 Years*. New York: Birch Lane Press, 1990.

Daly, Steve. *Dem Little Bums: The Nashua Dodgers*. Concord, NH: Plaidswede, 2002.

Devaney, John. *Gil Hodges: Baseball Miracle Man*. New York: Putnam, 1973.

Diamond, Arthur. *Jackie Robinson*. San Diego, CA: Lucent Books, 1992.

Dickson, Paul. *Leo Durocher: Baseball's Prodigal Son*. New York: Bloomsbury USA, 2017.

Doeden, Matt. *Sandy Koufax*. Minneapolis: Twenty-First Century Books, 2007.

Durocher, Leo, with Ed Linn. *Nice Guys Finish Last*. New York: Simon & Schuster, 1975.

Endsley, Brian M. *Finding the Left Arm of*

God: Sandy Koufax and the Los Angeles Dodgers, 1960–1963. Jefferson, NC: McFarland, 2015.

_____. *Koufax Throws a Curve: the Los Angeles Dodgers at the End of an Era, 1964–1966*. Jefferson, NC: McFarland, 2018.

Erskine, Carl. *Tales from the Dodgers' Dugout*. Champaign, IL: Sports Publishing, 2000.

Erskine, Carl, with Burton Rocks. *What I learned From Jackie Robinson: A Teammate's Reflections On and Off the Field*. New York: McGraw-Hill, 2005.

Eskenazi, Gerald. *Lip: A Biography of Leo Durocher*. New York: William Morrow, 1993.

Falkner, David. *Great Time Coming: The Life of Jackie Robinson, From Baseball to Birmingham*. New York: Simon & Schuster, 1995.

Ford, Carin T. *Jackie Robinson: "All I Ask is That You Respect Me as a Human Being."* Berkeley Heights, NJ: Enslow, 2005.

_____. *Jackie Robinson: Hero of Baseball*. Berkeley Heights, NJ: Enslow, 2006.

Frommer, Harvey. *Rickey & Robinson*. New York: Collier MacMillan, 1982.

Giordano, Geraldine. *Sandy Koufax*. New York: Rosen, 2003.

Golenbock, Peter. *Bums*. New York: Putnam's, 1984.

Gruver, Ed. *Koufax*. Dallas, TX: Taylor, 2000.

Hano, Arnold. *Sandy Koufax, Strikeout King*. New York, Putnam, 1964.

Hillstrom, Laurie Collier. *Jackie Robinson and the Integration of Baseball*. Detroit, MI: Omnigraphics, 2013.

Holmes, Tot. *Brooklyn's Best*. Gothenbert, NE: Holmes Publishing, 1988.

Honig, Donald. *The Man in the Dugout: Fifteen Big League Managers Speak Their Minds*. New York: Follett, 1977.

James, Bill. *Bill James' Guide to Baseball Managers, From 1870 to Today*. New York: Scribner's, 1997.

_____. *Historical Baseball Abstract*. New York: The Free Press, 2001.

Kahn, Roger. *Beyond the Boys of Summer*. New York: McGraw-Hill, 2005.

_____. *Rickey & Robinson: The True, Untold Story of the Integration of Baseball*. New York: Rodale, 2014.

Kashatus, William C. *Jackie and Campy: The Untold Story of Their Rocky Relationship and the Breaking of Baseball's Color Line*. Lincoln: University of Nebraska Press, 2014.

Koppett, Leonard. *The Man in the Dugout: Baseball's Top Managers and How They Got That Way*. Philadelphia: Temple University Press, 2000.

Koufax, Sandy, with Ed Linn. *Koufax*. New York: Viking Press, 1966.

Lamb, Chris. *Blackout: The Untold Story of Jackie Robinson's First Spring Training*. Lincoln: University of Nebraska Press, 2004.

Lanctot, Neil. *Campy: The Two Lives of Roy Campanella*. New York: Simon & Schuster, 2011.

Lasorda, Tommy. *Artful Dodger*. New York: Arbor House, 1985.

Leavy, Jane. *Sandy Koufax: A Lefty's Legacy*. New York: HarperCollins, 2002.

Linge, Mary Kay. *Jackie Robinson: A Biography*. Westport, CT: Greenwood Press, 2007.

Lipmen, David. *Mr. Baseball: The Story of Branch Rickey*. New York, Putnam, 1966.

Lowenfish, Lee. *Branch Rickey: Baseball's Ferocious Gentleman*. Lincoln: University of Nebraska Press, 2007.

Macht, Norman L. *Roy Campanella: Baseball Star*. New York: Chelsea House, 1996.

Mann, Arthur. *Branch Rickey: American in Action*. Boston: Houghton Mifflin, 1957.

Marshall, William. *Baseball's Pivotal Era, 1945–1951*. Lexington: University Press of Kentucky, 1999.

Marzano, Rudy. *The Last Years of the Brooklyn Dodgers: A History, 1950–1957*. Jefferson, NC: McFarland, 2008.

May, Julian. *Frank Robinson: Slugging Toward Glory*. Mankato, MN: Crestwood House, 1975.

_____. *Roy Campanella, Brave Man of Baseball*. Mankato, MN: Crestwood House, 1974.

McCullough, David. *The Pioneers: The Heroic Story of the Settlers Who Brought the American Ideal West*. New York: Simon & Schuster, 2019.

Mercer, Paul. *Jackie Robinson*. New York: Barnes & Noble, 2003.

Michael Fallon. *Dodgerland: Decadent Los Angeles and the 1977–78 Dodgers*.

Lincoln: University of Nebraska Press, 2016.

Nathanson, Mitchell. *God Almighty Hisself: The Life and Legacy of Dick Allen.* Philadelphia: University of Pennsylvania Press, 2016.

Ninfo, Bill. *Carl Furillo, The Forgotten Dodger.* Bloomington, IN: 1st Books Library, 2002.

Plaschke, Bill. *I Live for This!: Baseball's Last True Believer.* Boston: Houghton Mifflin, 2007.

Polner, Murray. *Branch Rickey: A Biography.* New York: Atheneum, 1982.

Pope, Edwin. *Baseball's Greatest Managers.* Garden City, NY: Doubleday, 1960.

Price, Sean. *Jackie Robinson: Breaking the Color Barrier.* Chicago: Raintree/Fusion, 2009.

Prince, Carl. *Brooklyn's Dodgers: The Bums, The Borough and the Best of Baseball, 1947–1957.* New York: Oxford University Press, 1996.

Rampersad, Arnold. *Jackie Robinson: A Biography.* New York: Knopf, 1997.

Reed, Ted. *Carl Furillo, Brooklyn Dodgers All-Star.* Jefferson, NC: McFarland, 2011.

Reiser, Howard. *Jackie Robinson: Baseball Pioneer.* New York: F. Watts, 1992.

Robinson, Jackie, edited by Charles Dexter. *Baseball Has Done It.* Philadelphia: Lippincott, 1964.

Robinson, Jackie, with Alfred Duckett. *Breakthrough to the Big League: The Story of Jackie Robinson.* New York: Harper & Row, 1965.

_____. *I Never Had it Made.* New York: Putnam, 1972.

Roseboro, John. *Glory Days with the Dodgers.* New York: Atheneum, 1978.

Russell, Patrick. *The Tommy Davis Story.* Garden City, NY: Doubleday, 1969.

Schneider, Russell J. *Frank Robinson: The Making of a Manager.* New York: Coward, McCann & Geoghegan, 1976.

Schoor, Gene. *Pee Wee Reese Story.* New York: J. Messner, 1956.

_____. *Roy Campanella, Man of Courage.* New York: Putnam, 1959.

Schraff, Anne E. *Jackie Robinson: An American Hero.* West Berlin, NJ: Townsend Press, 2008.

Schutz, J. Christopher. *Jackie Robinson: An Integrated Life.* Lanham, MD: Rowman & Littlefield, 2016.

Shapiro, Michael. *The Last Good Season.* New York: Doubleday, 2003.

Shapiro, Milton J. *Gil Hodges Story.* New York: Messner, 1960.

_____. *Jackie Robinson of the Brooklyn Dodgers.* New York: Messner, 1966.

_____. *Roy Campanella Story.* New York: Messner, 1958.

Simmons, Matt J. *Jackie Robinson: Breaking the Color Line in Baseball.* New York: Crabtree, 2014.

Simon, Scott. *Jackie Robinson and the Integration of Baseball.* Hoboken, NJ: J. Wiley & Sons, 2002.

Skipper, John C. *Frank Robinson: A Baseball Biography.* Jefferson, NC: McFarland, 2015.

Snider, Duke, with Bill Gilbert. *Duke of Flatbush.* New York: Kensington, 1988.

Stout, Glenn. *Jackie Robinson.* New York: Little, Brown, 2006.

Stout, Glenn, and Richard Johnson. *120 Years of Dodgers Baseball.* New York: Houghton Mifflin, 2004.

Sullivan, Neil. *The Dodgers Move West.* New York: Oxford University Press, 1987.

Tackach, James. *Roy Campanella.* New York: Chelsea House, 1991.

Testa, Judith Anne. *Sal Maglie: Baseball's Demon Barber.* DeKalb: Northern Illinois University Press, 2007.

Thorn, John, Pete Palmer, Michael Gershman, and Matthew Silverman. *Total Baseball.* Kingston, NY: Total Sports Publishing, 2001.

Tygiel, Jules. *Baseball's Great Experiment: Jackie Robinson and his Legacy.* New York: Oxford University Press, 1983.

Wills, Maury. *How to Steal a Pennant.* New York: Putnam, 1976.

_____. *On the Run: The Never Dull and Often Shocking Life of Maury Wills.* New York: Carroll & Graf, 1991.

Wills, Maury, with Steve Gardner. *It Pays to Steal.* Englewood Cliffs, N.J. Prentice-Hall, 1963.

Wilson, John R.M. *Jackie Robinson and the American Dilemma.* New York: Longman, 2010.

Winehouse, Irwin. *Duke Snider Story.* New York: J. Messner, 1964.

Young, Dick. *Roy Campanella.* New York: A. S. Barnes, 1952.

Zachter, Mort. *Gil Hodges: A Hall of Fame Life.* Lincoln: University of Nebraska Press, 2015.

Index

207